Springer Series on Social Work

Albert R. Roberts, PhD, Series Editor

Sophia F. Dziegielewski, PhD, LCSW, is a Professor in the School of Social Work, University of Central Florida, Orlando, FL. Prior to this appointment, Dr. Dziegielewski had faculty appointments in the School of Social Work, The University of Alabama, Tuscaloosa, AL; the Departments of Family and Preventive Medicine and Psychiatry at Meharry Medical College, Nashville, TN; The School of Social Work at the University of Tennessee, Nashville; and the U.S. Army Military College stationed at Fort Benning, GA. Her educational qualifications include an MSW and PhD in Social Work from Florida State University, Tallahassee, FL. Dr. Dziegielewski is a Licensed Clinical Social Worker and with her nursing background is firm on the importance of social workers learning more about prescription and herbal medications and the relationship of the use of these products with time-limited psychosocial interventions. She supports her research and practice activity with over 65 publications and over 200 recent workshops and community presentations on medications, herbal preparations, and mental health assessment documentation and treatment planning in today's managed-care environment.

Ana M. Leon, PhD, LCSW, is an Associate Professor in the School of Social Work, University of Central Florida, Orlando, FL. Over the past 22 years, Dr. Leon has had extensive experience in providing mental health services to individuals, families, and groups. Her experiences range from providing direct services in agency settings, psychiatric hospitals, and private practice to administrative positions in Departments of Psychiatry and mental health facilities. Although her experiences in mental health and psychiatry have included work with both adults and children, her major research interests have focused on psychiatric services for children and adolescents. As part of this interest, Dr. Leon has been instrumental in developing and implementing psychiatric inpatient and outpatient programs for conduct-disordered adolescents, and has served as a consultant for several local psychiatric hospitals. Dr. Leon has conducted numerous workshops for mental health professionals on interviewing, clinical documentation, juvenile offenders, clinical practice with Hispanic women, and assessing children and adolescents.

Social Work Practice and Psychopharmacology

Sophia F. Dziegielewski, PhD, LCSW
and Ana M. Leon, PhD, LCSW

 Springer Series on Social Work

Springer Publishing Company, Inc.
536 Broadway
New York, NY 10012-3955

Acquisitions Editor: Bill Tucker
Production Editor: Pamela Lankas
Cover design by Susan Hauley

01 02 03 04 05 / 5 4 3 2 1

Library of Congress Cataloging-in-Publication Data

Dziegielewski, Sophia F.
   Social work practice and medication use / Sophia F. Dziegielewski and Ana M. Leon.
       p. cm. — (Springer series on social work)
   Includes bibliographical references and index.
   ISBN 0-8261-1394-X
   1. Medical social work.   2. Pharmacology.   I. Leon, Ana.   II. Title   III. Series.
HV688.A2 D95 2001
362.1'0425—dc21   00-051574
                                                                            CIP

Printed in the United States of America by Sheridan Press

I would like to dedicate this book to my high school music teacher, William Garodnick. Through his unconditional support and guidance, he taught me if I believe in myself, all things are possible.

S.F.D.

I believe that life presents us with at least one angel ... I have been fortunate enough to have many angels who have provided me with strength, courage, and wings to fly. This book is dedicated to those angels, my mother Marcelina; my husband Pedro; my friends Claire and Merlin; and my mentor and wonderful friend, Sophia.

A.M.L.

Contents

Part III   Special Topics in Psychopharmacology and Social Work Practice

Preface

In this era of managed care, social work and many other disciplines
have been forced to examine treatment methods and modalities with
a new vigor. In order for social workers to survive in the physical
and mental health care arenas, it is clear that we must provide the most
effective and accountable care. This care must incorporate knowledge of
the medications that are being used to supplement therapeutic interventions. In this volume, we will provide an overview of issues and concerns
about medication that social workers will encounter in practice.

• **Why do social workers need to know about medication?**

Social workers traditionally have been expected to contribute to all
aspects of a client's life. Yet the newer forms of social work counseling such as short-term therapy and behavior-based interventions may
still come up short unless medications are considered as a viable
supplement to intervention. Medical social workers are expected to
understand the diagnostic criteria, usage, and side effects of the
medications provided in the context of the intervention.

The role of the social workers remains complex as they are often
called upon to advise on diagnostic criteria and on which medications
would be the best adjunct to the current therapy. Social workers
should not shy away from learning about current diagnostic guidelines
and the medications that are frequently used. Until recently, most of
the resources available in this area were written by other than social
work professionals and were considered "unfriendly" in terms of
correlating the information to the social work treatment regimen in
terms of moral and ethical issues.

- **Which social workers are involved in using medication information with their clients?**

All social workers are involved. Whether in private practice or agency settings, social workers have always been involved with medication and its effects on their clients. Although social workers do not prescribe medication, few professionals would debate the need for these professionals to be well versed in the matter in order to provide ethical, efficient, and effective services to their clients. Historically, social workers have been critical of the use of medications and have actually discouraged their use. This view must now be reconsidered because many clients not only request medication to supplement psychological interventions—they expect it. As social workers will undoubtedly encounter clients who are taking medication, their knowledge will in turn affect the counseling relationship. Social workers must know the basics of medications and how these drugs can affect the time-sensitive counseling environment.

- **As a member of an interdisciplinary team, what is the unique role of the social worker?**

Social work professionals spend quality time with their clients, so it is likely that they will be the first interdisciplinary team member to notice possible side effects or medication reactions. In this book special emphasis is placed on the role of the social worker regarding the use and misuse of medication. Although it is not meant to be all-inclusive, it does seek to present medication-prescribing considerations that will allow social workers to better serve their clients.

- **Do I have to know all medications and what they are used for?**

Of course not, but all professionals should attempt to learn all they can and to utilize this new information to help their clients. Medication has dramatically improved the treatment and intervention possibilities for numerous clients who might otherwise have spent their lives in psychiatric facilities struggling with mental illness. These mental-health medications help individuals respond to everyday life as well as to psychotherapeutic interventions. Knowing how to access information about medicinal products and having a basic understanding of what they mean is critical to promoting education to clients, families, and communities.

The use of medications has increased and so have the numbers of medication available. The *Physicians' Desk Reference*, 2000 (*PDR*, 2000) lists more than 4,000 medications, and there are more than 700 medications in the *Physicians' Desk Reference for Herbal Medicines* (*PDR for Herbal Medicines*, 2000). In addition there are innumerable over-the-counter products. No professional can be familiar with all of them, but it is crucial to know what medications a client is taking and how to research these medications.

- **What type of information should a social worker know about medication?**

Taking into account the vast array of medications in use today, this book will help the social worker: (a) establish a basis for understanding the use of medication with a primary focus on those used to improve mental health; and (b) provide basic information that will enable social work professionals to interpret, predict, and suggest environmental treatment strategy for clients who are taking medication as part of a therapeutic regimen.

- **Do I really need to know about medication, or can I depend on other professionals to teach clients?**

More than 98% of the social workers surveyed thought it was critical for successful social work practice to be educated about medications (Dziegielewski & Leon, 1998). Though all accredited social work programs generally offer at least one graduate-level course in psychopathology or clinical diagnosis, there are few textbooks available and only two address the influence of medication from the perspective of social work treatment. Most social workers agree that at some level education in the use and misuse of medication and its influence on the therapeutic process is a necessity (Bently, 1997; Dziegielewski, 1997, 1998). Many social work professionals and educators believe that such training should be incorporated into the curriculum provided by social work programs at both the graduate and undergraduate levels (Dziegielewski, 1997; Rowan & Dziegielewski, 1996).

- **How can I benefit directly from this book?**

This book can be used by social work professional both as a textbook and as a clinical resource. Considering that most social workers do not receive training in medication during their social work program, it provides an excellent practice resource for clinicians in the field. In Part I, general information is included that will prepare social workers to address the needs of clients who are taking medication. The use of medication is viewed as part of social work practice, and strategies for understanding its use are highlighted. Each chapter features a case study that exemplifies common practice principles. Societal myths and the obstacles they create are reviewed and how medications work, how they are related to brain function, and the role of neurochemicals are explored. An explanation of the difference between generic and brand names is presented along with medical terminology that is used in prescribing medications and in health care records. Basic rules for monitoring medication and compliance are provided along with tips for treatment planning and documentation.

Part II of the book outlines several mental-health diagnostic categories: schizophrenia, mood disorders, depression, bipolar disorders, and specific anxiety disorders including generalized anxiety disorder and obsessive compulsive disorder. Each chapter provides a case example, consideration in diagnosis, and the interventions utilized. Medications used to treat these disorders and relevant psychosocial interventions are outlined. Each chapter emphasizes the need for accurate treatment planning and documentation and offers suggestions to facilitate this process.

Several special topics are set forth in Part III, where consideration is given to understanding cultural diversity and working with children and older people. A chapter on herbal and medicinal products reminds the social worker of their increasing usage among clients. Unfortunately, many consumers are lulled into thinking that these products are safe because they are said to be natural. The authors remind the social worker that if a product is strong enough to create an action-reaction in the body, it is also strong enough to interact with other medications and produce undesirable side effects whether it is herbally or chemically based. Appendixes A and B provide resources to help social workers find useful information that can be shared with their clients about medications, and a sample evaluation form (Appendix C) is included to facilitate taking a medication history. Appendix D provides a glossary that serves as a quick reference for what may initially be unfamiliar terms.

The use of medication as a therapeutic modality constitutes a growing and changing field of science. Social workers must keep up-to-date with new trends and with how these medications can affect the client in the counseling relationship. To complete the advocacy and broker functions that are basic in the field of social work, an accurate assessment and referral process must be initiated with regard to medication. Professional social workers must assess the various types of medications a client is taking, be they prescription, alternative remedies, or over-the-counter medicines. Whether one takes the more radical stance of allowing limited prescription privileges for social workers as suggested by Dziegielewski (1997) or the more conservative role recommended by Bently (1997), it is clear that social workers must have at least a general knowledge of medications. All social workers should be familiar with side-effect profiles and dosage routines in order to assist clients in maintaining the most therapeutically productive intervention possible, and they must be able to recognize potential problems in order to refer the client for adequate or revised treatment.

REFERENCES

Bently, K. J. (1997). Should clinical social workers seek psychotropic medication prescription privileges?: No. In B. A. Thyer (Ed.), *Controversial issues in social work practice* (pp. 152–165). Boston: Allyn & Bacon.

Dziegielewski, S. F. (1997). Should clinical social workers seek psychotropic medication prescription privileges?: Yes. In B. A. Thyer (Ed.), *Controversial issues in social work practice* (pp. 152–165). Boston: Allyn & Bacon.

Dziegielewski, S. F. (1998). Psychopharmacology and social work practice: Introduction. *Research on Social Work Practice, 8,* 371–383.

Dziegielewski, S. F., & Leon, A. M. (1998, Winter). Psychopharmacology knowledge and use with social work professionals: A continuing education evaluation. *International Journal of Continuing Education, 1*(3), 31–40.

Physicians' Desk Reference. (2000). *Physicians' desk reference* (54th ed.). Montvale, NJ: Medical Economics Company.

Physicians' Desk Reference. (2000). *Physicians' desk reference for herbal medicines* (2nd ed.). Montvale, NJ: Medical Economics Company.

Rowan, D., & Dziegielewski, S. F. (1996, October). *Inclusion of psychopharmacological content in BSW curricula.* Paper presented at the 14th Annual BPD Conference, Portland, OR.

Acknowledgments

We would like to express our sincere gratitude for all the help we have received from the many practitioners and health educators across the United States. In particular, we would like to thank Kathryn Goldin, MD, for her thoughtful commentary on the initial chapters of the book. Because the use of medications to address mental health disorders is widespread, knowledge of this area has become practice necessity for social workers. These visionary professionals have acknowledged the importance of this information and their efforts to make this the best and most informative book in the area is sincerely appreciated.

Furthermore, the authors would like to thank all of the individuals who assisted with the production of this book. First, we would like to acknowledge Albert Roberts, DSW, the series editor, who has been a wonderful resource and inspiration for completing this project. Second, we would like to thank the production staff at Springer Publishing Company, who helped to edit the book. Last, we would like to thank Ursula Springer, whose motivating words of inspiration, dedication, and drive for excellence will never be forgotten.

Because the time and effort needed to complete a book imposes burdens on those who share our lives inside and outside the work environment, we would especially like to thank our families and friends who understood when we said, "We can't because we have to work on the BOOK."

PART I

Mental Health Medications: What Social Workers Need to Know

CHAPTER 1

Knowledge and Use of Medication

This book is designed to provide an overview of the medication issues and concerns that social workers will encounter in practice. The philosophy of the authors is simple: We believe that the knowledge and use of medications in the field of social work is necessary for ethical and competent social work practice. To assist the social worker in providing health and mental services, special emphasis is placed on the role of the social worker with regard to new trends in the field and the knowledge of medication use and misuse.

For the most part, the main focus of this book will be the medications that are used to treat mental health conditions; however, since so many other types of medications can be used as intervention supplements, some references to them will be presented. The authors do not claim to be experts on pharmacology. Instead this text is intended as a guide to assist social workers in the field so they can plan better for helping their clients. This chapter provides social work professionals with a historical as well as current perspective on the importance of the knowledge of medication usage and misuse as a means of initiating and furthering competent, ethical social work practice. It introduces the social worker to the wide array of the most popular medications in use today and provides a framework for knowing how medications can facilitate practice. Our approach is one of application and how those medications can directly impact social work practice.

MEDICATION AS PART OF SOCIAL WORK PRACTICE

As part of a health care team, the social worker is expected to assist clients and their families in taking charge of their lives while they are striving to improve their levels of physical health and mental health satisfaction and functioning. Traditional forms of social work intervention such as long-term therapies and insight-oriented methods have been questioned and no longer seem to provide the most cost-effective basis for intervention. Therefore, when counseling is provided, it is generally of a time-limited nature and utilizes methods that clearly establish the effectiveness of the intervention (Dziegielewski, 1996, 1997). Social workers and others in the helping professions must recognize that time limits as part of the intervention process. All social workers in practice will undoubtedly encounter clients who are taking medications that will subsequently affect the therapeutic counseling relationship. Because on the pressures inherent in counseling, social workers must know the basics of medication use, avoid its misuse, and understand how these medications are being used as an intervention modality in time-limited intervention.

Social workers practicing directly in the health and mental health arena frequently serve as part of an interdisciplinary team and often spend more clinical time with their clients. They are more likely, therefore, to the first team member to recognize the possible side effects or reactions to medication. In case management and in many other medical and mental health related practice areas, social workers are expected to understand the medications their clients are taking and to assist the client with compliance issues, pharmacy shopping, side-effect profiles, and insurance coverage. Due to the varied roles that social work professionals are expected to perform they must be knowledgeable about medications so they can interpret and suggest medication regimens and address related treatment issues with their clients. Social workers must actively provide advocacy and brokerage services in order to identify, implement, and monitor medication regimens.

ENVIRONMENTAL INFLUENCES: PHILOSOPHICAL DIRECTIVES AND TECHNOLOGICAL ADVANCES

Trying to balance the issues that clients face is difficult, particularly with regard to medication. It is especially problematic when considering so many philosophical directives and technological advances. Among the numerous pressures to provide accountable, efficient, and effective service is the encouragement of medications that are used as a form of intervention for clients suffering from many physical and mental health difficulties.

As with all counselors, social workers must be aware of the philosophical directives or environmental pressures that motivate a client to seek care. According to Walter (2000) advances in technology have changed our environment and have forced society to reexamine current roles and positions. The idea of simply taking a pill offers a "quick fix" to those who see it as an easy way to solve a problem. Many clients seek medications from their physician, therapist, or social worker as either a sole or adjunct remedy for treatment in mental health.

Primary care physicians and other professionals support this notion when they write a prescription without thoroughly examining other possibilities or additional interventions that would effectively complement medication use. The prevalence of this quick-fix mentality is evidenced in estimates from the Centers for Disease Control and Prevention and from the Federal Drug and Food Administration (FDA) showing that approximately 50 million unnecessary antibiotic prescriptions are written each year (Nordenberg, 1998). Many times individuals are placed on medications for problems that could be addressed at least in part by counseling strategy; however, referrals of this nature are rarely given during a brief office visit with the physician. For example, a client loses a loved one and is experiencing depression and difficulty adjusting to the life changes. She may ask for a medication to alleviate the symptoms presented by the crisis and is prescribed medication to get her through this period. The value of psychosocial interventions in the adjustment process is either overlooked or not emphasized enough in the total treatment strategy. It seems shortsighted to put a client on medication without her ever having been referred to a social worker to clarify or explore the difficulties she is experiencing. When the presenting psychosocial component is overlooked, the opportunity is missed for the client to learn new problem-solving and coping skills that may be of benefit in other similar situations.

As the first line of intervention, taking some type of medication to deal with problems is becoming common practice. Unfortunately, many clients want a quick and easy answer and believe that the simple act of taking a pill can be curative in itself. Many clients not only believe that the pill will help relieve their symptoms but also that it will eventually provide a simple and easy cure for what is ailing them. Many clients who visit a physician's office today expect some type of medication (Dziegielewski, 1998).

This misconception permeates our society and may be hard to dispel because medications do indeed offer help and can actually alleviate symptoms. There are still many professionals, however, who support the contention that mental health problems are often complex and require a multifaceted intervention approach. Relying solely on medications to control or cure mental health problems is not enough.

In the face of societal expectations that a pill alone can cure, social workers must become knowledgeable about the medications that are being prescribed. They must spend time educating clients, their family members, and other members of the health care team about the benefits of combining medication regimens with effective psychosocial strategies. This means using a multidimensional approach to provide the client with specific information on mental health problems and concerns and on how social and mental functioning is enhanced by the interdependent relationship of medication and psychosocial interventions. Simply stated, in the clinical practice environment social workers are now compelled to have a working knowledge of medications as a common form of mental health intervention whether they openly embrace medication use or not. In order to provide effective service, social workers must know the different types of medications, the specific uses of medications and clearly be able to distinguish side effect profiles as well as other problems that can affect the clients.

In addition to this philosophical directive, there have been many technological advances regarding medication and its effect on the brain. In the last few years scientists have learned more about the brain and the role of medications in treatment than ever before. A versatile three-pound maze of nerve and tissue, the brain is a virtual laboratory whose workings and chemical interactions determine the state of our mental health, down to the most complicated mood (Kotulak, 1997).

As a form of medical intervention, psychopharmacology is considered a relatively new intervention with its roots planted only in the last 40 to 45 years. There is so much new information regarding medications, and this needs to be combined with the "individual" or "unique" responses that can occur with use. Medication trials cannot cover every side effect a client might experience. For example, a client can have a serious reaction to a drug when taken with another drug that has never occurred in the medication trials before (Henkel, 1998). Even though trials of medications are conducted and monitored by the FDA, it is long after the medication has been used on the market that additional or true effects are known. As will be discussed later in this text, the clinical trials that are used to approve a drug initially remain limited, and it is not until afterwards when millions of individuals have used the product that a more accurate picture presents itself (Henkel, 1998). This is why post-marketing programs such as MedWatch have been developed. MedWatch was developed by the FDA as a reporting system to track adverse reactions to prescription and over-the-counter medications (Nordenberg, 1999). With MedWatch, information is put into a computer database where it is analyzed and tracked for occurrence of adverse reactions. Programs like this become effective when health professionals such as doctors, dentists, physicians and other counselors pass along information that will help detect any serious and adverse reactions so that they can be clearly documented and avoided in future use.

Therefore, knowledge of the philosophical directive, technological advances, and rapidly expanding information about the brain is essential. This is not to say that all social workers must have an in-depth knowledge of all the types of medications used in the professional helping relationship. An awareness of the types of medications available (particularly the mental health medications) as well as where and when to seek additional information in order to assist the client is considered an ethical and competent practice necessity (Dziegielewski, 1998).

The effects of these medications cannot be underestimated, whether prescribed, over-the-counter, or herbal or natural remedies. Medications are taken for a variety of reasons and are expected to assist with multiple health and mental health problems. The *Physicians' Desk Reference* has more than 3,000 pages of text that advertise more than 4,000 drugs by product and generic name (*PDR*, 2000). There are also more than 600 OTC products now available (Nordenberg, 1998), and an entire volume of *PDR* is dedicated to herbal medicines (*PDR for Herbal Medicines*, 2000). Medications, prescription and otherwise, are clearly being used in the therapeutic environment, and social work professionals must not only be aware of them but be willing to assist as part of the health care delivery team in monitoring and assisting clients who are using them.

MEDICATION AS A TREATMENT MODALITY

Many individuals may benefit tremendously from the use of psychotherapeutic medications. Regardless of the type of intervention, about 85% of people who are moderately anxious, frustrated, and distressed often get better regardless of the strategy employed or without formal intervention (Lambert, 1992). This statement has been questioned by Lazarus (1997) who believes this premise does not hold true for clients who fit into diagnostic categories like obsessive-compulsive or posttraumatic stress disorder, eating, sexual, and panic disorders, as well as several others. Dziegielewski (1991) highlighted this point with her research on family caregivers of persons with Alzheimer's disease.

In this randomized classic control group, several different treatment options were explored for the reduction of caregiver stress. The 40 participating caregivers were randomly assigned to three different treatment groups that were designed to help them improve their relationships with relatives who suffered from dementia. The study found that regardless of the type of social work intervention, the three psychosocial methods tested were all more effective in increasing caregiver satisfaction than that reported by the non-intervention control group. Although not statistically significant, a clinical difference was found in those who received a more structured approach to improving their relationships. The highest gains were made in the group that had clear goals and objectives for educating the relative about dementia and its related problems. This approach outlined clearly the importance of providing concrete information on the relative's mental health diagnosis and the medications being used by the institution where the relative resided. Families were eager to learn about the gains that could be expected with medication and how these related to their relatives' actions and subsequent performance.

To date, simple studies such as Dziegielewski's (1991) lend added support by providing more evidence for psychosocial interventions that can assist individuals who suffer from mental health difficulties. In addition to psychosocial intervention, particularly in more serious cases, medications continue to be used to supplement the treatment regimen (Schatzberg & Cole, 1991). The participants in Dziegielewski's (1991) study wanted more information about medication and wanted to know how and why they were being used. It is essential that social workers be versed in the common medications that their clients are using in order to help the individual and the family learn how environmental, situational, and other psychosocial factors can impact the intervention process.

One extremely important point is that like the psychosocial process, medication as an intervention should not be considered an exact science (Prufer, 1996). In terms of practice, this is where the use of medication and psychosocial interventions must be joined. Alone or together, neither can guarantee that the treatment rendered is exactly what a client needs. Since many clients are led to believe that medication does alleviate the symptoms and root causes of mental illness, social workers must take the lead in advocating a total package of mental health services that may include psychotherapeutic medication. Just as the experience and symptoms of mental illness vary, so too can the benefits that derive from any type of intervention, including the use of medication.

The effects of medication and response to it can vary depending on a host of factors: age, size, body weight, metabolism, race, gender, and whether generic or brand names are used. To complicate the matter, the same client will respond differently at other times in life or under different circumstances (the death of a loved one, for instance, as opposed to a general difficulty in getting to sleep). Response to medication in these events can vary widely, with some clients reporting mild temporary discomfort and others a more severe and long-lasting one.

For example, it is not uncommon when working in a mental health inpatient unit to see medication administered to reduce or eliminate violent or self-destructive behavior. The medication's sedative effect will calm one person immediately and may produce sleep; another client of similar age, weight, and height may remain extremely combative. In order to achieve the same result, the second client may require a subsequent dose. Why does this happen? There are no definitive or easy explanations for variability in client responses to medications. In many cases the combination of the client's unique biological system coupled with the variability of medications confirms that the use and application of medication is not an exact science.

Clinical trials are not comprehensive or inclusive enough to address adequately all medication-related problems, issues, and interactions that may develop (Henkel, 1998). In trials, drugs are studied only for the use intended by the pharmaceutical company that is researching it. Once a drug is on the market, many clients will be treated with the drug, some of whom do not have the condition for which it was originally tested and approved. These individuals may also be taking other medications, dietary supplements, and products that could interact with the drug and cause additional problems (Nordenberg, 1999).

Mosher (1999) warns of an "unholy alliance" when psychiatrists or other prescribers of medication are recruited by drug companies and persuaded to use a particular type of medication by drug company representatives who offer free services or rewards for prescribing the medication. Unfortunately, it is this alliance rather than the client's condition that dictates which prescriptions are written.

To best serve our clients, a dual perspective is recommended that takes into account the use of medications while not underestimating the political pressures that can influence prescribing patterns and counseling. Since neither psychosocial interventions nor the use of medication is an exact science, both types of intervention require professional application and ongoing monitoring. For all clients, medication as the sole modality of treatment is not recommended, because there are so many situational or environmental considerations that must be taken into account. At a recent workshop conducted by the senior author on medication and social work practice, one participant asked the following question: Since we have medications such as Prozac, why do we need to do psychosocial interventions at all? If medications are so successful, why not just give them the pill, monitor them, and send them home?

The reply was simple: When clients are put on an antidepressant medication as the sole modality of treatment, they may indeed get better. These medications are particularly good for endogenous or internal types of depression where the signs and symptoms of the illness can be adjusted within the body. But what about the environmental factors? If someone has been depressed for a long period of time, he or she has probably adjusted to a certain lifestyle and level of performance and so have individuals in the client's environment. Now that the client is feeling better, his or her mood may lift and he or she has more energy. The family must readjust or reframe the client's behavior. More energy more expectations may be placed upon him or her by family, friends, and employers. The client may feel lost and frustrated and not understand why things are changing so rapidly. To put it simply, the client may be healing and feeling better but what about the situational factors that make up his or her life? Mental illness and related disorders can affect the individual's total biopsychosocial and spiritual environment. While biological processes as in the case of depression are affected by the illness so are the psychological, social, and spiritual spheres of the client's life. Psychologically the client with a mental disorder encounters feelings of anxiety, self-doubt, frustration, hopelessness, inadequacy, and many other difficult emotions. Although medication may alleviate the physiological symptoms of mental illness the client oftentimes must learn to identify, understand, and resolve the psychological and emotional remnants of the illness. Psychosocial interventions in conjunction with medication can help the client with this process and can also assist the client in developing new coping skills to handle situations and stresses. A client's social and spiritual spheres also require the problem-solving processes inherent in counseling. It is not uncommon for individuals with mental disorders to create or experience alienation and isolation from friends, social supports systems, and their spiritual frame of reference. Again, medication can address biological symptoms, and psychosocial interventions can enhance and restore the client's social and spiritual functioning. What about the family members and others who now have higher expectations of performance? In this case the use of the medication can assist the client, but counseling for both the client and those in the environment remains essential for the continued success of the intervention process.

CASE EXAMPLE: JOHN

John came to the social worker on the recommendation of his physician. He reported that he felt sad, depressed, and alone ever since his wife threatened to leave him and end their ten-year marriage. Upon evaluation, it became clear to the social worker that John had the idea and a concrete and immediate plan for harming himself, and the social worker immediately sought admission to an inpatient facility for this client. The social worker handled both the outpatient and the inpatient admissions for the facility so she was able to follow John after his admission. John was immediately placed on an antidepressant medication. After one week in the hospital he reported that he was feeling better, and it was obvious to all who were treating him that his depression was indeed lifting. The social worker was not convinced. She remained concerned that John still had many personal issues regarding his marriage and family that remained problematic. He had made little progress in exploring alternate problem-solving strategies for handling the rejection and abandonment if his wife refused to continue the marriage. His wife did not visit him in the hospital and declined an invitation to meet with the social worker for counseling. John openly stated that he was sure he had to make his marriage work and convince his wife that they should stay together. After a brief interview with the psychiatrist John convinced him that he needed to go home on pass to talk to his wife under the supervision of his brother. He agreed to a trial three-hour pass, and his brother was to pick him up and drive him to and from the hospital. The social worker disagreed with this plan but eventually relented after documenting John's repeated statements that he would not harm himself and no longer had a plan or felt the need to end his life. He now believed that things could be better, and blamed much of what had happened between him and his wife on his depression. He was given the pass and his brother arrived as planned.

John never returned from his pass. His brother said that after fighting with his wife John said he was just going to run to the store to cool off and get a pack of cigarettes. He was found later that day locked in his car at a local shopping plaza having taken his own life with a gun. No one really knows what happened.

Cases like this are not unusual, particularly with the advent of medications that work quickly to relieve the signs and symptoms of depression. There have been many debates in the field about whether the newer antidepressants such as Prozac are related to higher suicide rates or whether higher suicide rates are related to the fact that the depression is lifting. Most professionals agree that a person is most likely to harm himself or herself when the depression starts to lift, for it is during this phase of treatment that the client has more energy and drive for all types of action. In cases such as this one it is important not to place blame. The social worker must not be lulled into believing that the underlying depression itself is no longer a problem just because the symptoms have abated. It is obvious that antidepressant medication can help individuals to feel better, but as a sole modality it may indeed fall short, as evidenced by what happened to John. This case reaffirms why social workers need to be aware of medications and how they affect clients during psychosocial interventions.

MEDICATION AS A FORM OF TREATMENT

Compared to other forms of treatment, prescription medications are newcomers, especially in the fight against mental illness. For social work professionals in the field, the last 30 years have been a whirlwind of activity that has turned the focus of mental health treatment from the traditional psychoanalytic approaches of counseling. This shift from long-term counseling is linked directly to a more descriptive method of mental health-care delivery that utilizes a biological or medical framework. It is supported by numerous medication-based studies, conducted primarily by drug companies, showing that medication alone can be a viable and often effective form of treatment. Managed care with its emphasis on quick stabilization, rapid assessments, and time-limited treatment has contributed to the increase in medication regimens as the sole intervention for mental health problems (Dziegielewski, 1998).

When medications are used as the solitary treatment modality, often they may fall short in addressing exogenous or external factors. Of all visits to primary health care providers, 70% to 80% are by individuals suffering from psycho-physiological illness (Corbin, Hanson, Happ, & Whitby, 1988). This proves the importance of recognizing the relationship between the psychological aspects of an illness and those that are physical, medical, or biological. In addition, although drugs may have a profound effect on cognition, mood, and behaviors they rarely change the underlying disease process (Schatzberg & Cole, 1991). A disease process is often influenced by situational and environmental stresses, and as described in the case example of John, there are many issues that cannot be defined or addressed easily. The use of medication can result in a false sense of security with regard to the "curative" nature of medicines. The studies that have been completed on the effectiveness of medication often foster unrealistic expectations about the benefits of medication.

Many professionals have questioned the assumption that these medications are profoundly effective particularly in treating mental health problems; and when medication is used as the sole method of treatment, core aspects of the disease and the resulting problems often go untreated (Gitlin, 1996).

There are several reasons that psychopharmacology is used as a primary treatment modality. First, medications are often used to treat acute short-term conditions because they alleviate symptoms (Gitlin, 1996). For example, aspirin can diminish the acute symptomatology of the flu by reducing fever and muscle ache, and antidepressants can lift depression. Second, medications can be used to prevent relapse. And third, they can prevent recurrence of the disorder (Gitlin, 1996). This is particularly important when clients can relapse into the same episode that the treatment was designed to alleviate. In addition, if a full course of a medication is not completed, it is often possible for the client to produce drug resistant bacteria. When taking an antibiotic, clients are usually instructed to continue the medication beyond the typical course of the illness to ensure that a full compliment of the medication has been delivered, to discourage relapse, and to prevent a recurrence. Unfortunately, the trend that results in discontinuance, as well as an eventual building of resistance for some bacteria to treatment has led to experts the world over advocating for ways to prolong the life of antibiotics as well as the development of new "miracle drugs" (Nordenburg, 1998).

In using medication as a treatment modality, there are three courses of therapy that are usually identified: acute, continuation, and maintenance (Gitlin, 1996). Acute treatment addresses the symptoms of an active problem or disorder such as taking lithium to reduce the active symptoms of mania. The continuation phase is designed to prevent relapse. The last course of therapy is maintenance. In the maintenance phase, prevention is emphasized, and medications are used as needed or as symptoms arise (acute treatment), or they can be given to prevent recurrences of the disorder (maintenance treatment). In maintenance treatment, a client is often encouraged to take ongoing doses of the medication to prevent a recurrence.

Social workers need to be aware of the basics of medication usage as a form of treatment. They must also know how it can affect the client, with or without *verbal therapy*. Today, most professionals agree that the current purpose of using medication as a treatment modality is twofold. First, individuals suffering from crippling mental illness can return to the community instead of spending years in hospitals. Second, it can help scientists to better understand mental illness and the etiology of mental and medical conditions. Medications are remarkable in that they have allowed us to cure some diseases, reduce suffering, and markedly improve the quality of life for individuals, but only when they are used correctly (Simonson, 1994).

PRESCRIPTION MEDICATIONS

When a client is prescribed a medication there are often two names listed.

Example: Prozac (flouxetine hydrochloride)

In this case the first name listed (Prozac), which represents a popular antidepressive medication, is the brand name of the medication. This name was chosen by the company (Lilly Research Laboratories) that produced the medication and originally petitioned the FDA for the patent. The second name, often put in parentheses, is the chemical name of the product. If a generic medication is available it will be referred to by the chemical name (see chapter 3, for a more in-depth explanation of the difference between brand names and generic medications). Although it may initially seem confusing to clients taking these medications, prescribers and other professional helpers may use either name when referring to a medication. For example, if a physician prescribes the brand-name medication Prozac and a generic equivalent were available, it would most likely be substituted. If a prescriber does not want the client to take a chemical equivalent, it would be specified that no substitutions should be permitted.

As will be explained further in chapter 3, it is critical to know the differences between whether a medication is biomedically equivalent and therapeutically equivalent. Drugs are considered biomedically equivalent by the FDA if they are chemically equivalent and deliver the same level of administered dose to the system (Haynes, Patterson, & Wade, 1992). This does not include what are sometimes referred to as "medication fringes." For example, ingredients such as coating and coloring or other additives that are not strictly part of the chemical make-up of the medication are not included as part of the chemical make-up of the medication and can be considered medication fringes. That is why many times clients will state that the biomedical equivalent of a brand name medication does not taste the same or is a different color when dissolved. The best example to illustrate this point is to think about taking an aspirin that is coated and one that is not. Although the ingredients are the same for both aspirins, the taste is not. If it sits in your mouth too long before swallowing, you most assuredly can taste the difference between the two pills, as the absence of the protective coating allows the ingredients to dissolve more quickly in the mouth. Therefore, the pills taste different, although they are said to be biochemically equivalent.

The second factor to be considered is if the medication is therapeutically equivalent. Medications are considered therapeutically equivalent if they provide the same efficacy and controls for toxicity (Haynes et al., 1992). The question posed here is, can the medication help the client achieve the same results, even if it is not chemically the same as another similar medication? If a medication is therapeutically equivalent, the same effect is achieved clinically (e.g., headache goes away) but the chemical ingredients are not exactly the same as the other medication. This is particularly important for some agencies in which money is allocated to purchase medications in bulk. This bulk purchase requires that certain therapeutically equivalent medications be purchased and used based on their cost-savings features (Haynes et al., 1992). Cost-effective measures often result in managed care companies changing medications that they deem too costly. In these cases social workers must not only be aware of such changes in the client's medication regimen, but also empower clients to advocate and negotiate with their physicians and insurance companies whenever possible that effective medications not be changed purely for economic reasons.

Reports have now surfaced showing that the cost of medications used to treat clients that suffer from mental health problems can be influenced by whether the client is treated on an inpatient basis (Mental Health Report, 1999a) or an outpatient basis (Mental Health Report, November, 1999). When receiving care under the auspice of a particular hospital or program, these individuals may have limited medications due to the cost factors involved. To facilitate treatment progress it has been argued that the newer brand-name medications need to be considered because although they are more expensive they can have fewer side effects. For social workers, the reality of the service provider's environment (i.e., company serving the client or insurance reimbursement requirements) in helping to get the best choice for the client in terms of medication available cannot be underestimated.

The fact that each individual is different and may require a slightly different compound of a medication to get relief has lead some prescribers and other health professionals to customize prescription medications by compounding (Nordenberg, 2000). *Compounding* can involve nothing more than crushing medications into a powder with a mortar bowl and pestle (a crushing tool) and later turning them into a liquid. In 1997, as part of the FDA Modernization Act, which defines the limits of compounding, this practice has become more common. Compounding prescription medications can be very helpful for those who have allergies to certain substances such as product fillers or dyes or for individuals who cannot swallow tablets or capsules and need a liquid form (Nordenberg, 2000). Regardless, of the purpose compounding can be useful but since the compound itself has not been subject to the testing required of all approved drugs by the FDA, it should be used with caution. According to Nordenberg (2000) whenever possible the FDA would recommend that an approved drug be used before a compound is attempted.

For more information on pharmacy compounding, try the FDA's Web site at: www.fda.gov/cder/pharmcomp/

Another important area of concern with prescription medications is the possibility of a medication error occurring. With the entire prescription process there is room for error of all types (Zellmer, 1993). Errors can happen anywhere in the medication process and can occur as early as when the prescription is first read or written. To stress the seriousness of these errors some professionals are requesting that clients be given the actual medication on discharge from a facility, rather than a prescription (Johnson et al., 1996). The most common examples of medication errors include: illegible handwriting, improper transcription, inaccurate dosage calculation, and inappropriate abbreviations used in prescribing and labeling errors (ASHP Report, 1993). Recently, drug product nomenclature of look-alike and sound-alike names can lead to prescriptions being filled incorrectly (Allan, Barker, Malloy, & Heller, 1995). Tracking of this problem has revealed that filling the prescription with the wrong medication is much too often an occurrence for comfort and can result in dangerous health situations for clients (Allan et al., 1995; Cohen, 1994). To track medication errors and interaction effects one of the latest advancements involves the creation of a databases that detect drug interaction effects, allergies, contraindications, side effects, duplicate therapy as well as ensuring the safety and efficacy of the medications used (De Angelo, 2000). It is hoped that services such as these Internet connections can serve to reduce medical and prescribing errors protecting the client.

Social workers also need to be actively involved in medication compliance. Many times medication errors occur because clients are not compliant and do not adhere to the medication regime outlined. There can be numerous reasons for this from being instructed to take several prescriptions at different times throughout the day, to ambiguous prescribing principles (ASHP Report, 1993). For example, if a prescription is given twice a day (BID) what exactly does that mean? Does the client take the medication every 8 hours or when awakening and before going to sleep? Physicians often disagree about the exactness of these prescribed schedules; therefore it is not uncommon for clients to be confused. In addition, clients may be unsure of what aspects of the medication or treatment regime are most important to learn (Airaksinen, Ahonen, & Enlund, 1993). When clients first begin medication they are often confused about instructions to lower or increase their dosage depending on the feelings or symptoms presented. In these cases clients do not trust their own feelings and may either take too much or too little needed medication.

The American Society of Hospital Pharmacists (ASHP) recommends that the best way to approach the problem of medication errors is through the use of an interdisciplinary team approach. Social workers, who generally are part of these teams, need to examine and exemplify their role.

There are several things social work professionals can do to assist the team in this process. First, they can help in recognizing and reporting medication errors. Second, while spending quality time with the client they can ask about and monitor client responses to the medications they have been given. Particularly noting side effect profiles, excessive sleepiness, and impaired functioning. Third, social workers can help to note any particular problems with dosing schedules or other noncompliance issues that may result. Fourth, they can help with educating the client and family members to all the considerations that should be noted when using medications (Bently & Walsh, 1996). When the social worker cannot offer an immediate response to a medication question the information should be obtained and provided to the client at the next session. Last, social workers need to help clients learn about the medications that they are taking. They need to provide clients with a general understanding of how the medications work and encourage clients to develop a sense of entitlement and comfort in seeking medication information from the physician or the local pharmacist (Airaksinen, Ahonen, & Enlund, 1993).

NONPRESCRIPTION MEDICATIONS

Health care social workers are well versed in prescription medication; however, too little emphasis is placed on use of nonprescription (over-the-counter [OTC]) medications in the professional helping environment. Today, more and more nonprescription medications are becoming available to clients. The reader will note that many of the concerns that were expressed in this chapter in regard to the prescription medications will often apply to the nonprescription medications as well. After all, a considerable number of these OTC medications were previously known as prescription medications. To date, there are over 600 products now available without a prescription (Nordenberg, 1998), ranging from heartburn medications to nicotine patches. Clients may often assume that a nonprescription medication cannot be harmful, but nothing could be further from the truth. They can produce powerful side effects and negative interactions with other prescription and nonprescription drugs.

In the past, little attention was paid to OTC medications. However, the number and type of these medications now available to clients has grown tremendously. This increase is closely related to the trend for self-treatment and gives clients or consumers of health care the ability to direct, implement and thus control their own course of treatment. Because more people want to self-diagnose and monitor their own treatment some pharmacies have adapted services such as Healthwatch and have installed blood pressure machines in their stores (Ralston, 2000). According to the 1992 Heller Research Group study, 85% of Americans felt it was important that over-the-counter medications be available to relieve minor medical problems (Heller, 1993). This demand and the expected profits have encouraged drug manufacturers to switch from prescription to nonprescription. In implementing this change it is essential that the labels of these medications have simple and easily understood directions so that self-diagnosis and self-treatment is possible for most adults.

The reason for choosing an OTC medication instead of a prescription medication should not be based on the strength of the medication. Over-the-counter medications can be just as powerful as prescription ones, however, they are generally dispensed at lower doses (Nordenberg, 1998). Social workers need to be aware of and dispel the myth that increased amounts of a medication can be more effective. It can actually make it worse because at times mixing OTC and prescription medications can be a dangerous combination without the client ever suspecting the problems that can occur from such a combination.

The use of over-the-counter medications can be a significant problem with older people, who make up 13% of the population according to the National Center for Health Services Research and Health Care Technology estimates. Adults over the age of 65 purchase 30% of all prescription drugs and 40% of all nonprescription drugs. Two-thirds of adults over 65 use one or more drugs daily and older persons use an average of three prescription and nonprescription drugs at any given time (Beizer, 1994; Cohen, 2000). "Start low and go slow" is a well-known precaution when working with older individuals because of adverse drug reactions in this population. In patients 60 and older, about 51% of deaths occur from adverse drug reactions (Cohen, 2000).

The sheer numbers and increasing trend to use these medications in today's health care environment compel social workers not to underestimate, neglect, or minimize the effects of these medications in the treatment process. These medications, similar to prescription drugs, can easily interact or cause toxicity when used in conjunction with other medications. The social worker's awareness and knowledge of the effects that OTC medications can have on the therapeutic environment is essential.

COMPLEMENTARY HEALTH CARE AND
HERBAL REMEDIES

The authors believe that any discussion of medications in today's practice environment would not be complete if it did not include herbal treatments and remedies. The knowledge of herbal medication is so important that an entire chapter is dedicated to it. Herbal medications and remedies are not new, although interest has waxed and waned and dates back extensively. The resurgence of interest, however, is clearly documented (*PDR for Herbal Medicines*, 1999; Reaves, 2000).

Today a significant number of Americans are self-medicating with a combination of nonprescription and herbal medicines. Often herbal remedies and treatments are being used that can interact with prescription and nonprescription medications, and the U.S. Food and Drug administration does not regulate herbal medications that are used as dietary supplements. This permits commercial preparation without monitoring these products, allowing the potency of the product to vary considerably. With the lack of regulation that ensures standardization, it is possible that some herbs contain no pharmacological ingredients at all. If individuals report effects from these inactive ingredients, it can be related to placebo effects or the vague claims that are used in the advertisements of the product. Some herbs can contain active pharmacological ingredients that can be toxic and standards of quality often vary from one manufacturer to another or from one batch of the product to another. The loophole that allows manufacturers of herbal and dietary supplements a great deal of leeway in making unsubstantiated health claims is the 1994 Dietary Supplement Health and Education Act (DSHEA). Under DSHEA, complementary medicines can be labeled and sold as dietary supplements and remain exempt from the strict pharmacological regulations as their prescription and OTC counterparts (Murphy, 1999).

The United States lacks a regulatory system for herbal products, particularly those that are marketed as food and dietary supplements (Herbal Drugs: Medicines or Food Supplements, 2000; Zink & Chaffin, 1998). Since "no legal standards are applied to their harvesting, processing or packaging, the possibilities of poor quality, adulteration, contamination and varying strengths must be kept in mind" when evaluating their use with clients (Zink & Chaffin, 1998, p. 1133). This information is essential for the social worker especially since clients may be lulled into believing that products claiming to be "natural and safe" actually are. These new products with their so-called "natural ingredients" have the potential to depreciate mental health problems and inadvertently minimize the need for and advantages of counseling. However, it should never be assumed that something is safe because it is natural; these remedies can interact adversely with other pharmaceutical agents. The client and the social worker both can benefit from always remembering that any medication that is strong enough to help also has the power to hurt, if not taken correctly. Therefore, any medication (herbal or otherwise) that is strong enough to produce a therapeutic benefit can also produce an unexpected side effect. Taking a medication correctly can avoid adverse reactions and provide the greatest benefit (Nordenberg, 1997).

Nonprescription and herbal remedies will be discussed further in this text. These types of medications are especially relevant to social work practice as they reflect a pattern of clients taking charge of their own health and health needs. Social work professionals have long encouraged the process of self-determination and client empowerment. The uneducated, misinformed, or unaware client may unwittingly cause harm to himself or herself without the necessary information to determine if the medication is safe, indicated, and appropriate for a specific situation. Therefore, social workers need to ask clients about past and current medication use and accept the responsibility to help clients explore medication related issues that clearly impact their health and wellness and can also impede the psychosocial intervention process. In the field of professional social work, it appears that psychopharmacology is a flourishing area of practice that continues to expand and is generating a resurgence of interest and debate.

THE ROLE OF THE SOCIAL WORK PROFESSIONAL

Social workers have historically been active in working with psychiatrists, primary care physicians, and other health professionals who are involved in most aspects of psychiatric treatment, including the monitoring and dispensing of medications (Cohen, 1994). Although the exact role that social workers perform can vary, it generally involves encouraging medication compliance, monitoring side effects, and educating and assisting clients and their families about medication use (Bently, 1997; Bently & Walsh, 1998; Dziegielewski, 1998).

One issue that should not be overlooked and that differentiates social workers from other professionals is based primarily on the inclusion of the "person in situation" or "person in environment perspective" that has long since been part of the professional foundation of social work. This core concept enables social workers to understand clients within a biopsychosocial and spiritual framework and allows the practitioner to integrate medication regimens and related issues into the helping process. Understanding and appreciating the client's total situation has identified the social worker as a valuable team member who is often called upon to assist other professionals in understanding the psychosocial and spiritual dynamics that surround medication use and abuse.

Today, the actual role the social work professional should assume in this area continues to cause controversy within the profession. Some social workers believe that understanding medications and assisting clients who are taking them is an essential aspect of the social worker's professional role (Bently, 1997), whereas others advocate an even more openly active and directive role in medication knowledge and use that includes advocating for social workers to receive limited prescription privileges (Dziegielewski, 1997).

It is obvious that in today's environment there is less emphasis on psychosocial models and interventions as the sole treatment modality. An understanding of conjoint psychopharmacology and counseling has become a practice reality for the social work professional. In addition, the role of the social worker can add an important component to the use of medications by introducing how medications can and are often influenced by environmental and other psychosocial and spiritual factors. These environmental factors are of particular importance when addressing medication use and compliance issues in the health care environment.

SUMMARY AND FUTURE CONSIDERATIONS

Knowledge of medications has become a practice necessity for social workers. The social worker may be the first to recognize (a) the need for medication changes or adjustments; (b) side effects related to the medications being taken; (c) the need to assess and monitor a client; and (d) which medications might work best and have not yet been prescribed. These expectations can be a particular problem for rural health care social workers who may be unable to get the professional support and additional information needed. Professional social workers are important to the inter-disciplinary team and can assist in providing improved communication, coordination, and referral between primary health, mental health, and community-based programs (Van Hook, 1996).

Medications in use today include more than prescription drugs. There are numerous alternative medicines and treatment strategies that are gaining in popularity. Social workers encounter clients who want to rely less on traditional medications and more on alternative or holistic preparations. These alternate approaches may include acupuncture, exercise, nutrition, and herbal medicines (Lee & Carlin, 1997).

Although the FDA can basically monitor many of the claims made for traditional medicines, the client has easy access to these alternative medicines, and self-medicating is a practice reality. The medical community and the FDA often discourage the use of alternate medications, but interest and use continues to rise (Ullman, 1993). The medical climate is also changing, and physicians are becoming more aware of alternate medicine. In the future it may be common practice to include alternative strategies as part of the treatment regimen for clients.

In order to complete the advocacy and broker functions basic in the field of social work, an accurate assessment and referral process must be assumed with regard to the use of medication. Professional social workers must consider the various types of medications a client is taking, whether they are prescription, alternative, or over-the-counter remedies. Whether the more radical stance is taken to actually provide enough education to enable limited prescription privileges as suggested by Dziegielewski (1997) or the more conservative role is adopted, as suggested by Bently (1997), it is clear that social workers must have at minimum a general knowledge of medications. All social workers must be familiar with side effect profiles, dosage routines, and compliance issues in order to assist clients in obtaining and maintaining the most therapeutically productive treatment possible. Social workers must be able to recognize potential problem areas in order to refer the client for adequate or revised treatment.

This chapter is not meant to be all-inclusive of the concerns that social workers may have with regard to medication. It is written in the hope that it will provide basic information for the health and mental health social worker and that it will encourage the social worker to seek and learn more in this area. We will next provide a simple overview of how medications work.

REFERENCES

Airaksinen, M., Ahonen, R., & Enlund, H. (1993). Drug information for pharmacies: Desire for more spontaneous information. *Medical Care, 31,* 846–850.
Allan, E. L., Barker, K. N., Malloy, M. J., & Heller, W. M. (1995). Dispensing errors and counseling in community practice. *American Pharmacy, NS35,* 25–33.
American Society of Hospital Pharmacies Report. (1993). ASHP guidelines on preventing medication errors in hospitals. *American Journal of Hospital Pharmacy, 50,* 305–314.
Beizer, J. L. (1994). Medications and the aging body: Alteration as a function of age. *Generations, XVIII*(2), 13–18.
Bently, K. J. (1997). Should clinical social workers seek psychotropic medication prescription privileges?: No. In B. A. Thyer (Ed.), *Controversial issues in social work practice* (pp. 152–165). Boston: Allyn & Bacon.
Bently, K. J., & Walsh, J. (1996). *The social worker and psychotropic medication: Toward effective collaboration with mental health clients, families, and providers.* Pacific Grove, CA: Brooks/Cole.
Cohen, M. R. (1994). Medication errors: Second-guessing and soundalike generic names. *Nursing, 94,* 29.
Cohen, S. J. (2000). Avoiding adverse reactions—effective lower dose drug therapies for older patients. *Geriatrics, 55*(2), 54–56.
Corbin, L., Hanson, R., Happ, S., & Whitby, A. (1988). Somatoform disorders. *Journal of Psychosocial Nursing, 26,* 31–34.
De Angelo, M. (2000). Internet solution reduces medical errors. *Health Management Technology, 21*(2), 20.
Dziegielewski, S. F. (1991). Social group work with family members who have a relative suffering from dementia: A controlled evaluation. *Research on Social Work Practice, 1,* 4, 358–370.
Dziegielewski, S. F. (1996). Managed care principles: The need for social work in the health care environment. *Crisis Intervention, 3,* 97–111.
Dziegielewski, S. F. (1997). Should clinical social workers seek psychotropic medication prescription privileges?: Yes. In B. A. Thyer (Ed.), *Controversial issues in social work practice* (pp. 152–165). Boston: Allyn & Bacon.
Dziegielewski, S. F. (1998). *The changing face of health care social work; Professional practice in the era of managed care.* New York: Springer.
Dziegielewski, S. F. (1998). Psychopharmacology and social work practice: Introduction. *Research on Social Work Practice, 8,* 371–383.
Gitlin, M. J. (1996). *The psychotherapist guide to psychopharmacology* (2nd ed.). New York: Free Press.
Haynes, L. M., Patterson, A. A., & Wade, S. U. (1992). Drug information service for drug product procurement in veterans' affairs health-care system:

Preliminary experience. *American Journal of Hospital Pharmacy, 49*, 595–598.

Herbal drugs: Medicines or food supplements? (2000, January). *Manufacturing Chemist, 16,* 27.

Heller, W. M. (1993). Initial responses to recommendations of the blue-ribbon committee on generic medicines. *American Journal of Hospital Pharmacy, 50,* 318–321.

Henkel, J. (1998). Reporting adverse reactions and other product problems. *FDA Consumer, 32*(6), 7–15.

Johnson, K. B., Butta, J. K., Donohue, P. K., Glenn, D. J., & Holtzman, N. A. (1996). Discharging patients with prescriptions instead of medications: Sequelae in a teaching hospital. *Pediatrics, 97,* 481–496.

Kotulak, R. (1997). *Inside the brain: Revolutionary discoveries of how the mind works.* Kansas City, MO: Andrews McMeel.

Lambert, M. J. (1992). Psychotherapy outcome research: Implications for integrative and eclectic therapists. In J. C. Cross & M. R. Goldfried (Eds.), *Handbook of psychotherapy integration* (pp. 94–129). New York: Basic Books.

Lazarus, A. A. (1997). *Brief but comprehensive psychotherapy: The multi-modal way.* New York: Springer Publishing Co.

Lee, K., & Carlin, P. (1997). Should you try mind-body medicine? *Health, 1,* 77–78.

Mental Health Report. (1999a, October 29). VP Gore pledges support for mental health parity (p. 166). Silver Spring, MD: Business Publishers.

Mental Health Report. (1999b, November 12). Outpatients face higher hurdle to getting new antipsychotics (p. 174). Silver Spring, MD: Business Publishers.

Miller, R. S., Weideman, G. H., & Linn, L. (1980). Prescribing psychotropic drugs: Whose responsibility? *Social Work in Health Care, 6,* 51–61.

Mosher, L. R. (1999, September/October). Are psychiatrists betraying their patients? *Psychology Today, 32,* 40–41; 80.

Murphy, J. M. (1999). Preoperative considerations with herbal medicines. *AORN Journal, 69,* 1, 174.

Nordenberg, T. (1997). New drug label spells it out simply. *FDA Consumer, 32,* 29–32.

Nordenberg, T. (1998). Miracle drugs vs. super bugs: Preserving the usefulness of antibiotics. *FDA Consumer, 32*(6), 23–25.

Nordenberg, T. (1999, September–October). When is a medical product too risky? *FDA Consumer,* 8–13.

Physicians' Desk Reference. (2000). *Physicians' desk reference* (54th ed.). Montvale, NJ: Medical Economics.

Physicians' Desk Reference. (2000). *Physicians' desk reference for herbal medicines* (2nd ed.). Montvale, NJ: Medical Economics.

Prufer, D. (1996, April). Is your medicine safe? What pharmacists don't tell you. *Good Housekeeping, 222,* 137–138.

Ralston, J. (2000). Beyond pill pushing: How shoppers' drug mart positions itself above the pharmacy fray. *Marketing, 105*(12), 19.

Reaves, J. (2000, January 6). If you choose the herbal life, it is buyer beware. *Times Daily* (n.d.).

Schatzberg, A. F., & Cole, J. O. (1991). *Manual of clinical psychopharmacology* (2nd ed.). Washington, DC: American Psychiatric Press.

Simonson, W. (1994). Maximizing the benefits of drug therapy for older people— and minimizing the risks: Quality of life is the key. *Generations, XVIII*(2), 5–7.

Ullman, D. (1993). Renegade remedies? The medical establishment is turning a blind—and biased eye—to the alternative-medicine boom. *Utne Reader, 60,* 42–44.

Van Hook, M. P. (1996). Challenges to identifying and treating women with depression in rural primary care. *Social Work in Health Care, 23*(3), 73–92.

Walter, K. (2000). Will teenagers disappear? *Time, 55,* 60.

Zellmer, W. A. (1993). Medication error versus medication misadventure— what's in a name? *American Journal of Hospital Pharmacy, 50,* 315–317.

Zink, T., & Chaffin, J. (1998). Herbal health products: What family physicians need to know. *American Family Physician, 58,* 1133–1140.

CHAPTER 2

Understanding How Medications Work

This chapter will highlight basic biomedical knowledge that is essential for understanding the use of medication and the role it plays in the psychosocial intervention. Fundamental issues about the brain and the nervous system are also discussed in a practical manner that is relevant to social work. In this chapter, we advocate that all healthcare professionals learn how to communicate effectively with clients who are taking prescribed medications (FDA Consumer, 1997).

The abundance of information now available to the nonprofessional can result in conflicting information that is available to the lay public and increases the possibility of misinterpretation. Social workers must acquire a working knowledge of how medications should and do work. It is important to recognize that the self-help information available on the Internet gives clients easier access to information about medication and that the Internet has become a supplier for prescription and nonprescription drugs and herbal remedies with no physician's visit necessary (Associated Press, 1998). This type of access reinforces the consumer's right to control one's own health and mental health, but ensuring competent and effective use of medications then becomes a more complicated challenge (Friebert & Greely, 1999). Although client self-determination is encouraged, it is important to remind the client to approach with caution any information they obtain from newspapers, television, or the Internet (Larkin, 1996), as some of these claims may be unsubstantiated. Clients must learn to investigate carefully whether a particular medication is appropriate for their specific and unique situation. The role of the social worker is central to helping clients secure and interpret accurate and relevant product information. Social workers should make it their responsibility to help clients obtain the most up-to-date information available and assist them in determining the credibility of the information. This empowers clients to determine if the medication in question is appropriate for them.

CASE EXAMPLE: JOAN

Joan, a 30-year-old single parent with little free time or extra money, began to experience flu-like symptoms. They were not severe enough to keep her home from work, and she decided against a trip to the physician because she was concerned about the co-payment required by her insurance company. She stopped at the pharmacy and decided that some type of cough-and-cold medicine might relieve her headache and runny nose. The preparation she bought was a standard over-the-counter cough preparation. When she finally got home Joan was feeling rather tired and decided that increasing the dosage might help her sleep. She took two full tablespoons of the medication and went to bed, but about an hour later she started feeling sicker. Her head throbbed, she began feeling nauseous, and then vomited. She tried but could not fall asleep, her palms were sweating, and her heart raced. Afraid of what was happening, she went into the kitchen and reread the label. The directions read two teaspoons, and she realized she had taken more than double the prescribed dose for adults. There was also a warning of drug interaction with certain types of antidepressants and advice to contact a physician before using the medicine. Joan was taking such a medication—Prozac—that her physician had prescribed for Joan's depression and to control her appetite. She called her neighbor to help with the children and was taken to the hospital for assessment and treatment.

Fortunately for Joan there were no serious repercussions, but cases like this are not uncommon. She probably experienced a serious side effect: first from overdosing and then by combining a cold preparation with another medication that it specifically warned against. She did not read the directions carefully and compounded the problem by using a common household tablespoon, which is not standardized in size.

Unfortunately, many people like Joan are lulled into a false sense of security that over-the-counter preparations are safe because they are sold without a prescription and are available at any pharmacy. And many are not aware that over-the-counter preparations can produce an interaction.

According to the Food and Drug Administration (FDA), 50% of all consumers simply do not take medicine as prescribed or they take it without proper professional supervision. One reason cited for this trend is that too many people (primarily women) neglect their own health because of busy schedules and a lack of time (Friebert & Greely, 1999).

MEDICATIONS, EMOTIONS, AND THE BRAIN

It is beyond the scope of this chapter to explain the basic anatomy and physiology of the brain, but there are numerous medications that directly affect brain function. The 1990s are recognized as a period of major progress in this field and though research has uncovered valuable information it is still in its infancy stage. As we learn more about the effect of medications on brain processes we will better understand its complexity and versatility. Research has substantiated the importance of viewing human beings from a holistic approach because of the interdependent relationship between mind, body, and emotions.

Most social workers are not trained in the biomedical aspects of the brain, but it is essential that as practitioners they gain a general working knowledge of this organ and how it affects a client's physical and mental states. For this purpose, we will provide a brief review and specifically address the role and function of the neuron. This chapter is meant to highlight the synergy between brain processes, medications, and the psychosocial counseling relationship.

In every respect, the brain is the most intricate organ of the human body. Two of the most astounding and profound discoveries to come out of research are (a) how the brain uses information from the environment to shape how it functions; and (b) how the brain must go through crucial periods of specific stimulation in order to develop abilities such as language, smell, vision, muscle control, and reasoning (Kotulak, 1997). In light of these discoveries, it is not surprising that our personality traits, thought processes, and behaviors are linked and greatly influenced by the way our brain functions.

There has been considerable debate among scientific professionals about whether mental illness is biological or organic in nature (Kotulak, 1997). Although this question is by no means settled, it appears that aspects of both are involved. Through brain-mapping and biochemistry we can identify and link emotions and behaviors to specific areas of the brain (Kotulak, 1997). It is now known that certain mental health conditions and the dysfunctional behaviors that result can be directly linked to chemical activity within certain areas of the brain. For example, in paranoia clients may experience feelings that result in the distorted perception that someone is out to get them or wants to harm them. It now appears that these feelings and emotions can be traced directly to the brain and its neurochemicals. The neurochemicals and the interactions that occur within the brain can clearly be linked to other mental health behaviors as well.

NEURONS, NEUROTRANSMITTERS, AND BRAIN ACTIVITY

To understand the relationship between the brain and emotions, behaviors and feelings, some description of the neuron is necessary. The neuron, which is the basic functional unit of the nervous system, is a highly specialized cell responsible for signal transduction and information processing (Coyle & Enna, 1998). Basically the neuron serves one primary purpose and that is to receive, conduct, and transmit signals to the other cells. The signals are transmitted from cell to cell at specialized contact sites called synapses, which are the gaps between neurons. Messages are transmitted within the brain in two ways: electrically and chemically. Electrical impulses are limited because they cannot bridge the synapse so creation and continuation of the messages is dependent on chemical messengers. Chemical messengers are often referred to as neurochemicals or neurotransmitters. Actually, the words "neurochemical" and "neurotransmitter" are often used interchangeably. To explore the relationship between the brain and emotions, further understanding the development process of the neurotransmitter is important because these chemicals are synthesized within the neuron from precursors that are brought in by outside cells. Enzymes within the neuron break down the precursor and ultimately form the neurotransmitter.

Although social workers do not have to be experts in neurochemicals or neurotransmission, a basic understanding of this function can clarify the primary role that neurotransmitters play in creating or minimizing the symptoms that clients exhibit. According to Coyle and Enna (1998), knowledge of the basic neurotransmitters and the principles of neurochemical transmissions provides a context for understanding how and why brain activity is influenced. Actually, some knowledge about the role of the neurotransmitter is essential because it is these chemicals that are basically responsible for the connection of all communication in the brain. Communication within the brain starts with an electrical impulse that is initiated or triggered by sound. This impulse causes the neuron to release a chemical into the synapse. Since the electrical impulse that has been created cannot bridge the synaptic gap, the neurotransmitters act as chemical messengers to create the connection that completes the unification process. The presence of the chemical in the receptor sparks an electrical impulse in the neuron, and the sequence continues until a thought, a feeling, or a behavior is initiated (Coyle & Enna, 1998).

For example, we know there is a relationship between a common neurochemical called serotonin and depressive symptoms. We have learned that serotonin is a relatively simple neurochemical that appears vital to the brain's regulation of many bodily functions such as sleep, appetite, muscular activity, breathing, and blood circulation, and abnormal secretion levels have been blamed for a large number of mental and physical problems, including depression, obsessive-compulsive disorder, and panic disorder (Hickling, 2000). A depressed individual desperately tries to control feelings that may be the result of internal causes (endogenous factors) rather than environmental causes (exogenous factors). When released, serotonin will fit into a specifically shaped receptor, diminishing the emotional and behavioral manifestations of the client's depressive mood. Marano (1999) warns that this process might not be as simple as it seems. He believes evidence exists to indicate that a neurodegenerative process can occur in cases of recurrent depression. The previous structure and function of brain cells are affected, resulting in the destruction of nerve cell connections, which in turn can precipitate further cognitive decline. Serotonin is just one of numerous chemical messengers at work, but researchers will continue to discover new and different neurochemicals that influence thoughts, emotions, and behaviors. As of 1993, at least 50 neurotransmitters related directly to health and emotions had been identified. The complexity of the brain is evident in the discovery of new receptor sites as well. Recently, as many as 16 different serotonin receptor sites in various parts of the brain have been identified, all modulating different basic drives and emotions (Kotulak, 1997). See Table 2.1 for a description of several classic neurotransmitters and their primary relationships to symptomology.

These chemical messengers and their receptor targets regulate basic feelings and emotions and are naturally designed to work together. We used to believe that only one neurochemical was needed to enhance the neurotransmission, but we now know that more than one neurotransmitter is involved in the response–action pattern, a process referred to as colocalization (Lehne & Scott, 1996). In colocalization, the neurochemicals work together to excite the same receptor site, helping to fine-tune the neurotransmission process. For example, dopamine (another neurochemical

TABLE 2.1   Selected Neurotransmitters and Applications

Neurotransmitter	Mental health indications
Dopamine	Psychosis
Norepinephrine	Depression
Serotonin	Depression
Acetycholine	Dementia (Alzheimer's disease, Parkinson's disease)
GABA	Anxiety, sedation, muscle relaxation
Glutamate	Anesthesia

*Selected information adapted from Coyle and Enna (1998).

often involved in mental responses) and serotonin have been shown to play a decisive role in maintaining improved mental health. Historically, when examining the development of psychosis, the neurochemical dopamine was indicated as the primary neurochemical involved in this behavior. Now we know the psychosis does not appear to be related to dopamine alone, but rather to some type of interaction (colocalization) between serotonin and other neurochemicals. Exactly how these chemicals respond to environmental factors to influence the development of psychosis is unknown.

Greater understanding of the use of these neurochemicals and the newer medications that enhance this response is helping to maximize what we know about the brain, thereby enabling the restoration of normal brain chemistry. When a neurotransmitter's level is too high or too low (by as little as 5 or 10%), it can affect the way other neurotransmitters work (Kotulak, 1997) and can trigger a major chemical chain reaction that affects or contributes to a range of mental health behaviors.

Neurochemicals bind at the awaiting receptor sites, and scientists are eager to understand what happens when this binding takes place. Many scientists believe that the receptor is like a closed door and the neurochemical is the key. When binding occurs the door opens. For example, one such "door" has been identified as the 5HT1 serotonin receptor, which affects aggression, mood, and appetite. Receptor 5HT3 plays a role in learning and memory as well as in nausea and vomiting (Kotulak, 1997). Other identified receptors are 5HT2 and 5HT1c, which we know, relate directly to psychosis, depression, alcohol abuse, and mood. By understanding this process we can understand the action–reaction that results. Although the role of the neurotransmitters and the dynamic processes at the receptor sites remain a complicated process, further study of the brain will illuminate this complex process.

In this chapter, we have discussed the role of neurochemicals in the brain as it relates primarily to mental health. Keep in mind, however, that the neurochemicals related to mental health actually make up only a small portion of all neurochemicals in the brain. Some of the general neurotransmitters found in 75 to 90% of all neurotransmissions are glutamate, gama-aminobutyric acid (GABA), and glycine. Many professionals agree that of all of the general neurotransmitters GABA plays a large part in mental health reactions. It has been identified as essential in exciting reactions and initiating many of the chemical transmissions (Coyle & Enna, 1998).

The neurotransmitters that are involved in mental health responses and behavior are less common and are found in approximately 2% of the synapses of the brain (Kotulak, 1997). The most common are norepinephrine, serotonin, and, dopamine.

Although this information may seem somewhat technical for social workers, it is important, as part of an interdisciplinary team, that they understand the use and application of these terms. A basic ability of understanding the brain and how neurochemicals influence behavior will help social workers assist clients, and their families contribute. Understanding how pharmacological interventions affect the client will enable the social worker to participate in discussions and gain credibility as someone who is aware of the purpose, use, benefit, and side-effect profiles of medications. The bottom-line for mental health and health care social workers is that they need to be aware of how different parts of the brain utilize different neurotransmitters. A basic understanding of the process can help the social worker to realize that although there are many different purposes for neurotransmitters, they are all synthesized, stored, released, and inactivated by the same general process.

The role of the neurotransmitter is essential in either exciting a response or inhibiting one. Understanding the role of the brain, the neuron, the neurotransmitter and what happens at the receptor sites can help in delineating how specific responses are generated, encouraged or discouraged through the use of medications. This understanding can be enhanced only by careful observation, taking into account the uniqueness of the individual client served (Henkel, 1998). Because the side effects and the way a client may respond to the medication can differ, monitoring these potential responses by social workers can be invaluable. The professional's role is essential in understanding, relating, and recommending what they believe to be the best course of action for the client based on his or her reaction to medication that is being used as part of the intervention process. For a more detailed presentation of the role of the mental health and the health care social worker in the area of mental health and medication usage see the application chapters in Parts II and III of this text.

REVITALIZATION OF THE BRAIN

Social workers who deal with older people who suffer from brain deterioration are often frustrated by their inability to help their clients. Feelings of helplessness and hopelessness are worsened when the client's family and friends believe that little can be done to help the loved one recover, especially when brain damage and deterioration is suspected. The hopelessness that accompanies these types of illnesses has been a disincentive for many social workers entering the field. All that may be about to change.

One of the biggest problems with the neuron is that this highly specialized cell does not replace itself, which has obvious clinical implications when dealing with a damaged central nervous system (Coyle & Enna, 1998).

The brain's power to heal itself, however, has brought new hope and better understanding for working with clients who suffer from organic brain damage or injury. We now understand that brain deterioration does not always result in total nonfunctioning. Although much of the research is still experimental, scientists are now convinced that there are many hormones and other chemicals that can nurture and sustain brain cells.

According to Kotulak (1997) there are several significant findings with regard to repair and renewal of the brain. Hormones such as estrogen, progesterone, testosterone, and growth hormones can be important factors in maintaining many types of brain cells. It is believed that these hormones may become the most powerful form of treatment to prevent debilitating conditions such as Alzheimer's, Parkinson's, and other degenerative diseases. Estogren, for example, was previously believed to be a female hormone related primarily to reproduction, but we now know that estrogen is present in both the male and female brain. Because of its unique biological ability to enter most cells, it is active in many communications between the brain and the rest of the body.

Certain brain chemicals called neurotrophic factors can also keep brain cells healthy and receptive. When these neurotrophic factors diminish and stop working so do the brain cells that they nourish. Studies are now being conducted to see if new brain cells can be grown to replenish those that are no longer functioning.

Brain cells, like muscles, need exercise or stimulation in order to remain healthy and functioning. Growth is not limited to childhood, and with stimulation, experience-based learning can continue throughout life. The act of learning is now considered a powerful preventive of brain degeneration because it excites the production of connections between the brain cells. These connections make it easier to withstand the destructive forces that accompany a debilitating disease.

Recently the results were revealed of a 30-year federally funded study that examined more than 8,000 Japanese American men who were heavy coffee drinkers. The study suggested that in some way caffeine may contribute to protecting against the nerve cell destruction that leads to Parkinson's disease. Parkinson's involves the gradual deterioration of nerve cell clusters that make the chemical dopamine, which helps control muscle movements. There is speculation that caffeine might actually increase dopamine levels in the human body, thereby decreasing the likelihood of developing the disease ("Preventing Parkinson's," 2000).

THE BRAIN, NEUROCHEMICALS, AND SOCIAL WORK PRACTICE

The last 10 years have brought a new understanding of the brain and how it relates to health, mental health, and maintaining wellness. We are not only learning what it means to keep a brain in balance, but we are experimenting with ways to create and maintain that balance. The neurons (brain cells) receive, analyze, coordinate, and transmit information. Researchers now know that some of these connections can grow stronger with learning and weaker when not utilized. The development of a biological profile that identifies those individuals who are at risk for mental health illness is probably not far off. We can measure chemical markers for twenty neurotransmitters including serotonin, dopamine, and noradrenaline. The development of computer-generated biological profiles holds promise that these profiles can be used to target and ultimately to treat mental health problems.

The actions and reactions within the brain are complex, and it follows that medications designed for one purpose can affect something else. As an example, psychiatrists have discovered that drugs designed to treat schizophrenia can also be useful in manic depression. Although the exact response and pattern is not known, it appears to be related to a common biochemical pathway where the combination of neurochemicals and medication can also inhibit the development of psychosis (Foreman, 2000).

It is important to remember that the brain and the neuroconnections within the human body are not always linked with negative feelings or behaviors. There is also a link with pleasurable feelings such as happiness and satisfaction. The emphasis, however, remains on studying the negative behaviors that clients experience rather than the positive ones, because it is the negative behaviors that interfere or impair social and occupational functioning.

Social workers should have a basic understanding of the brain and its effect and influence on personality traits (e.g., paranoid feelings, obsessive thoughts), feelings, emotions, and behaviors. This sensitivity is enhanced when we acknowledge the role neurochemical activity can have in developing and influencing so many of our most basic personality traits. It becomes clear that how an individual develops, who he or she becomes, and how he or she behaves, is related to how the brain functions and the reactions that appear to be produced by different molecules working on different brain structures (Kotulak, 1997).

It is essential to understand the effect these medications can have because they do more than simply sedate. For example, Clozaril, which was designed to treat psychosis, not only reduces explosive aggression, but also helps to clear psychotic thoughts. The antipsychotic drugs were formerly called the major sedatives because clients became lethargic, sleepy, apathetic, and nonsexual. These side effects often resulted in a client's discontinuing or refusing to take medication. Fortunately, the new generation of psychotropic medications do not work that way. At a conference for mental health practitioners one of the authors compared these newer medications to a guided missile that targets the source of difficulty within the brain. Scientific advances and psychopharmacological efforts have enabled researchers to better understand the brain and the resulting medications perform with more accuracy and less severe side effects than previous generations of drugs (Mental Health Report, 1999).

An increased knowledge of brain biochemistry can assist social workers in learning and understanding how brain cells interact with each other in patterned and characteristic ways. It is estimated that there are more than 100 trillion possible interconnections. The responses that result from these connections are too numerous to count and each is finely tuned, which results in a large repertoire of cognitive, affective, and behavioral capacities.

A course on human anatomy and physiology with special emphasis on the study of the brain is recommended in order to prepare for effective practice. Recognizing that this task is beyond the scope of this book, we have summarized what we believe to be essential knowledge for understanding how clients are affected by medications.

A basic knowledge of the anatomy of the brain and an understanding of how thought and emotions develop will enable social workers to be more effective when dealing with clients who are on medication.

DEPENDENCE VERSUS CHOICE

FEAR OF ADDICTION

Most professionals agree that there are biological and biochemical processes that can increase the possibility of medication dependence. Many clients avoid using medications whenever possible because they fear that they will become addicted, but the reality is quite different. When using medication there is a continuum of use that goes beyond the simplistic notion that "the medication either worked or it didn't." Certain drugs in themselves present unique properties that determine how often they will be taken.

When a medication is said to be reinforcing, it refers to how much pleasure results from taking the medication. The more reinforcing or pleasurable the effects of the medication, the more likely clients will continue to take them, increasing the likelihood of physical dependence. For example, many professionals complain about the difficulty that can occur when a client is placed on a medication, begins to feel better, and subsequently refuses to address the underlying issues that caused or contributed to the mental condition in the first place. If the medication is capable of controlling the outward symptoms, the client may view psychosocial intervention as unnecessary and accept the medication as the sole modality for intervention. After all, it is easier and oftentimes more cost-effective to simply take a pill that makes you feel better than to struggle with uncomfortable issues in the therapeutic relationship.

On the other hand, many drugs have properties that can result in overall therapeutic effects and side effects that are unique to the individual and that are the result of many complex processes (Schwartz, 1998). The uniqueness of the individual response can affect the pleasure gained from these drugs, can be less immediate, more diluted or more of an acquired taste, or may result in side effects that are unacceptable to the client. If a prescribed or self-introduced medication is somewhat reinforcing yet produces side effects that are not tolerable, the client will avoid it. Drugs that affect the body in this way are clearly less addictive and less likely to cause dependence. As an example, many cases have been brought to the attention of professional counselors with regard to Prozac, which was originally approved by the FDA to treat severe depression. Though effective in treating depression, the use of Prozac can result in sexual disinterest and in some individuals actual sexual dysfunction (*Physician's Desk Reference*, 1999, 2000), which in turn causes strained marital and other interpersonal relations. If the medication is used as the sole modality for treatment, the premise is that relationship factors may not be adequately addressed. In addition, the client may blame himself incorrectly and be too embarrassed to report the side effects that he is experiencing. This can result in the client's discontinuing the medication and avoiding the sexual issues that have developed, which further complicates the relationships, and treatment as well. Therefore, the uniqueness of the individual and the subsequent identification of side-effect profiles can be critical in promoting the overall health and well-being of the client.

ADDICTION TO OVER-THE-COUNTER MEDICATIONS

Clients do not become dependent on prescription drugs only; dependence and addiction can also occur with over-the-counter drugs. Many individuals take over-the-counter drugs regularly, perhaps even daily, without thinking about the relationship between these drugs and other health factors. Because these medications are easy to purchase and readily available, there is a misconception that they cannot do harm. Among the most frequently used OTC drugs, nonsteroidal, anti-inflammatory drugs such as aspirin or ibuprofen are not always harmless. These NSAIDs can cause stomach bleeding and ulcers and can disrupt normal kidney functioning (Mayo Clinic, January 6, 2000).

There is one major difference with over-the-counter drugs: addiction does not rest with getting high from the medication, but rather stems from taking the medication longer than expected and developing a need to continue taking it. Addiction can be defined as simply "abstinence syndrome." If an individual experiences physical or psychological withdrawal symptoms upon discontinuance, addiction has occurred. In the case of caffeine, for instance, an individual who has not had her morning coffee or tea develops a headache. Chances are that this person is addicted. Ingesting a caffeinated beverage will reduce the pain more quickly than an aspirin because the body is craving the drug and will only be satisfied by taking it. See Table 2.2 for over-the-counter medications that may seem safe but that can be addictive if overused.

The social work professional with a solid knowledge of medication usage and misuse can also help clients integrate situational or environmental concerns that may not be listed in the PDR. Furthermore, the role of nonprescription medications and their effects on the body, especially in terms of the potential for addiction, should not be underestimated. Wilson (1992) gives the following advice for using medications wisely:

1.   Always read the label on a new bottle or package. For prescription medications, be sure that the pharmacist gives the client a written synopsis of the drug including what it is used for and what the side effects are. In this area the pharmacist can be invaluable by answering questions regarding the cost of medications, by clarifying dosages, and by addressing concerns that the client may have with regard to continuing the medication (*PDR for Nonprescription Drugs*, 1997). Manufacturers are always updating ingredients, so be sure to read the printouts or bottles in order to help the client understand what it means. Always check the list of ingredients, the warnings, and the expiration date. Expiration dates are very important to note, because many times the manufacturer will not guarantee that the ingredients remain in an active state after that date. If there are two

---

TABLE 2.2   Over-the-Counter Medications with a High Potential for Addiction

Nasal sprays: Topical decongestants can be habit-forming.

Laxatives: Labels clearly warn that these preparations can be addictive if overused.

Eye drops: Designed to "get the red out," but rebound effect can occur.

Stay-awake pills: Generally contain concentrated amounts of caffeine, a powerful and addictive stimulant.

Sleeping pills: Most of these have anti-allergy components that can cause sleepiness.

Cough syrups with codeine: Some pharmacies still allow cough syrups with codeine to be sold over the counter.

---

expiration dates, consider the earlier one the expiration date. If the product is outdated, it should be thrown away immediately either by flushing the medication down the toilet, returning it to the pharmacy for disposal, or by ensuring that it cannot be used improperly if found.

2.   Warn clients to limit the dose to the amount and dosage specified in the product directions. This is particularly important for those who practice self-medication. Clients should have a clear understanding of the medications, accompanied by simple, written, easy-to-use directions. In some cases, such as with older people, a chart or table to accompany written directions would be useful. It could indicate when the medication is to be taken throughout the day and would allow the client to check off the daily doses as taken. Another suggestion is for social workers to advise clients to use egg cartons to dispense their daily doses. Remind clients never to skip a dose, share medicines, or take other medications without knowing what they are taking and what effects it may have. Social workers need to remind their clients to always keep a record of what is being taken including herbal preparations, over-the-counter, and prescription medications. Clients will not remember every medication especially when they are nervous, not feeling well, or under pressure. Be sure your clients have a list of the medications they are taking and that they update it regularly.

3.   It's important to empower clients and their families by either asking or helping them to ask relevant questions related to medication use. Clients should know the name of the medicine, why they are taking it, how it should be taken, and whether a generic is available. They should also know how long to take the medication and what foods or beverages to avoid while taking it. In this rapidly changing field and with a vast number of drugs available, social workers are encouraged to help clients seek out further information especially on side effects and the potential for adverse reactions between medications.

4.   When clients suspect they are taking too much of an over-the-counter preparation, they probably are. Advise them that it is possible to become addicted to a nonprescription medication. Clients should consult their primary physicians when physiological symptoms of dependence are suspected and should work towards terminating use of the medication. Oftentimes, convincing them to stop buying the product or to place it out of reach is the most simple and effective solution. Social workers should encourage clients to keep a log indicating the frequency, dosage, time of day, and the stresses that precipitate use of the medication. In this way,

they will become more aware of the habits and patterns that trigger their dependency.

5.   Educate your clients about addiction. If they are finding it difficult to give up or if they justify why they are using it frequently, explain that the problem can become more serious and that they should not be embarrassed to ask for help. This is especially important with over-the-counter remedies because they do not require a prescription and many clients do not know they can be addictive. Integrating basic education and support into the therapeutic relationship can help to address the client's and family's concerns and can facilitate the intervention process and help medications work more effectively.

ROUTES OF ADMINISTRATION

The route of administration can influence whether a client will take a medication and for how long. Some methods of taking medications are very reinforcing or convenient (Goode, 1992a). For example, oral adminis-tration of a pill and nasal administration (snorting or sniffing) are clearly convenient, but the actual rewards or reinforcement are generally delayed. When a client needs immediate assistance, these methods may not be as desirable as a quicker, more direct method.

Two forms of ingestion that are more immediate, and therefore more reinforcing, are intravenous injection and oral filtration (smoking) (Goode, 1992a). If a client is extremely agitated and hostile and is threatening to do harm, a sedative antipsychotic administered via injection is usually the best plan of action. When time is of the essence, the oral route may not be feasible. The intravenous injection is much more immediate and delivers the medication very quickly, allowing for faster control of the symptomology.

Knowledge of depot preparations (long-acting, injectable medications) also can be invaluable when working with chronic clients who need long-term therapy or who are difficult in terms of compliance (Lehne & Scott, 1996).

Smoking is another fast route of administration. Its quick delivery may be why smoking can be such a seductive prospect for many users, whether the drug of choice is nicotine or crack cocaine. It is obvious that the potential for addiction is much greater when a highly addictive drug can be taken in convenient fashion. Many professionals consider the immediate reinforcement of intravenous injection and oral filtration a major contributing factor in the increased use of illegal drugs such as crack cocaine and heroin.

It is clear that there is a link between a medication's routes of administration, its reinforcing nature, and the immediate results it produces. However, we cannot underestimate cultural and social factors that play an important role in a client's pattern of medication use and misuse (Goode, 1992a). Clients are individuals with unique experiences, belief systems, ideas, concerns, and patterns of behavior that will influence why, how, and when the medication taken. It is imperative that the social worker understand the client's cultural, religious, and social influences, because these may determine how an individual perceives medication usage and compliance. When clients trust the social worker, they are more likely to comply by following the routine and taking their medication. As a profession, social work has always stressed the importance of the "person-in-environment" perspective wherein practitioners view clients through a cultural lens. This framework is an integral component of the intervention and ensures that any medication difficulties related to cultural or religious beliefs are addressed.

FACTORS RELATING TO MEDICATION AVAILABILITY AND PRICING

Pharmaceuticals are a $40-billion-a-year enterprise in the United States with an additional $7 billion spent on over-the-counter drugs (Goode, 1992b). The use of herbal medication has also increased with an estimated $2 billion in preparations, extracts, and teas (Brevoort, 1997). It is estimated that three out of every four doctor's visits result in prescriptions and that approximately 2.8 billion prescriptions were written in 1999 alone (Friebert & Greeley, 1999). This in turn relates to the power of the pharmaceutical company in setting prescription prices. As some clients are able to purchase their own prescription medications for a lower price at a veterinarian office rather than at a pharmacy because the pharmaceutical companies charge less if the same medication is for animals as opposed to people (Fourneir, 2000).

SELF-HELP AND THE INTERNET: DECIPHERING AND USING MEDICAL INFORMATION

There is a massive amount of information available to the consumer that describes the risks and benefits of medication. Technology provides easy access to information, and the public's interest and desire to find out more is at an all-time high. Clients are asking more involved questions and those in the helping services are expected to have the answers. Social work professionals must be able to help clients and their families view objectively the information received. In examining the information it is essential to question the reliability of information retrieved from on-line services or from the Internet. With the growth of computer technology and access to this type of on-line service, many clients are using the Internet as a source of information. To assist clients in determining the reliability of the information gathered from these various sources, the FDA and others familiar with medical offerings suggest the following guidelines (Larkin, 1996):

1.   Who maintains the site? Government or university-based Web sites are recommended for the most scientifically sound information. Private sources may have their own entrepreneurial agenda for promoting or marketing a product that may not be appropriate for every client. This is particularly important when reading and interpreting information on herbal remedies that are offered for preventive or therapeutic purposes as foods or dietary supplements. The FDA does not generally monitor these products and the claims they make (Zink & Chaffin, 1998).

2.   Is there a professional body responsible for reviewing the Web site's contents? Do the professionals who review the site have a direct connection to the site (i.e., are they employees at the site) or are they independent professionals? Who will review contents from a more objective perspective? Are references made to professional journals or researchers that can support the claims being made? Can the professionals, researchers, or scientists that review the site be contacted and is there an address where they can be contacted for additional information or clarification?

3.   Is there a link to other sources of information that can support or supplement what is provided in the site? Be sure these referral sources are reputable and well established, because many companies set up professional-looking Web pages but may not be accurately representing the product they are advertising.

4.   How often is the site updated? With the rapidly changing mental health field and the increasing information resulting from research and scientific advances during the last decade, all sites that describe medications or other medical information should be updated at least monthly.

As Henkel (1998) described, much of what we know about reactions to medication has been learned from its use on the market.

5.   Does the site supplement medical information with any type of multimedia presentation that facilitates understanding of the product? This presentation should not be the only way the medical information is presented as it might lead to a limited presentation of the required information.

6.   Does the site charge a fee for access? Before paying such a fee, determine if such a service is more worthwhile to pay for than the many sites that are free of charge. Paying for information does not guarantee that the information is proven, worthwhile, or appropriate for the client. Social workers should warn clients to be cautious of products that advertise a miracle cure or promises that a pill can cure or solve their problems. Any claims of this nature should be scrutinized thoroughly.

It is not surprising that technological advances have resulted in a surge of self-help interventions, particularly in the area of health and wellness, and that it will continue. What is most frightening is that many clients will take over-the-counter medications or herbal treatments and not inform their health-care worker. It is common to think that herbal preparations are "natural and safe" and therefore harmless, and clients will take these preparations because they believe it will lead to improved health. This can be extremely problematic because many of these medications and treatments can interact with prescription medications. For example, some herbal preparations can become toxic when taken with certain drugs, and fatal herb-drug interactions can occur (Fugh-Bergman, 2000; Mayo Clinic, March 6, 2000). All social workers are reminded to encourage clients to write down all their medications and treatments and the source of their information on the product. This information should later be shared with the health-care provider or the interdisciplinary team in order to determine whether the product is indicated for a particular client and whether it is compatible with the client's medical, mental, social, and environmental situation.

SUMMARY AND CONCLUSIONS

Understanding how medications work is a necessity for effective social work practice in today's healthcare environment. The last ten years have brought about unprecedented gains in knowledge and application with regard to the brain and its role in mental illness. These gains are going to continue and eventually science will become so sophisticated that medication or neurochemical influencing will have a greater impact on mental health practice. The challenge for social work practitioners will be twofold: First, social workers must stay current on medication and neurochemical research and findings; and second, they must ensure that all clients benefit from these scientific gains regardless of their ability to pay.

It is important to recall the lessons that were learned from prior misuse of medication, specifically Fenfluramine (approved in 1973) and Redux (approved in 1996) and other potentially deadly diet pills. These pills were distributed and prescribed repeatedly even after numerous warnings that not enough was known about them. The FDA approved Fenfluramine as safe for short-term use in 1973, under the assumption that the medication would be prescribed for individuals who were severely obese and not responding to other forms of treatment. This was not the case, however, and many physicians readily obliged and dispensed prescriptions to individuals who were not obese but who were seeking a quick fix for their weight problems. Furthermore, studies supported that the combination of two drugs—fenfluramine and phentermine when taken together called fen/phen—would help shed the pounds faster with fewer side effects. Although the FDA never approved the combined use of these drugs, it became one of the hottest-selling remedies for weight control in the drug industry.

Later Redux was approved in 1996, and it was not long before 2.5 million prescriptions had been written and the number of people exposed to the drug rose to 60 million worldwide. The news was shattering in July of that same year when Mayo Clinic researchers reported serious heart-valve damage in Fenfluramine and Redux user. Eventually 30% of the 291 users of the drug combination fen/phen reported the same problems (Golden, 1997), and combination use of the drug was prohibited and Redux was recalled. Golden (1997) brings up some interesting points when he questions who should be held accountable for serious errors of this type. The FDA in particular is to blame for approving it, given that initially it received five votes in favor of approval and three against and considering that researchers had serious misgivings. The drug companies that produced, tested, and marketed the drug knowing that more research was needed are responsible too, as well as the physicians and weight-control programs that eagerly dispensed them to individuals that the drugs were never intended for. Some blame can be placed on the media that advertised and promoted the drugs as a miracle, and on the clients, who so desperately wanted to lose weight. Regardless of where the blame is placed, consumers were harmed and professionals who are supposed to act in the best interests of the client lost credibility. As social workers, we need to look carefully at the benefits and limitations of medications, always remembering that medication prescription is not an exact science and reminding our clients of the fact. This requires that we become more aware of how medications work, the effects they can have on individuals, and ways to more effectively educate our clients about the use and misuse of these drugs.

REFERENCES

Associated Press. (1998, January 17). Drugs online—no doctor visit needed. *Orlando Sentinel*, p. A24.

Brevoort, P. (1997). *Overview of the U.S. botanical market.* Drug Information Association, Third Conference on Botanicals, Washington, DC.

Coyle, J. T., & Enna, S. J. (1998). Overview of neuropsychopharmacology. In S. J. Enna & J. T. Coyle (Eds.), *Pharmacological management of neurological and psychiatric disorders* (pp. 1–24). New York: McGraw-Hill.

FDA Consumer. (1997). Plan will give consumers better prescription drug information. *Author, 31*(3), 2.

Foreman, J. (2000, March 25). Health sense: Treatments for manic depression are improving. *Boston Globe*, p. A4.

Fourneir, R. (2000, June 14). Gore promises more money for health. *Orlando Sentinal* p. B1.

Friebert, E., & Greeley, A. (1999). Taking time to use medicines wisely. *FDA Consumer, 33*(5), 30–31.

Fugh-Bergman, A. (2000). Herbs-drug interactions. *Lancet, 355*, 134–145.

Golden, F. (1997, September 29). Who is to blame for Redux and Fenfluramine? *Time, 150*(13), 78–79.

Goode, E. (1992a). Addiction and dependence. In E. Goode (Ed.), *Drugs, society and behavior 91/92* (pp. 40–44). Guilford, CT: Dushkin Publishing Group.

Goode, E. (1992b). The economy of drug use. In E. Goode (Ed.), *Drugs, society and behavior 91/92* (pp. 168–169). Guilford, CT: Dushkin Publishing Group.

Henkel, J. (1998). Reporting adverse reactions and other product problems. *FDA Consumer, 32*(6), 7–15.

Hickling, L. (2000, May 11). Questions persist concerning Prozac's role in suicide risk. *Health News, 3*.

Kotulak, R. (1997). *Inside the brain: Revolutionary discoveries of how the mind works.* Kansas City, MO: Andrews McMeel.

Larkin, M. (1996). Health information on line. *FDA Consumer, 30*(5), 21–24.

Lehne, R. A., & Scott, D. (1996). Psychopharmacology. In V. B. Carson & E. N. Arnold (Eds.), *Mental health nursing: The nurse-patient journey.* Philadelphia: W. B. Saunders.

Mayo Clinic. (2000, March 6). Herb-drug interaction—Natural not always safe. *Mayo Foundation for Education and Research*, p. 6.

Mayo Clinic. (2000, January 6). NSAID's: Helpful, but serious side effects. *Mayo Foundation for Medical Education and Research*, p. 4.

Marano, E. H. (1999, March/April). Depression: Beyond serotonin. *Psychology Today, 32*, 30–36, 72–75.

Mental Health Report. (1999, October 29). VP Gore pledges support for mental health parity (p. 166). Silver Spring, MD: Business Publishers.

Physicians' Desk Reference. (1999). *Physicians' desk reference* (53rd ed.). Montvale, NJ: Medical Economics.

Physicians' Desk Reference. (2000). *Physicians' desk reference* (54th ed.). Montvale, NJ: Medical Economics.

Physicians' Desk Reference. (1997). *Physicians' desk reference for nonprescription drugs* (18th ed.). Montvale, NJ: Medical Economics.

Preventing Parkinson's: Study says caffeine may prevent disease. (2000, 24 May). *Journal of the American Medical Association.*

Schwartz, J. B. (1998). Clinical pharmacology. In W. R. Hazzard, J. P. Blass, W. H. Ettinger, J. B. Halter, & J. G. Ouslander (Eds.), *Principles of geriatric medicine and gerontology* (4th ed., pp. 303–331). New York: McGraw-Hill.

Wilson, J. (1992). Hooked on over-the-counter drugs. In E. Goode (Ed.), *Drugs, society and behavior 91/92* (pp. 136–138). Guilford, CT: Dushkin Publishing Group.

Zink, T., & Chaffin, J. (1998). Herbal health products: What physicians need to know. *American Family Physician, 58*, 1133–1140.

CHAPTER 3

Interpreting and Using Medication Information

U nderstanding the medical aspects of psychopharmacologic interventions can be very intimidating for many social work professionals. Professional social workers generally do not receive this training in their undergraduate or graduate education, thus any skills acquired in this area must be derived from on-the-job training within the agency setting or through continuing education (Dziegielewski, 1999). Although continuing education might indeed be beneficial, often it is not provided by a professional social worker. The benefits of receiving this training from a professional social worker are many including the fact that she is more likely to be sensitive to the "person in situation" or "person in environment" stance that has long been the foundation of social work activities.

Despite the lack of formal and extensive training in medication usage and misuse, social workers frequently provide services to clients who are on psychotropic medications and are required to integrate medication information into the assessment, working phase, and termination phases of the helping relationship. Social workers should be familiar with basic medical terminology, including the differences between generic and brand name medications. Acquiring this basic knowledge can ensure that social work professionals are proficient in accurately assessing, documenting, and integrating a client's medication history into the counseling relationship.

GENERIC VERSUS BRAND NAMES: IS THERE REALLY A DIFFERENCE?

A sweet-voiced elderly woman describes what it is like to live on a fixed income of $658 a month. She relates how she places her six pill bottles on her kitchen

49

table, then decides which ones she can afford to refill, which pills she will have
to take every other day, and which ones she will do without. (Serafini, 2000a, p. 1)

The cost of medication is not only a personal issue but a political one
as well. According to political observations, the cost of medication has
become so high that desperate measures are needed to examine the situation
and plans made to address and combat these costs (Serafini, 2000a). With
medication costs rising and changes in insurance reimbursement patterns,
social workers are often faced with the dilemma of whether a client should
use a generic medication or a brand name. The most obvious way to cut
these costs is to substitute generic medications for the more expensive
brand names if they are available.

Although switching sounds simple enough, there are many issues that
need to be addressed in order for social workers to help clients make
educated decisions. Clients are sometimes unsure and unable to determine
whether there is a difference between the brand name and the generic
medications, and whether one medication might actually be more effective
than the other. Those decisions and who actually makes them can be
complicated. For many clients, however, the decision is based on the fact
that they cannot afford the brand-name medication, or they are simply
given the generic without being consulted. Since many companies such
as the Veterans Administration and military-based pharmacies are now
buying medications in bulk, replacing brand-name medication with the
cheaper generic alternatives is becoming common practice.

If one accepts the cost-saving incentive to switch from a brand name
to a generic brand, the rationale is simple. On the surface, it is clear that
the generic medications are less expensive and are generally considered
as equally effective therapeutically as the brand name. For others the
selection process may be predetermined by insurance reimbursements that
dictate which medications are included in the plan's formulary and paid
for under a current health care plan. Regardless of the reason for using
or changing to a generic medication, many clients and professionals do
not understand what the difference between the two really is. It is unfortunate that the desire to save costs at times overrides the necessity for
efficiency and effectiveness.

WHY THE GENERIC DRUG IS LESS EXPENSIVE

The creation of a brand-name medication starts with original research,
testing, and marketing investments that can be quite costly for the manufac-

turer (Heidari, 2000). In recognition of this, when the Food and Drug Administration (FDA) approves the medication it approves a time period reflective of the patent, which stipulates that for a certain period of time no generic drugs can be created that will utilize the same ingredients under the original patent. There is a general format that manufacturers and the FDA follow before a medication is approved in Box 1.

APPROVAL PROCESS FOR BRAND-NAME PRESCRIPTION MEDICATIONS

Brand-name drug is developed
Drug company conducts testing and submits results to the FDA
Receives time-limited patent with exclusive production rights from
  FDA
Time-limit ends and patent expires
Application for the generic drugs can now be filed and approved

---

In the past, the approval process was not clear, and the FDA became the focus of critical attention. In 1989 it was accused of accepting "gratuities" from the pharmaceutical companies to approve new brand-name medications more expeditiously (Heller, 1993).

Currently, the FDA is indeed reviewing drugs more quickly. "It used to be that the review period—after the pharmaceutical company studies the drug, writes up the report, and sends a gigantic packet of information to the FDA took about two to three years to complete . . . now it takes 12 months" (Nordenburg, 1999). The FDA attributes this to having more people working within the review process. This additional support staff is needed to ensure the continuation of shorter drug-review time periods. Furthermore, representatives of the FDA argue that the actual clinical trial time for testing is now longer. There will be more controlled testing of the drugs and manufactures will be expected to include women, older patients, people with kidney filtering problems, and other population groups that were not included in the previous testing process.

As a matter of general protocol, a generic drug cannot be developed until the brand name manufacturer's patent has expired. This time period is an important incentive for the manufacturer because no generic copies can be created during this time. This allows the brand-name manufacturer an exclusive market for a period of time. The fact that a generic drug cannot be produced until the patent on the brand name expires could be considered the manufacturer's reward for the expensive process of creating the original drug. A second issue with this approval process is that it seems some manufacturers have been allowed to extend their patent or reward time on the grounds that more extensive and lengthy testing periods are required. Serafini (2000b) warns that this appears to go against the Drug Price Competition and Patent Term Restoration Act (the Hatch-Waxman Act). The fear is that extending patent protection periods for brand-name medication manufacturers will lead to higher medication costs because there will be no competition from the generic drugs (Banta, 2000).

Generic drugs, which are always called by their chemical name, are created only after the patent for the brand-name medication has expired and are merely less expensive copies of the brand-name medication (Watson-Heidari, 2000). The use of this chemical name can cause some confusion because the brand name (which is different) is generally discarded and may not appear on the pill bottle at all. The chemical names are not nearly as catchy and easy to remember as the brand name, and confusion is a likely result.

The Federal Trade Commission reports that to date generic versions are available for about one-half of all the medications on the market (Watson-Heidari, 2000). Since the production cost of a generic drug is so much less, there may be several different manufacturers seeking approval of these generic medications when the brand-name patent expires. Creating the generic is much less expensive because the FDA requires only that the generic have the same active ingredients, strength, and dosage of the brand-name medication it duplicates (Heidari, 2000). Almost all initial testing and marketing information carries over to the generic manufacturer, because the generic drug is said to be a copy and duplicate testing on a biochemically similar drug is not nearly as intensive or expensive.

The comparison for equivalence between the generic and the brand-name drug is a statistical one. Generic drugs must be at least 20% similar to the standard drug when plasma levels are measured (Public Citizen's Health Research Group, 1993). In general, there should be an overall deviation of not more than 10% between generic and brand-name products. Simply stated, "It has always been our position, there is no difference between generic and brand-name drugs on the odds that there will be something found wrong with the amount of active ingredient or the purity" (Public Citizen Health Research Group, 1993, p. 679).

Keeping this information in mind, are brand-name and generic medications truly equivalent? From a statistical perspective they are. Generic drugs are required to have the same active ingredients, dose, and strength as the brand name they replicate. Although the cheaper price is attractive, many health care prescribers still prefer to use the brand-name medication whenever possible. Unfortunately, there is little concern for whether the client can afford the brand-name medication and whether it will be covered by medical insurance. It is critical for social workers to encourage clients and family members to talk with the prescriber about budgetary restrictions, so that an informed decision can be made about whether the more expensive brand names or generic brands are better for the client.

Furthermore, clients should be aware of some of the differences with the "no frills" generic medication. Since the FDA requires only that the chemical composition of active ingredients be the same, the color, shape, size, and taste of the generic medication may be different. It is these inactive ingredients that hold the pill together or maintain its shape (Heidari, 2000). These differences may be visible to the client and switching from a brand name to a generic medication could actually cause confusion about which medication to take or even trigger a psychotic reaction unanticipated by the intervention team. Other clients may be upset by a switch from brand name to generic (with or without their consent) and might worry about different or additional side effects.

Professionals should educate their clients about the differences between generic and brand-name medications so that an educated choice can be made and clients will not think of the pill as something different or less effective. There are laws in virtually all states that allow pharmacists to substitute generic drugs for many brand-name products. Some states actually require that a generic must be substituted if it is available (Heidari, 2000). If a client does not want a generic medication or if the provider does not want the client to have one, the prescription should state this specifically. The social worker should check to see that the prescriber has written the words "dispense as written" or "do not substitute" so that the pharmacist is required to fill the prescription with the brand-name product requested.

Asking questions about insurance and medication reimbursement is critical when working with clients or their family members. This generally means helping the clients read pamphlets that outline their insurance coverage or helping them call the insurance benefits office. Simply helping clients determine what, when, and under what circumstances medication will be covered by insurance will help them make informed self-care decisions. Although this information is crucial, using this information as the primary consideration for prescribing should never be considered standard practice. To let the cost completely determine prescribing patterns is contradictory to the real purpose of using medications. Medications are part of the treatment strategy expected to assist with establishing efficiency and effectiveness for the medical or mental health condition being treated. As practice reality, and no matter how disturbing it is to take cost into consideration it is relevant to a client's decision. If clients cannot afford to pay for the medication they will try to cut corners or simply avoid taking the medication altogether. These issues are important ones in deciding whether to use a generic medication or a brand name and should always be considered within the therapeutic decision-making process.

MYTHS ABOUT MEDICATION

There are several societal myths with regard to the use of medications to assist those who suffer from physical health and mental health problems.

> Myth 1: Physicians and other health care professionals are familiar with most if not all of the medications on the market, and there is extensive research to explain how the medication will affect the client who is using it.

It is true that most physicians and other mental health professionals have an overall awareness of certain drugs, particularly the medications that would fall in the categories of their own specialty. It is not uncommon, however, for prescribing professionals to have to look up medications that they do not regularly use or come across in practice in order to determine their value and effect on the client. Given the available prescription, over-the-counter, and herbal medicines, competent and ethical practice requires that professionals be able to identify interactive effects produced by these medications. This is especially important when the client is taking other medications at the same time that can interact, diminish, or augment the effect of the original medication.

> Myth 2: The medication a client is prescribed is based on a careful evaluation, utilizing previous research that establishes the correct therapeutic dose that will be needed to address the client's problem.

Many times the medication prescriber does not know exactly what dosage of medication to prescribe for a particular client. It is not uncommon to try different dosages and several different types of medications before the most beneficial and effective medication with the fewest side effects is identified. This is further complicated by the fact that although a drug can produce effects, some drugs may vary in their effect and actual reason for use based on the dosage prescribed (Eisenbauer, 1998). For example, lower doses of antidepressants may be used for some types of neurological pain where higher doses are used in the treatment of depression.

Finding the right medication for a client rests on two premises. First, an individual's biological and physiological system is unique, metabolizing and reacting to medication in a singular manner. Older clients, for instance, can present a real challenge for the clinician (Eisenbauer, 1998). These clients tend to have a slower metabolism and organ functions than younger adults (Dziegielewski & Harrison, 1996). When this is combined with chronic medical conditions and multiple drug prescriptions, a complex situation can result. In general, as people age they lose muscle tissue and gain fat tissue, and major organs such as the liver and kidney begin to slow down (Williams, 1997). Age-related factors such as organ absorption and changes in drug metabolism as a drug passes through the intestine and liver can affect overall response to a medication (Schwartz, 1998). This makes prescribing medication with this population especially unpredictable and supports the adage "Go slow and dose low" when prescribing medications to older clients (Schwartz, 1998; Williams, 1997).

The second premise is that medications simply may not react the same in all individuals, and some individuals respond better to certain types of medications than others. Variables of age, body size, body chemistry, habits, and diet can influence the way a specific medication affects the client. Consequently, while general guidelines for prescribing medications exist, prescribers must also remain flexible in individualizing dosing regimens for each client.

IMPORTANT TERMINOLOGY FOR MONITORING MEDICATION

Some common terms in medication dosing and monitoring that the professional social worker should be aware of include: medication half-life, drug potency, the therapeutic index, and drug tolerance.

A medication's half-life is the amount of time it takes for one-half of a drug's peak plasma level to be metabolized and excreted from the body (Kaplan & Sadock, 1990). The half-life of a drug is defined as the time it takes the amount of the drug in the body to be decreased by half (Schwartz, 1998, p. 311). In other words, if the half-life of a medication is estimated to be 4 hours, the peak concentration of the medication within a client's system occurs within 4 hours of ingestion. After 4 hours the level of medication in a client's system continues to decrease by another 50% of the original amount. In 8 hours, the medication in the client's system is reduced by another 50% and so on. The original 50% that was left continues to be divided so that 12 hours after taking the medicine 87.5% would be left. Although this calculation may be confusing, the basic point is that many medications remain in the system long after the medication is taken. This has serious implications for clients who combine medications or who begin another medication before the first drug has left the system, which creates the potential for hazardous reactions.

A computation of medication half-life can assist the health care team in determining how much medication is actually left in the client's system and how this residual amount can effect present and subsequent treatments. A distinction is made between a short-acting medication that is eliminated more quickly from the system and a long-acting one where the drug can stay in the system for a much longer period of time.

Potency refers to the relative dose needed to achieve a certain effect (Kaplan & Sadock, 1990). For example, haloperidol (Haldol), a drug used to treat psychosis, is a high-potency medication because the dose needed to produce a therapeutic effect (5 mg) is much lower than its counterpart chlorpromazine (Thorazine). Thorazine requires a much higher dose (100 mg) to achieve the same effect. Understanding medication potency helps to explain why doses are given in such different levels for clients. These dosages can be very confusing and difficult to predict for the layperson who does not understand medication potency. Family members can also be confused when the dosage requirements for a loved one vary from a high-potency to a low-potency medication or vice-versa.

Knowledge of the therapeutic index is also essential for professional social workers, because this is the relative measure of a drug's toxicity or safety level for the client. Clients may also develop drug tolerance or lower levels of responsiveness to a medication over a period of time. The development of tolerance is associated most often with the client's physical dependence on the medication. In these cases clients must take the drug regularly in order to prevent the usually uncomfortable symptoms related to withdrawal (Kaplan & Sadock, 1990).

Professional social workers are often involved in helping to establish and monitor a client's medication regimen. Therefore, a working knowledge of medications helps the social worker to prepare for potential problems related to medication usage and misuse. The role of the social worker is an essential one and often consists of educating clients and their families on basic issues related to medication use. A common problem noted by medical social workers in the field is a lack of awareness among clients on basic and commonsense principles of medication usage (Dziegielewski, 1998). For example, some clients may be unaware that a time-release medication should never be chewed. These medications are coated so that part of the medication is released first, and the remainder is released later when the additional inclusive coating breaks. Chewing this type of medication defeats the purpose of a time-release dosage, yet clients are seldom reminded not to do so because it is assumed they know. Social workers should never assume that clients are clear about medications and time needs to be allotted for instruction about how to take the medications and why it is important to take them as directed. Clients must also be informed that those medications that are capsulated cannot be reduced by splitting.

A second and more common example of misdosing can occur when a client is not instructed properly on how to take a scored tablet. Many medications are expensive, particularly those required for maintaining mental health. In a desperate attempt to save money clients may try to split tablet medications in half. Oftentimes health professionals may look at dosage information and agree that in practice this should work. The client splits the pill thinking that he is getting half the prescribed dose, unaware that there is no uniform dose distribution in a non-scored tablet. The amount of medication in each side of a split nonscored tablet cannot be determined. Every attempt should be made to ensure that the client knows the importance of only splitting medication tablets that have been scored. Such a simple mistake could cause serious problems in the client's medication regimen that might not be easily detected by the client, the prescribing professional, or the health care interdisciplinary team.

Dosing problems that may not seem obvious to most professionals are the problems that occur with liquid medications. Most clients will simply use a kitchen spoon, but all spoons are not the same size. Common tableware teaspoons come in various sizes, from 2.5 milliliters (ml) to

9.5 milliliters. The average measurement for a teaspoon is set at the 5 ml mark (Kurtzweil, 1994); and, using everyday tableware does not guarantee accurate dosages. To assist consumers there are various types of standardized measuring devices available including hypodermic and oral syringes, oral droppers, cylindrical dosing spoons, and plastic medicine cups.

A simple explanation or demonstration of how to measure liquid medicines would prevent dosing problems. When using instruments such as oral syringes, remind the client and family members to remove the cap in order to prevent injury from swallowing it (Kurtzweil, 1994).

Consumers and professionals traditionally have been led to believe that the dosing cup used in inpatient or residential settings is an accurate and effective way to ensure that the client is receiving the correct medication. There have been several cases of mislabeling that have caused the FDA to survey drug companies and to recall these products from time to time when they have not met the standard (Kurtzweil, 1994). The role of the health professional is essential in educating the consumer about the problems that can occur in dosing and in helping to identify problems that may be related to manufacturer error that need to be reported to the FDA for correction.

TIPS FOR HELPING CLIENTS WHO TAKE LIQUID MEDICATIONS*

1. Remind the client to remove caps from hypodermic or oral syringes, and if not needed throw them away prior to giving the medication to anyone.
2. Use only the plastic dosing cup that comes with the product; don't use one from another product.
3. Do not use tableware spoons to measure liquid medication, as there is too much variability in dosing.
4. Read the directions for proper cleaning and handling techniques.

*Suggestions adapted from Kurtzweil (1994).

It is important that social workers stay abreast of medical terminology and jargon. To read and interpret medical records, social workers need to be aware of the symbols and abbreviations commonly used in the medical profession and how these terms are applied in the health and mental health care of clients. Table 3.1 provides examples of medical abbreviations that are often used in the health care environment.

MEDWATCH: HOW TO FILE A PROFESSIONAL OR CONSUMER REPORT

MedWatch is a program sponsored by the FDA that looks directly at post-marketing surveillance. Through this program health care professionals can share information on products that identify safety concerns and that may require formalized action (Henkel, 1998; 1999). Since the actual initial testing for side-effects of medication before it is released on the market is limited, programs such as MedWatch allow for follow-up on medication reactions that take place once it is on the market.

Program MedWatch has four purposes. First, to clarify the parameters of what should be reported to the FDA. Second, to increase awareness about serious reactions caused by drugs or medical devices. Third, to help make it easier to report adverse drug reactions. Fourth, to give the health community a continuous feedback mechanism for reporting product safety issues (Henkel, 1999).

The major criterion for filing a report is belief or evidence that a serious adverse reaction has occurred (Henkel, 1999). Generally, the type of reaction to report is one that was not evident during initial drug trials and was not expected to be a common side effect and, therefore, does not appear in the product handout. The reporter is not required to demonstrate or substantiate an actual reaction, yet the reporter needs to believe it has occurred and that future incidents are possible. Since the FDA will proba-bly ask for technical follow-up information on each of these reports, it prefers that a trained health care professional, rather than a client, make the actual reports. A post-marketing safety evaluator examines information from MedWatch reports, and according to Henkel (1999) once the adverse effect has been identified the FDA can take the following actions:

- Issue medical alerts: These information or product alerts can provide valuable product safety information to physicians, pharmacists, and other health professionals, as well as to trade and media groups.
- Require label changes: The manufacturer may have to add or change product information and put it on all current product labels.

TABLE 3.1   Medical Abbreviations

Abbreviation	General meaning (English)
ad	to; up to
ad lib	as desired
aq	water
f	female
fl dr	fluid dram
fl oz	fluid ounce
mg	milligram
ml	milliliter
mm	mill imeter
os	mouth
oz	ounce
pt	pint
qt	quart
s̄	without
sc	subcutaneously
abs feb	without fever
ac	before eating
adhib	to be administered
alt dieb	every other day
alt hor	every other hour
alt noc	every other night
bal	bath
bp	blood pressure
c̄	with
tm	tomorrow morning
tn	tomorrow night
cont rem	let the medicines be continued
D	give
d	day
/d	daily (per day)
hn	tonight
hs	at bedtime
ind	daily
pr	through the rectum
prn	as needed
pv	through the vagina
qh	every hour
q 2h	every two hours
q 3h	every three hours
qid	four times a day
tid	three times daily
tin	three times a night

TABLE 3.1 *(continued)*

Abbreviation	General meaning (English)
a	before
add	add
bid	twice daily
bin	twice a night
ddin d	from day to day
dos	dose
emp	as directed
gtt	a drop, drops
liq	a solution
pc	after meals
sig	write; let it be labeled
ss	a half
tab	a tablet

- Create prominent or boxed warnings on packaging and product information: The FDA can require that these warnings be placed in a prominent place so that physicians, health care professionals, and consumers are aware of their existence.
- Product withdrawals: When warranted, the FDA has the power to require the company to withdraw its product permanently from the marketplace.

An immediate report to MedWatch is considered warranted if one of more of the following occurs:

- Death: If you believe that using a medication or medical device is the suspected cause of a client's death
- Life-threatening hazard: If a client was at risk of death due to the adverse reaction or if it is suspected that continued use of a product could cause death (e.g., pacemaker failure of an intravenous pump that could cause excessive drug dosing)
- Hospitalization: If a client is admitted to a hospital because of a severe reaction to a prescribed medication
- Disability: If the adverse reaction results in a significant or permanent change in a person's previous level of functioning

- Birth defects, stillbirth, miscarriage, or birth with disease: If a client is exposed to a medication or medical device that leads to any of these problems in the birthing process
- Intervention: If a client needs intervention to avoid permanent damage

---

FILING A MEDWATCH REPORT

A MedWatch report can be filed by mail, fax, or online.

By mail: Use the postage-paid MedWatch form, which includes the address. To get a copy of the form call MedWatch at 1-800-332-1088, and one will be sent by mail or fax.

By fax: The fax number for MedWatch is 1-800-332-0178. Be sure to use the form. Any serious or adverse reaction can also be reported to the product manufacturer who by law is required to report it to the FDA.

Online: Go to the MedWatch website at www.fda.gov/medwatch/ and follow the directions for submitting a report electronically.

ISSUES IN MEDICATION USE

Mental health and health care social workers need to be aware of several issues that can assist in monitoring their clients who are taking medications. Social workers can empower clients to gain the confidence to ask questions of the prescriber and to verify that the medication that has been prescribed is the best one for them. Often clients rely on the professional judgment of their physicians, pharmacists, and other professionals who prescribe and dispense medications, but forget that the prescribers cannot always account for the reaction a client may have. It is critical that professionals listen carefully and encourage clients to express what they are experiencing. Clients need to be reminded that ultimately they must be aware of their own bodies and reactions that may occur. It is the client that will reap the rewards or suffer the consequences of the medication. If a client is well educated and aware on the properties and possible side effects of medications he or she can be the first to identify adverse reactions.

IDENTIFYING REACTIONS AND SIDE EFFECTS

Social workers should be aware of the expected general reactions outlined for a medication by becoming familiar with the precautions that apply to each drug. This means that a basic knowledge on referencing medications in the *Physicians' Desk Reference* (PDR) is needed. This book can provide all the manufacturers' data on testing and side effects (PDR, 2000). A call to the local pharmacy will yield information on nonprescription medications as will bottle or package inserts. *Physicians' Desk Reference: For Nonprescription Medications* (1997) may also be helpful. It provides pictures and clear explanations of the medications and possible adverse reactions similar to the PDR for prescription medications.

In addition to these resources, oftentimes the pharmacist can provide printed information to clients that is more user-friendly than the descriptions in the *PDR*. Clients must be encouraged to read these inserts completely before beginning their medication regimens.

TAPERING MEDICATIONS

A common question that clients ask is in regard to reducing their medications. It is always best to refer this question immediately to the prescriber because of the complications that can result from discontinuing or reducing the level of certain drugs. Clients should be cautioned on the perils of stopping medication abruptly or weaning off medication without medical advice and monitoring. For example, Xanax, which is used to control anxiety, should never be discontinued suddenly because of the risk of seizures. If a social worker is unfamiliar with the actual effects of discontinuing or tapering off a medication, it is considered standard practice to refer the client appropriately before encouraging reduction or discontinuance of any medication.

Tapering a medication requires constant monitoring, and there are no firm rules for all medications. If a client states that they are going to discontinue a medication without seeking medical advice, it is best to recommend a slow tapering process, decreasing by about 10 to 15% of the medication given each day. When a plan for tapering has been established by the prescriber, the social worker can assist the client in identifying any side effects during the weaning period.

EXPIRATION DATES

If asked about using medications that are past the expiration date, the social worker should advise the client to call the pharmacy before discarding the medication. Many times pharmacists stamp their own expiration date, and generally it expires before the one assigned by the manufacturer (Prufer, 1996). This practice can be costly for the client who can't afford to purchase new medication when the old one appears to have expired. At the same time, clients should be reminded that old medications could prove ineffective and may be discarded after consultation with the pharmacist. If there are two dates on a prescription bottle, the earlier is the one most likely put there by the drug manufacturer and is the one that should be followed. Care should always be taken when disposing of medications. Remind clients that it is better to flush them down the toilet than to simply throw them in the trash.

TAKING A MEDICATION HISTORY

As part of the assessment process, the social worker is expected to take a medication history that includes information on the client's patterns of medication use, preference, and abuse. Identifying patterns of high risk or potential for medication abuse allows the social worker to share information with the medication prescriber who in turn can anticipate possible problems and determine the most effective medication and dosage. When taking a medication history, it is important to include all medications that have been taken, including prescription and nonprescription drugs and drugs for chronic conditions. The social worker should also ask about any herbal medications and treatments and nontraditional drugs that are assumed by clients to be "safe." A client may take aspirin for arthritis pain and not consider it important enough to mention. Recording aspirin as one of the client's medications is important, however, because it can interact with certain blood pressure or anticoagulant medications (Coumadin), diabetes medications (diabenese), or mood stabilizers such as valporic acid (*PDR*, 2000).

It is also important to make note of substances that clients would not consider worth mentioning. For example, caffeine has been noted to decrease the antipsychotic effects of medications. Cigarette smoking has been linked to decreased levels of antidepressant and antipsychotic medications in the blood. Over-the-counter medications should also be documented, particularly antacids that may lead to decreased absorption of the antipsychotic medications. Needless to say, it is important to document all medications and herbal products that a client is taking, even the ones that may not be considered real medications including any over-the-counter medications, vitamins, and diet supplements.

Careful documentation is essential. Medications that are currently being taken should be distinguished from those that have been taken in the past. Generally, a time frame of at least three months is recommended for documentation of past medication use. Because most individuals may have trouble remembering, especially those who have taken multiple medications, it is important to be supportive and allow the client to search for any medication bottles or prescriptions that will provide accurate information for documentation purposes.

LEARNING AND ASSESSMENT ACTIVITY

Create a client medication file box. Complete a medication assessment for each client and an index card to record subsequent medication information. Write down all the medications your client is currently taking on a 3″ × 5″ index card. Describe the purpose of the medication, how the drug works, the side effects, the dosage the client is receiving and the expected dosage range, and any precautions that must be taken. List how the client feels the medication is benefiting him or her, what side effects have been experienced, and how are side effects to be handled. This activity helps the social worker assist clients in tracking medication changes that may affect the clients' treatment progress.

Professional social workers are not usually responsible for documenting the medication history. We cannot emphasize enough the importance of keeping careful records and documentation that supports the service a member of the interdisciplinary team provides. It is anticipated that the increased emphasis on effective treatment and outcome by managed care and regulatory organizations will require social workers and other mental health professionals to include specific medication-therapy information in counseling documentation.

DOCUMENTATION

Social workers have always relied on some form of documentation of client situations and problems. While the formats have changed, documentation for maintaining case continuity remains a professional priority

(Dziegielewski, 1998; Kagle, 1995). Record-keeping provides the health and mental health care social worker with a map of where the client and worker have traveled in their intervention journey. Understanding and recording the client's problems, the counseling and medication interventions used, and the client's progress enables the social worker to assess the interventions, to recommend adjustments in medications, and to make necessary changes in the counseling strategies.

PROBLEM-ORIENTED RECORD-KEEPING

Of the various types of record-keeping, health care facilities frequently use a problem-oriented format. Developed first in medical settings, this type of record-keeping was used to encourage interdisciplinary collaboration and to train medical professionals (Weed, 1969). Working in interdisciplinary health care and mental health settings, social workers find that problem-oriented record-keeping enables them to comply with the facility's documentation requirements.

Problem-oriented recording emphasizes worker accountability through brief and concise documentation of client problems, services or interventions provided, and client responses. With its emphasis on brevity and its numerous formats, problem-oriented recording is compatible with the increase in client caseloads, rapid assessments, and time-limited treatment (Dziegielewski, 1998). By taking brief, informative notes, healthcare social workers are able to provide comprehensive summaries of a client's treatment progress. One of the most popular formats for problem-oriented recording is the Subjective-Objective-Assessment+Plan (SOAP). In this format, the social worker uses the S (Subjective) to record the data relevant to the client's request for service. The O (Objective) includes observable and measurable criteria related to the problem, symptoms, behaviors, and quotes as reported by the client or as observed by the worker are included as objective data. The A (Assessment) is the social worker's assessment of the underlying problems and the development of a *DSM-IV* (American Psychiatric Association, 1994) diagnostic formulation. In P (Plan) the worker records how treatment objectives will be carried out, areas for future interventions, and specific referrals to other services required by the client. In some health care agencies, workers have added components to clarify the problem further. By adding I (Implementation) and E (Evaluation), social workers are able to identify specific actions related to intervention implementation and the worker's evaluation of progress after intervention.

Another popular problem-oriented recording format used in many healthcare facilities today is the DAP (data, assessment, and plan) format. A brief format, the DAP encourages healthcare social workers and other professionals to identify only the most salient elements of a worker's client contact. Using the *D* (Data), social workers record objective client data and client statements related to the presenting problem and the focus of the therapeutic contact. The *A* (Assessment) is used to record the social worker's interventions, the client's reactions to the interventions, and the worker's assessment of the client's overall progress. Specific information on all tasks, actions, or plans related to the presenting problem and to be carried out by either the client or the worker is recorded under *P* (Plan). Information is also recorded here on issues related to the presenting problem that will be explored at the next session and the specific date and time of the next appointment.

It is essential that social work practitioners ask clients on a regular basis about the positive and adverse effects of their mental health medications. Social workers and other mental health professionals should not assume that clients are not experiencing any issues of noncompliance or other difficulties related to their adjustment to the medications. At every session it is important to ask the following questions.

1. Is the client still taking the medication as prescribed?
2. Did the client make any changes in dosage or frequency directions?
3. When was the last time the client took the medication?
4. Were there any interruptions in the medication?
5. Has the client noticed any positive or negative effects from the medication?
6. Is the client clear on what the medication is supposed to accomplish?
7. How does the client feel now about taking medication?

In addition, the client should be given opportunities to ask questions about the medication and to express any other concerns not covered by the social work practitioner. By asking these questions and having the client explain his or her understanding of the medication therapy, the social worker helps the client increase his or her compliance with the medication regimen and ultimately achieve success in treatment. Addressing these questions also provides important information that is documented in the client's record and is available to the medication prescriber and other health care team members for coordinating and maximizing the client's treatment.

The primary care physician or the nurses are generally assigned the responsibility for documenting the progress note. According to Ouslander, Osterweil, and Morley (1998), the following information must be clearly documented in order to accurately monitor medications:

1. Assessment of the clinical effectiveness of the drug and identification of side effects
2. Periodic measurement of various clinical parameters (e.g., pulse, blood pressure, postural blood pressure)
3. Periodic laboratory studies (p. 378)

The most valuable contribution the social worker can make is to provide other team members with information and to document how the client appears to be responding to the medication. For example, a client has been prescribed a medication to be taken PRN (only as required or needed). During visits with the client the social worker becomes concerned as the client complains that she is in so much pain she is taking the medication regularly every two to four hours. The social worker should immediately document this information and share it with the intervention team. This information is essential in making the best decisions for the client. In this case, the information presented will help the team and prescriber decide if this is the best way to administer the medication, if the medication is really needed on a regular basis or another stronger medication might be more beneficial, and if there is potential for abuse or dependence.

The key to documenting medication and counseling strategies is to maintain brevity yet to provide informative data. Only the most salient issues relevant to client care and progress should be recorded. Information should focus directly on the content covered in therapeutic sessions and on the interplay of the client's progress with the medication and counseling interventions. It is equally important for the social work professional to include the medication and counseling strategies in the primary treatment plan. Always link the therapeutic interventions to the original problems, goals, and objectives.

Providing brief, accurate, and informative documentation that includes both counseling and medication interventions requires skill and training. Social workers must learn to document important information that will assist the medication prescriber and other health care and mental health team members in providing the most effective interventions for clients. This requires that vital client information gathered during the assessment, diagnostic impressions, and intervention recommendations be presented in documentation that clearly identifies the client's problems, signs and symptoms, and past and current mental health and medication history. While the specific type of documentation format used by social workers will often be determined by the agency setting, social workers should closely examine the format of choice and learn to integrate biopsychosocial and spiritual information that will be helpful in understanding the client and assist in formulating an effective intervention strategy.

With so much emphasis on outcome, it is essential that social workers learn to include objective measures that will help to evaluate the effects of medication and counseling therapies on the clients. Some of these measures are standardized scales, surveys, and instruments such as the Beck Depression Inventory, or the Hudson Self-Esteem Scale. These tools provide empirical data that identifies changes over the course of medication and counseling interventions and are especially important in today's health care practice environment, which emphasizes treatment efficacy and accountability. It is extremely important that social workers become familiar with and integrate measurement instruments in their practice and in their documentation to determine if treatment interventions have impacted baseline behaviors and problems (Dziegielewski, 1997). Gathering data throughout a client's course of treatment enables both the social worker and the client to see whether progress has been made and provides regulatory agencies with tangible objective evidence of client progress or decompensation.

By using a holistic framework that stresses the client's biopsychosocial factors, social workers play an important role in the efficient delivery of interdisciplinary health care services. As part of the health care team, social workers can use record-keeping to communicate effectively and collaborate with other interdisciplinary team members on client progress and problems. Providing accurate, up-to-date, and informative records is vital to the coordinated health care planning efforts of the entire team and most important to ensuring the client's health.

SUMMARY AND CONCLUSIONS

Social workers are often involved in medication regimens, and the more knowledge they have in the area, the more equipped they will be to handle potential problems. The role of the social worker in medication usage is an essential one, if only to educate clients on some of the issues that other professionals avoid or neglect mentioning. One problem often noted in the field by medical social workers is the lack of awareness of actual pill-taking behaviors. Even the most educated clients may be unaware that a time-release medication should never be chewed or split in half. A similar problem can occur if a client breaks a tablet that is not scored in an attempt to save money. If the tablet is not scored there is no guarantee that the medication is distributed equally throughout the tablet.

The role of the social worker in helping to understand, educate, monitor, and document issues surrounding the use of medications is an important one. Social workers need to be aware of medication interactions and help clients prepare for and avoid negative reactions to medication. Like most physicians and other prescribers of medication, it is unrealistic to expect social workers to know about every medication a client is taking. It is not unreasonable, however, to expect them to find out the necessary medication information and to become familiar with effects and adverse reactions. Using the *Physicians' Desk Reference* and other similar resources can assist in gathering available manufacturers' data on the testing and side-effect profiles of the medications in question (*PDR*, 2000). The *Physicians' Desk Reference for Over-the-Counter Medications* may also be of assistance (*PDR OTC*, 1998). If this is not available, a call to the local pharmacy can provide information package inserts.

The social worker is essential both as a direct provider and as a member of the interdisciplinary team in helping to verify information about the medications the client is taking. Although careful monitoring of drug therapy is not considered the primary role of the social worker, assisting in this process is. Social workers can identify medications that might be unnecessary or inappropriate and assist in documenting the efficacy of the drug, because many clients do not explore the appropriateness of their medication.

Social workers are now often expected to assist with taking an initial medication history. It is important to remember that an accurate and responsible history should also explore the possibility for abuse. When the potential for abuse is high, social workers can note this and prepare the team to be aware and avoid possible problems for the client. When taking a medication history, include prescription and nonprescription drugs and drugs for chronic conditions that may not seem worth mentioning.

It is important to document all medications and substances that a client is taking including caffeine, nicotine, and over-the-counter medications.

It is predicted that in the future with the financial crunch and the blurring of roles in managed care, social workers and other disciplines will be held accountable for this very important responsibility (Dziegielewski, 1998).

REFERENCES

American Psychiatric Association. (1994). *Diagnostic and statistical manual of mental disorders* (4th ed.). Washington, DC: American Psychiatric Press.

Banta, D. (2000). Increase in global access to essential drugs sought (medical news and perspectives). *Journal of the American Medical Association, 283, 3,* 321.

Dziegielewski, S. F. (1997). Should clinical social workers seek psychotropic medication prescription privileges?: Yes. In B. A. Thyer (Ed.), *Controversial issues in social work practice* (pp. 152–165). Boston: Allyn & Bacon.

Dziegielewski, S. F. (1998). *The changing face of health care social work; Professional practice in the era of managed care.* New York: Springer.

Dziegielewski, S. F., & Harrison, D. F. (1996). Social work practice with the aged. In D. F. Harrison, B. A. Thyer, & J. S. Wodarski (Eds.), *Cultural diversity and social work practice* (2nd ed., pp. 138–175). Springfield, IL: Charles C Thomas.

Eisenhauer, L. A. (1998). Variations in patient responses to drug therapy: The role of pharmacodynamics and pharmacokinetics. In L. A. Eisenhauer & M. A. Murphy (Eds.), *Pharmacotherapeutics & advanced nursing practice* (pp. 53–66). New York: McGraw-Hill.

Heller, W. M. (1993). Initial responses to recommendations of the blue-ribbon committee on generic medicines. *American Journal of Hospital Pharmacy, 50,* 318–321.

Henkel, J. (1998). Reporting adverse reactions and other product problems. *FDA Consumer, 32*(6), 7–15.

Henkel, J. (1999). Monitoring medical product safety. *Consumer's Research Magazine, 82*(2), 27–28.

Kagle, J. D. (1995). Recording. In *Encyclopedia of social work* (19th ed., Vol. 2, pp. 2027–2033). Washington, DC: NASW Press.

Kaplan, H. I., & Sadock, B. J. (1990). *Pocket handbook of clinical psychiatry.* Baltimore, MD: Williams & Wilkins.

Kurtzweil, P. (1994). Liquid medication and dosing devices. *FDA Consumer, 28*(8), 6–9.

Nordenberg, T. (1999). When is a medical product too risky: An interview with FDA's top drug official. *FDA Consumer, 33*(5), 8–13.

Ouslander, J. G., Osterweil, D., & Morley, J. (1998). *Medical care in the nursing home* (2nd ed.). New York: McGraw-Hill.

Physicians' Desk Reference. (1998). *Physicians' desk reference: For nonprescription drugs* (18th ed.). Montvale, NJ: Medical Economics.

Physicians' Desk Reference. (2000). *Physicians' desk reference* (54th ed.). Montvale, NJ: Medical Economics.

Prufer, D. (1996, April). Is your medicine safe? What pharmacists don't tell you. *Good Housekeeping, 222,* 137–138.

Public Citizen's Health Research Group. (1993). *Worst pills best pills II.* Washington, DC: Public Citizens' Health Research Group.

Serafini, M. W. (2000a). Campaign medicine. *National Journal, 32*(2), 86.

Serafini, M. W. (2000b). No easy prescriptions on no-name drugs. *National Journal, 32*(8), 548.

Schwartz, J. B. (1998). Clinical pharmacology. In J. P. Blass, W. H. Ettinger, J. B. Halter, W. R. Hazard, & J. G. Ouslander (Eds.), *Principles of geriatric medicine and gerontology.* New York: McGraw-Hill.

Watson-Heidari, T. (2000, July/August). Generics for smart shoppers. *Humana Active Outlook,* p. 11.

Weed, L. (1969). *Medical records, medical evaluation, and patient care.* Cleveland, OH: Case Western Reserve University Press.

Williams, R. D. (1997, Sept.–Oct.). Medications and older adults. *FDA Consumer, 31*(6), 15–18.

PART II

Mental Health Conditions, Psychopharmacology, and Social Work Practice

Chapter 4

Treatment of Major Depression: Social Work Intervention

This chapter is designed to provide an overview of the medication issues and concerns that social workers will encounter when participating in the treatment of clients who suffer from depression. Because medication is often used as part of the intervention process, it has become a practice necessity for social workers to have a basic knowledge with regard to medication usage and misuse. This chapter includes information about major depression, the medications used to treat this disorder, short- and long-term efficacy, side effects, and other important considerations designed to increase the effectiveness of these social work intervention strategies.

For many social work practitioners, clients who report symptoms of depression are commonplace. It is reported that approximately 23% of the population will suffer from depression at some point in their lifetime (Marano, 1999). These symptoms are reported so frequently during routine medical visits and throughout the course of psychological treatment that many in the medical community have come to refer to depression as the "common cold of mental health." It is estimated that 1.5 million people receive treatment for unipolar illness each year and another 4.5 to 7.5 million go untreated (Merck Research Laboratories, 1992). Unfortunately, approximately 50% to 80% of clients who seek treatment for their depression will go unrecognized or misdiagnosed (Higgins, 1994). Furthermore, although depression can involve serious deficits in functioning, most cases are considered less severe with approximately 25% of all depressed individuals receiving inpatient mental health treatment. The remaining clients go directly to outpatient or other private practice medical settings (Merck Research Laboratories, 1992). In the primary care medical setting, up to 30% of all clients report having depressive symptoms (Tierney, McPhee, & Papadakis, 1997).

For the medical practitioner, clients suffering from depression may be especially frustrating to deal with as their complaints—generally somatic in nature—usually result in negative medical examinations that reveal no physical causes for the problem. This multifaceted disorder provides fertile ground for misunderstandings and frustration on the part of both health care providers and the clients. To complicate the matter, about 70% of those who have suffered from depression once can expect a recurrence (Resnick & Carson, 1996).

One of the biggest problems for many clinical professionals who work with these clients is the lack of clarity and problems in semantics in defining what the term depression actually means. For many individuals, depression can mean feeling sad, blue, or down in the dumps, whereas for others there are clearly established criteria that reflect consistent patterns, signs, and symptoms relative to a mood disorder (Gitlin, 1996). Furthermore, some form of depression (also referred to as dysphoric mood) is present in virtually all mental health conditions. The only possible exceptions to this are clients who suffer from mania, certain forms of schizophrenia, or dementia (Gitlin, 1996).

In addition, feelings of depression can often be overstated or understated because they reflect the definition and standards of normalcy within an individual's unique social and environmental context. As a first step toward acquiring effective treatment, a clear, concise, psychosocial-criteria-based diagnostic standard must be applied. All diagnostic interpretations must be sensitive to the influence of cultural and stress-related environmental and social factors.

CASE EXAMPLE: JEAN

Jean, a 70-year-old female, was admitted to the hospital after being evaluated for several medical conditions that included a fractured left hip with extensive bruising to the area and to the left side of her body. She and her family reported to the attending physician that they were expecting a short rehabilitative stay at the hospital, and a social work consult was generated to determine if she could continue living at home after stabilization or whether a temporary rehabilitation facility would be needed.

During the interview, Jean was alert and oriented and did not appear to be in any type of physical distress. Her affect (the outward expression of her mood) appeared flat, although she did warm up considerably when engaged. Her speech was clear, and she responded appropriately to all questions. During assessment, Jean talked about many events in her life. She stated that she had been raised in a rural area of Georgia, and she described her relationship with her family as a close one while growing up. Her father was a Baptist minister, and the family often spent a great deal of time praying together. She said that she had always felt very close to the church, and her greatest disappointment was that she no longer found comfort in organized religion. When asked further about this, Jean stated that her husband had died ten years ago, and after his death she felt as though she had lost all hope. Since that time, she had little if any contact with her family and often felt she was alone, without any connection except her memories. She confided that oftentimes she did not want to get out of bed and would stay there for days at a time. After not eating for a few days she would become fearful that she would die and that her death might be perceived as suicide in her expected afterlife. Not wishing to cause her own death, Jean ate everything she could find to avoid starvation. She said she always answered the phone if family members called because she did not want to be a burden to them. She worried that if she did not answer the phone her family might come to check on her thinking that she was dead. Although she acknowledged that there had always been times in her life when she didn't want to live anymore, she felt that her current feelings were more intense than before. She stated that she had fallen and fractured her hip after having a bad dream in which she was afraid her bed would swallow her up and she would never wake up. In her fear, she ran from her bedroom and tripped in the dark. When the client was asked directly if she was feeling suicidal, she stated no, but that she just wished that she could die to join her husband.

After interviewing the client to arrange her discharge plan, the social worker became very concerned because the client was obviously very depressed and most probably could not handle her own needs at home without assistance. Prior to meeting with the social worker, the client had not been assessed for depression nor had she gotten a psychiatric examination. It was obvious to the social worker that Jean was depressed, and that she had intense ambivalence about her desire to end her life. Based on this interview, the social worker requested a delay in discharge and an immediate psychiatric consultation. After the consult, however, the client was immediately placed on a low-dose antidepressant and discharged the next day. This course of action disturbed the social worker, because she had expressed concerns that the client was showing classic signs of depression and might not be able to handle the daily activities of living independently at home until the medication lifted her mood. After extensive debate with the team about an appropriate discharge plan, the social worker went to the client and shared her perceptions and concerns related to Jean's depression. The client agreed that she was depressed, and because she did not want to be alone agreed to placement in an assisted-living facility. The social worker was relieved by this decision, and she talked with the housing supervisor and arranged for a counselor to see the client in the facility. The client was grateful for the intervention and completed a no-suicide contract to be implemented upon discharge.

Situations like this are becoming much more common for social workers. Many individuals, particularly older people, are uncomfortable revealing their feelings of depression to a physician. This makes the role of the social worker essential in exploring mental health issues, especially those related to depression. Many of the newer antidepressant medications work quickly in lifting depression, so becoming aware of the quick response time is important because depressed individuals are more likely to harm themselves once they feel better and have more energy. The increased energy allows the individual to consider acting on suicidal thoughts or feelings. As illustrated in this case, prescribing medication without counseling or while quickly discharging clients from inpatient hospitals may unintentionally deprive these clients of the proper care and attention to address and reduce the depression and put clients in a potentially dangerous situation.

DEPRESSION: FORMING THE DIAGNOSTIC IMPRESSION

Two classification systems are often used for diagnostic and billing purposes by social workers who counsel clients who have mental health disorders. One was developed by the World Health Organization, which sponsored the *International Classification of Diseases*; and the other by the American Psychiatric Association (1994), which publishes the *Diagnostic and Statistical Manual of Mental Disorders* (*DSM-IV*).

In the past, social work practitioners often had difficulty establishing and separating the diagnostic criteria for major depression and other disorders, because the manuals differed and classification criteria did not overlap. This is no longer the case: The *DSM-IV* diagnostic categories are clearly related to the ICD-9 and ICD-10 (American Psychiatric Association, 1994). Most social workers can now concentrate primarily on defining the pharmacological treatment considerations for major depression as described in the *DSM-IV*. To support and substantiate diagnostic categories as described in the *DSM-IV*, mood disorder field trials were implemented that investigated the reliability and validity of the diagnostic categories established (Keller, Klein, Hirschfield Kocsis, McCullough, Miller, First, Holzer, Keitner, Marin, & Shea, 1995; Keller, Hanks, & Klein, 1996). This resulted in research support for the classification system of the major depressive episode. Table 4.1 lists and briefly describes this mental health disorder as outlined by the diagnostic framework within the *DSM-IV* (American Psychiatric Association, 1994). The table also delineates the specifiers used to categorize the type and course of the unipolar depressive mental disorder.

To date, two types of major depression have been postulated. The first is often referred to as endogenous or melancholic depression. In this type of major depression, symptoms of depressed mood are related directly to internal biologic factors such as neurotransmitter dysfunction (Kaplan & Sadock, 1990; Tierney et al., 1997). Electroconvulsive therapy (ECT), referred to historically as shock treatments, is often considered an endogenous treatment. Here, direct (biologic) stimulation of the neurotransmission process is the treatment strategy. Similar to ECT, antidepressant medications also are successful in lifting endogenous depression, with the major difference that they affect the neurochemical pathways chemically rather than electrically (Maxmen & Ward, 1995).

In the second type of major depression, a link generally exists between characterological, personal, or neurotic responses and precipitating events. This form of exogenous or environmental depression is often referred to as reactive depression, and its signs and symptoms are related directly to psychosocial factors or stresses such as divorce, unemployment, or injury (Tierney, McPhee, & Papdakis, 1997). Furthermore, Tierney et al. (1997) caution clinicians to differentiate between normal grief symptoms, which at first resemble major depression, and actual depression symptomatology. They believe that grief and sadness are normal responses to loss, whereas depression is not. In depression, the survivor feels a marked sense of worthlessness and guilt, but with grief individual self-esteem remains intact. From a practitioner's perspective, clients who are experiencing normal grief seem to provoke sympathy or sadness in service providers, but clients who report general signs of depression are often met with frustration and irritation (Tierney et al., 1997).

TABLE 4.1   Description of Major Depressive Disorders

296.2x
Major depressive disorder: single episode (presence of a single major depressive episode)

296.3x Major depressive disorder:
Recurrent (presence of two or more major depressive episodes)

Major depressive disorder criteria:

A: There must be a **major depressive episode** that has been present during the same 2-week period and that represents a change from a previous level of functioning, plus five other associated features (e.g., appetite disturbance, significant and unintentional weight loss or gain, sleep disturbance, fatigue, reduced ability to think or concentrate, diminished interest or pleasure in all activities, persistent thoughts of death or suicide).

B: This mood disorder cannot be better accounted for by another mental health disorder such as schizophrenia, schizophreniform disorder, delusional disorder, or psychotic disorder not otherwise specified.

C: There has never been another type of **mood episode** experienced such as manic episode, mixed episode, or hypomanic episode. If a history of these other "mood-like episodes" is reported, occurrence must be related to substance use, be treatment related or due to a general medical condition.

Specifiers describing major depressive disorder: recurrent

1.   Longitudinal: These specifiers are used to describe remission patterns. The two types include: with full interepisode recovery (i.e., full remission has been attained between the two most recent episodes); and without full interepisode recovery (i.e., when remission was not attained between the two most recent episodes).

2.   Seasonal pattern specifier: These specifiers link a time of year or season directly to the depressive episode. The term seasonal affective disorder (SAD) is often used to describe this type of depression.

3.   With melancholic features: These features can occur at anytime throughout the depressive episodes: loss of pleasure in almost all activities and lack of reactivity to pleasurable stimuli. In addition, three or more of the following are present: distinct quality of depressed mood, early-morning worsening, marked psychomotor agitation or retardation, disturbance in appetite with weight gain or loss, and excessive, inappropriate guilt.

4.   With atypical features: Within this specifier there are incongruent findings to some of the established criteria (e.g., mood brightens when exposed to a pleasant event, or unusual features related to the condition exist such as overeating, oversleeping, or patterns of hypersubjectivity to rejection).

Mental health diagnostic categories are summarized from the information presented in the *DSM-IV* classification system (American Psychiatric Association, 1994).

Whether depression is endogenous (related to internal causes) or exogenous (related to external or environmental causes) or a combination of both, the first clinical feature usually presented in major depression is dysphoria (a disturbance in mood) or anhedonia (a loss of pleasure or interest) (Maxmen & Ward, 1995). In anhedonia, there is a pervasive loss of interest or ability to experience pleasure in normally enjoyable activities. Depressed individuals present with a wide range of complaints that include withdrawal from normally pleasurable or interesting activities, feelings of guilt, the inability to concentrate, feelings of worthlessness, somatic complaints, feelings of anxiety, chronic fatigue, and loss of sexual desire. As with any mental health problem, an accurate diagnosis of major depressive disorder requires that the client's cognitive, behavioral, and somatic complaints be clearly documented.

When documenting major depressive disorder (described in Table 4.1), the *DSM-IV* (American Psychiatric Association, 1994) establishes diagnostic codes. If a client is diagnosed with major depressive disorder (single episode or recurrent), the following coding scheme needs to outlined:

1.   For the diagnosis major depressive disorder, the first three digits are always 296.
Major depressive disorder B 296.xx

2.   The fourth digit denotes whether it is a single (denoted with the number 2) or recurrent (denoted with a 3) major depressive episode.
Major Depressive Disorder
296.2x Single / 296.3x Recurrent

3.   The fifth digit indicates the severity:

296.x.1 mild severity	296.x.2 moderate severity
296.x.3 severe without psychotic features	296.x.4 severe with psychotic features
296.x.5 in partial remission	296.x.6 in full remission
296.x.0 if unspecified	

The other specifiers for the major depressive disorder (with melancholic features, with postpartum onset, etc.) cannot be coded within the numbering system. They are to be written out and listed after the official diagnosis.

MEDICATION INTERVENTION FOR DEPRESSION

Most professionals agree that normal life situations and developmental phases can create feelings of sadness or depressed moods in everyone. A depressed mood only becomes pathological when the magnitude or duration of the experience exceeds normal limits taking into account the precipitating event (Merck Research Laboratories, 1992). Therefore, all antidepressant medications are primarily used to treat individuals who suffer significantly enough from depressed mood to be classified as pathological. The person who will respond best to these types of medications is someone who suffers from more than just the "blues." A prolonged depressed mood that does not appear to respond to short-term brief psychotherapy or crisis intervention and that interferes with a person's family life, and mental, physical, job, and social functioning indicates the need for antidepressant medication (Rush, 1993; Shindul-Rothschild & Rothschild, 1998). Studies clearly support that the neurochemical-based treatments for depression such as antidepressant medications and ECT are effective in lifting depressed moods. Controlled studies using neurochemically based treatments specifically for the treatment of major depression indicated that 78% of the depressed individuals improved with ECT, and 70% with the newer antidepressants medications (Maxmen & Ward, 1995). In practice, it is estimated that 50% of individuals who take antidepressant medicines report feeling better or achieve complete remission. In addition, antidepressant medications can be used to treat related conditions such as obsessive compulsive disorder and overwhelming anxiety (Brophy, 1991). Antidepressants are often used to treat excessive anxiety since they can block the symptoms of panic including rapid heartbeat, terror, dizziness, chest pains, nausea, and breathing problems.

Generally, the antidepressant drugs can be classified into three major groups: (a) the tricyclic antidepressants, (b) the monoamine oxidase inhibitors, and (c) the newer generation antidepressant drugs such as the serotonin-selective reuptake inhibitors (SSRIs) (Brophy, 1991; Tierney et al., 1997). The popularity of these drugs, especially the newer-generation antidepressants, has risen dramatically. It is questionable, however, why the trend to medicate all depressive symptoms continues to rise, especially after current medical treatment guidelines have recommended that depression associated with reactive or external environmental pressures do not call for drug therapy. Perhaps what complicates matters for practitioners is that some clients present symptoms reflective of both endogenous and reaction depression (Maxmen & Ward, 1995). According to the 1997 recommended treatment guidelines postulated by *Current Medical Diagnosis and Treatment* (36th edition), this type of depression is better treated with psychotherapy and the passage of time (as cited in Tierney et al., 1997). Based on these treatment guidelines, however, drug therapy is recommended for individuals with a first-generation family history of major depression or a history of previous or recurrent episodes.

TRICYCLIC ANTIDEPRESSANT AND CHEMICALLY SIMILAR MEDICATIONS

The first major groups of antidepressant medications are the *tricyclics*, also known as the TCAs. Discovered in the late 1950s, these drugs are considered the oldest in the treatment of depression and have historically been used as the first line of medication intervention for the treatment of unipolar depression (Austrian, 1995). The side-effect profile that accompanies this group of medications, however, has recently caused them to fall into disfavor. For years, these medications were often considered the first choice for the client who suffers from depressed mood. Today, however, the antidepressant medications known as the selective serotonin inhibitors (SSRIs), and the selective serotonin norepinephrine inhibitors (SSNRIs) are often considered as the first-line medications.

The *tricyclic* medications inhibit the uptake of neurotransmitters such as serotonin, norepinephrine, and dopamine (Larkin, 1993). Generally, these medications are dosed at approximately 25–50 mg a day and increased by 25–50 mg every several days until the client has adapted gradually to side effects (Maxmen & Ward, 1995; PDR, 2000). When a client takes these medications peak concentrations of the drug are usually reached between 2 and 8 hours, but may extend to between 10 and 12 hours (*Physician's Desk Reference*, 2000). For most clients, a trial of at least 10 to 14 days is usually needed to get a full therapeutic dose, and this full effect might not occur for up to 6 weeks (Austrian, 1995). Since short-term effectiveness is noticeable in most clients within two to four weeks, it can be evaluated through changes in blood levels. An increase in the medication is appropriate if the client has not experienced any changes in symptoms and is reporting minimal side effects (Gitlin, 1996). Establishing an adequate course of treatment is considered essential for this classification of medications, especially since the most common cause of treatment failure is an inadequate trial of the medication (Tierney et al., 1997).

Examples of Tricyclics

Drug	Sedative effect	Dosage range
Elavil (amitriptyline)	Strong sedative	150–300 mg a day
Tofranil (imipramine)	Moderate sedative	150–300 mg a day
Pamelor/Aventyl (nortriptyline)	Mild sedative	50–150 mg a day
Norpramin/Pertofrane (desipramine)	Mild sedative	100–300 mg a day

The newest drug in this category, sometimes referred to as a heterocyclic:

*Asendin (amoxapine)	Mild/moderate sedation	150–450 mg a day

*Watch for tardive dyskinesia as this antidepressant can create substantive neuroleptic activity. Ranges are approximate. These values were taken from Shindul-Rothschild & Rothschild (1998).

Tricyclic medications have many side effects due to binding to multiple unrelated receptors (Kent, 2000). Therefore, monitoring the client who is placed on a tricyclic medication should be done carefully and depends on whether this type of medication was effective previously or whether the client can handle the side effects. The most common side effects include constipation, urinary retention, dry mouth, sedation, postural hypotension, cravings for sweets, and weight gain (Gitlin, 1996; Kent, 2000). Though tricyclic medications can decrease the symptoms of depression, social workers need to educate their clients on the potential long-term effects of these drugs. Some of these side effects, which vary from client to client, need to be identified and monitored while the client adjusts physio-logically and psychologically to the medication. Special consideration should be given to tricyclic medications such as clomipramine (Anafranil) since its powerful nature can cause typical tricyclic side effects, epileptic seizures, and serious sexual side effects (Gitlin, 1996). Of greatest concern to social workers who have clients taking tricyclic medications is that these medications can be lethal in overdose. This is probably the reason that many prescribers now seem to steer away from them, especially since individuals who are severely depressed generally need increased and prolonged dosages (Fugh-Bergman, 2000).

Possible Side Effects of Tricyclics

Complications
- Reactions may vary
- Can complicate heart problems
- Sweating, dryness of the mouth, headache
- Increased appetite for sweets
- Weight gain, unpleasant taste in mouth
- Difficulty urinating, changes in sexual desire
- Decrease in sexual ability
- Muscle twitches, fatigue, and weakness

Interactions
- thyroid hormones
- antihypertensive medications
- oral contraceptives, alcohol
- some blood coagulants, tobacco
- some sleeping medications
- antipsychotic medications
- diuretics, aspirin, vitamin C
- antihistamines, bicarbonate of soda

MONOAMINE OXIDASE INHIBITORS

MAO inhibitors are another group of antidepressant medications that have historically been used to treat major depressive disorders. Currently, this classification of medications is considered a second-line or third-line treatment of depression (Brophy, 1991; Tierney et al., 1997). There are times however, that this group of drugs can be utilized as the first line of treatment for depression of an atypical nature (Tierney et al., 1997). Generally, these medications with their dangerous treatment-effect profiles should only be considered after the tricyclic or the newer classifications of antidepressants have been tried (Tierney et al., 1997).

These drugs work by blocking the enzyme monoamine oxidase, which blocks the uptake of monoamines (Gitlin, 1996). Monoamines are chemicals that are responsible for stimulating effects that occur in the central nervous system. By blocking this uptake, more monamines remain available to the system. As these drugs carry a risk for serious reaction, clients should be warned about the high potential for interaction with other medications (Kent, 2000; Larkin, 1993). The social worker should remind clients to provide the prescriber with a complete account of the different medications they are currently taking as well as any medications taken in the last few weeks. Since the interaction potential is high, clients who are taking other medications should be assessed to determine whether this type of medication should be used at all. These medications also can have serious toxic side effects related to dietary intake and clients should be required to observe certain dietary restrictions and abstain from certain drug products (Lehne & Scott, 1996; Merck Research Laboratories, 1992; *PDR*, 2000; Tierney et al., 1997). Foods and vegetables to be avoided include: most cheese products (except cottage cheese, cream cheese, and fresh yogurt), any fermented or aged meats such as salami or bologna, liver of all types, pickled herring, broad bean pods and Chinese pea pods, meat and yeast extracts, raisins, pineapples, bananas, and chocolate. Beverages to be avoided include red wine, beer, ale, vermouth, cognac, sherry, and coffee. Drug products to be avoided include products containing phenylpropanolamine, phenylephrine, meperidine, dextromethorphan, and pseudoephedrine. Because of the presence of many of these compounds in over-the-counter cold and allergy preparations (*Physicians' Desk Reference*, 1997), it is essential that clients know about these ingredients and about the overall toxicity that can occur through drug interactions. Information on which dietary and drug products to avoid is essential since the MAO inhibitors (those marketed for the treatment of depression) leave the client vulnerable to exogenous amines (e.g., the tyramine in food items).

Recommendations to assist social work professionals working with clients on MAO-type medications include: (a) use of this medication should be reevaluated if the client has trouble understanding, following, or maintaining the dietary and medication compound restrictions; (b) ongoing education in regard to the dietary restrictions and the availability of many over-the-counter compounds that cannot be tolerated needs to be reinforced (Craig, 1995); (c) the client should be warned against taking or discontinuing any additional medications without knowing the possible interaction or withdrawal effects (Craig, 1995); and (d) the client needs to be made aware of the "wash out" time (2–3 weeks) that is required if there are plans to switch from one medication in this category of antidepressants to another, particularly when the change involves taking a newer generation antidepressant such as an SSRI (Tierney et al., 1997).

Examples of MAOIs

Drug	Dosage
Nardil (phenelzine)	45–90 mg a day

Eldepryl (selegiline)   20–50 mg a day
Parnate (tranylcypromine)   30–50 mg a day

Nardil and Parnate are the two most commonly used medications of this type (Lehne & Scott, 1996).

MAOIs: Most Common Side Effects and Possible Medication Interactions

- Dizziness and rapid heart rate when changing position (especially from sitting to standing)
- Interaction with certain food additives especially monosodium glutamate (MSG)
- Interaction with over-the-counter cold and allergy preparations, antihistamines, amphetamines, insulin, narcotics, and antiparkinsonian medications
- Reactions may not appear for several hours and can include rapid heart rate, high blood pressure, seizures, stroke, or coma

Despite their antidepressant efficacy, MAO inhibitors are not used as often as the other groups of antidepressants. Early observations suggested that MAO inhibitors were not as effective for clients with severe depression and that its side effects were serious and at times life-threatening (Gitlin, 1996). Both these concerns overshadowed later information that indicated that this group of antidepressants is effective in the treatment of both typical and atypical depression. With the development of the newer antidepressants, the MAO inhibitors have become the third choice of antidepressants and still generate concern related to hypertension as one of its major side effects. When this group of drugs is prescribed, clients should be carefully educated about the importance of avoiding foods containing tyramine (herring, aged cheese, salami) or sympathomimetic drugs (cocaine, amphetamines, decongestants) (Maxmen & Ward, 1995).

THE NEWER ANTIDEPRESSANT MEDICATIONS

Compared to other forms of antidepressant medication treatment, the SSRI's and other newer compounds identified to treat depression such as venlafaxine, mirtazapine, nefazodone and reboxetine are newcomers in the fight against mental disorders (Kent, 2000). This classification of antidepressants has rapidly become the most prominent form of antidepressant medication used today. For example, Prozac (fluoxetine), which was first approved in 1987, has now become one of the most popular antidepressants in use today (Jann, Jenike, & Liberman, 1994). With the advent of this medication and its ability to target the neurochemical serotonin, it is not surprising that numerous other similar medications such as Zoloft, Paxil, Celexa, and Luvox, soon followed ("Beyond Depression," 1999). Some professionals fear that the trend of prescribing an antidepressant immediately before any other type of intervention will discourage alternate and equally effective forms of treatment. Many fear that these newer antidepressants will become "as familiar as Kleenex and as socially acceptable as spring water" (Cowley, 1994, p. 41).

In this era of managed care, much of the traditional therapeutic work that was usually provided by the psychiatrist is now being funneled into the primary care environment. Over the last few years, there have been numerous concerns that primary care physicians and other specialists who prescribe antidepressants may lack information on medication effectiveness and side effects and that they are encouraging little or no verbal or sociopsychological intervention to supplement the use of medication. In a 1993 study, researchers at the Rand Corporation found that fewer than half the general practitioners who prescribed antidepressant medications spent 3 minutes or more discussing the problems that led to the depressive symptoms (cited in Cowley, 1994). In addition, researchers Rushton, Clark, and Freed (2000) found that primary care physicians prescribed medication for the treatment of childhood depression before they referred the child to any type of specialist for evaluation and intervention. Although these physicians reported no additional training in the area, they reported an increased level of comfort in prescribing medications for depression. It is clear that prescribers feel pressured to prescribe medications immediately for depression, and the effects that these medications can have on any future intervention remains questionable.

SELECTIVE SEROTONIN REUPTAKE INHIBITORS

There are several different types of medications that fall into the classification of selective serotonin reuptake inhibitors (SSRIs), which are commonly referred to as the second generation antidepressants. In the literature, they are almost always referred to by the acronym SSRIs. The SSRIs—fluoxetine (Prozac), sertraline (Zoloft), paroxetine (Paxil), fluvoxamine

(Luvox), and citalopram (Celexa)—work by inhibiting the reuptake of the neurochemical serotonin (Kent, 2000) and preventing the nerve cells from reabsorbing this neurotransmitter, thereby increasing its presence at the synapses in the central nervous system (Jann, Jenike, & Liberman, 1994; Lemonick, 1997).

Introduced in 1988, Prozac is the oldest in the SSRI class and is still the most commonly prescribed (Morris, 1999). Prozac is a highly successful antidepressant that has revolutionized the treatment of depression because of its ability to raise serotonin levels in the brain. Increased availability of this neurochemical has been directly related to addressing effectively the symptoms prevalent in depression, and Prozac was recently approved to treat obsessive-compulsive disorder and the eating disorder bulimia. Prozac and the other SSRIs are also considered the medication of choice for working with depressed older individuals because of fewer side effects than the tricyclic medications (Haider & Miller, 1993). In 1999 Prozac was endorsed by the FDA as being especially effective for geriatric depression (Hussar, 2000).

The SSRIs have been found to have fewer side effects than the older classes of antidepressants. The most common side effects of SSRIs include gastrointestinal complaints, nervousness and agitation, sexual dysfunction, and weight gain with long-term use (Kent, 2000). Being aware of these side effects is important because many times the discomfort will lead the client to stop taking the medication. Most professionals know that one of the greatest dangers in using tricyclic medications is that an overdose is often lethal; this is not the case with Prozac and the other SSRIs (Morris, 1999).

Selective Serotonin Reuptake Inhibitors

Drug	Maximum daily dosage
fluoxetine (Prozac)	80 mg
paroxetine hydrochloride (Paxil)	50 mg
sertraline (Zoloft)	200 mg
fluvoxamine (Luvox)	200–300 mg
citalopram (Celexa)	40 mg

Dosage information verified with *PDR*, 2000.

OTHER NEWER ANTIDEPRESSANTS

Although the SSRIs are said to have revolutionized the treatment of depression, there are several new medications that have gained in popularity. These medications are said to be equivalent to the SSRIs or even better in terms of efficacy (Kent, 2000). These newer antidepressant medications differ from the SSRIs in their mechanism of action. Since action is achieved differently, the side effect profiles also differ, and this second classification of drugs have improved side-effect profiles.

It is beyond the scope and intent of this book to explain the precise action of these newer medications. Simply stated, they differ from the SSRIs because they activate other neurochemicals as well as serotonin and do so differently depending on dosage. These newer medications differ from the SSRIs and in many ways improve upon them.

Two popular medications in this category are venlafaxine (Effexor) and nefazodone (Serzone). These medications are known as serotonin noradrenergic reuptake inhibitors, and the acronym for this classification is SNaRIs. Effexor is particularly convenient for clients because it comes in an extended release version, which allows the client who may have difficulty complying with multiple dosing to take the medication only once a day (Kent, 2000). For the older client with impaired liver or kidney functioning, both Effexor and Serzone must be cautiously used since this type of impairment may not allow the medication to be absorbed and filtered properly (Kent, 2000). Mirtazapine (Remron) is a noradrenergic and specific serotonergic antidepressant (NaSSA). The same warning applies for use with older people in terms of decreased liver and kidney function. Because Remeron is so new to the market and long-term studies have not been thoroughly documented, physicians who prescribe this medication should periodically evaluate the long-term use of this medication for the individual client (*PDR*, 2000). Reboxetine—which is so new it is not listed in the *PDR* 2000—selectively inhibits the neurochemical norepinephrine reuptake without inhibiting other neurochemicals such as serotonin or dopamine and is referred to as a NaRI (Kent, 2000; Moller, 2000). In preliminary studies this medication appears to be particularly effective in treating severe depression by improving negative self-perceptions and motivation (Kent, 2000).

Given these newer medications, the number of studies on drug trials that compare types of medication should be increased and refined. Social workers should keep in mind that all drug trials, especially the ones that have negative outcomes, might not be reported. Based on previous research on this category of newer antidepressants, and despite all the methodological issues relative to limited testing of client responses, there are probably only minimal differences in clinical efficacy among these four newer antidepressants (Kent, 2000).

Other Newer Antidepressants

Drug	Type of antidepressant	Maximum daily dosage
Effexor (venlafaxine HCl)	SNaRI	375 mg
Serzone (nefazodone)	SNaRI	600 mg
Remron (mirtazapine)	NaSSA	45 mg
Reboxetine	NaRI	12 mg

Maximum recommended daily doses might vary slightly based on the source. These values were taken from Shindul-Rothschild & Rothschild (1998); for Reboxetine, Kent (2000).

SIDE-EFFECT PROFILES WITH THE NEWER ANTIDEPRESSANTS

A major advantage to using the SSRIs is that a gradual dosage increase is not required to reach a therapeutic level. Most of the side effects caused by this group of medications are typically mild and tend to disappear within 1 to 2 weeks. The exception is the serious sexual side effects that are experienced by 20% to 60% of clients (Gitlin, 1996; Labbate, 1999). These sexual disorders can be long-term and include decreased libido or arousal and difficulties with erections and with reaching orgasms (Marano, 1999). Clients who experience sexual side effects should be informed that normal sexual functioning may return after the individual's system adjusts to the medication. Prescribing additional medications may be helpful in alleviating sexual side effects. For example, in one study, sildenafil (Viagra) was found to be effective in increasing sexual arousal in women taking SSRI antidepressants (Psychopharmacology Update, 2000). Social workers should be aware that several of these supplemental types of treatments are available.

One medication in particular shows promise for those clients who experience sexual side effects with the SSRI drugs. Studies of nefazadone (Serzone) reveal that only mild side effects occurred, none of which included sexual disinterest or sexual disorders (Austrian, 1995). Another consideration when working with clients who are on an SSRI is ensuring that an MAO inhibitor is not prescribed concurrently, because the interaction between the two drugs will cause a potentially fatal reaction known as serotonin syndrome (Gitlin, 1996). In serotonin overdose reactions, most individuals develop nausea and vomiting and can become very ill. The reader is referred to the case study involving this condition as described in chapter 9.

Possible Side Effects of the Newer Antidepressant Medications

- restlessness, agitation, dizziness, dry mouth
- difficulty sleeping, headache, nausea, vomiting
- constipation, change in weight, tremor, confusion
- rash, itching, seizures, sexual disinterest
- possible weight gain, suicide potential
- postural hypotension, possible decrease in fertility

DRUG INTERACTIONS

To avoid drug interactions with the newer antidepressants, it is critical that a comprehensive history be taken of all the substances that a client is taking. The history should always include prescription and over-the-counter medications, alcohol, herbals, nutritional supplements, and illegal substances. For example, many clients may not be aware of potential interactions between Prozac and an over-the-counter cough remedy that contains dextromethorphan, which can increase reactions such as dizziness, sedation, and confusion (Morris, 1999). Saint-John's-wort, an herbal preparation often used to treat depression, should never be used in conjunction with the newer antidepressants, especially the SSRIs (Morris, 1999). Taking this herbal medication with an antidepressant can raise serotonin levels to the point where toxicity may result in serotonin syndrome. Another herbal preparation that can cause interaction effects is Panax ginseng, which when combined with antidepressants, may cause manic symptoms (Fugh-Bergman, 2000). Both the social worker and the client need to be aware of adverse effects that may occur from combining over-the-counter and herbal products with prescription medication used to treat depression.

SPECIAL ISSUES

RELAPSE AND INCREASE RISK OF SUICIDE

One issue of particular concern for social work professionals with any of the newer antidepressant medications is the increased risk of suicide (Teicher, Glod, & Cole, 1990). In the past, results of research studies have been mixed. Some clearly support a correlation between the use of these medications (Jann et al., 1994; Kapur, Mieczkowski, & Mann, 1992). Others state "there is at present no convincing or consistent evidence that particular classes of psychotropic drugs provoke suicidal behavior in predisposed individuals" (Baldwin, 2000, p. 61). Regardless of the controversy (deVane, 1994; Gitlin, 1996; Hamilton & Opler, 1992; Mann & Kapur, 1991; Tollefson, Ramphey, Beasley, Enas, & Potvin, 1994), social workers who work with depressed clients who are taking medications need to clearly assess and address suicidal behaviors. It is important to remember that these medications are still fairly new and more testing is needed before there are finite answers. Until that time, social workers are advised to err on the side of caution. Antidepressant medications work very effectively in treating endogenous types of depression and result in positive mood changes that are usually visible within 2 to 6 weeks. Depressed clients are most vulnerable when they have more energy to act on their negative thoughts and feelings. As a rule of practice, it is recommended that when a client is taking any of the antidepressant medications, especially those in the newer category (SSRIs and others) he or she should be completely assessed for suicidal ideation and intent. Because hospitals and other mental health facilities continue to discharge clients after very short stays, social workers are in a position to recognize, assess and actively address any potential suicidal situations that may emerge prior to the client's leaving the hospital or facility. For those social workers in private practice, this means that the potential for suicide must be carefully assessed when a client is referred directly from a psychiatric hospitalization. This means asking the client directly if he or she is having any suicidal thoughts and has access to means, and determining whether a concrete plan exists. Whatever the severity of suicidal ideation, a no-suicide contract should be initiated directly with the client and maintained in the client's record.

The strength of social work intervention is in the planning and preparation for a client's return to his or her environment. When making arrangements for discharge planning, the social worker should be aware that significant others may not be ready for the positive changes in the client's mood. The absence of visible depressive symptoms may give the client and family members a false sense of total recuperation. Family members, employers, and coworkers may expect the client to resume normal family and occupational activities, resulting in emotional overload for the client. Many times clients do not respond as actively to these expectations as they did in the past, which may result in frustration for the client and other members of the environmental support system.

There are inherent risks that once symptoms of depression lift clients may want to discontinue their medication regimen. While clients have the right to self-determination (Hepworth & Larsen, 1993) in medication and other aspects of their treatment, it is the social worker's responsibility to educate the client about the triggers and risk of relapse. Clients should be advised to stay on antidepressants for a minimum of 16 to 20 weeks or until the stressors in their lives are under control (Maxmen & Ward, 1995). With the newer antidepressants and their mild side effects, psychiatrists are recommending that clients with severe and frequent episodes stay on those medications for longer periods of time. Whenever a client stops using antidepressants, extreme caution should be taken to ensure that the process is done gradually and is monitored along the way. This is especially true for the tricyclics, which may cause severe withdrawal symptoms that include nausea and sleeping problems if stopped abruptly. Because the risk of depression increases at certain times of the year (holidays and anniversary dates, for instance), social workers should work closely with their clients to select the least disruptive time to begin decreasing the medication. Clients should be aware that they have the option to return to earlier dosages if depressive symptoms reappear.

As clients prepare to discontinue the use of antidepressants, social workers should keep the following in mind: (a) encourage and reinforce the client's awareness and identification of recurring depressive symptoms; (b) ensure that the client has a good support system; (c) encourage the client to continue counseling even after discontinuing medication; (d) help the client develop a plan of action for the possible return of depressive symptoms; and (e) involve family and significant others in the early identification of relapse.

WOMEN, DEPRESSION, AND BREAST-FEEDING

Many of the clients who suffer from depression and who are taking one or more medications for this condition are women (Stowe et al., 2000). When working with women of childbearing age, social workers should remind the clients to discuss with their prescribers the possibility of transmitting antidepressant medications to an infant via breast milk. The majority of studies have shown that if a woman is taking antidepressant medications, particularly the SSRIs, the amount of this substance found in the milk is very low to undetectable (Stowe et al., 2000). Though research does not appear to show a direct correlation between medication in the milk and an infant's behavior, the client should still be advised that these medications are fairly new on the market and that conclusive and long-term effects have yet to be determined. Caution should be used when a woman is deciding whether to continue taking antidepressant medications during pregnancy and whether to breast-feed her infant.

WOMEN, DEPRESSION, HIV, AND AIDS

Depression is a common symptom when a client is diagnosed as HIV positive or with AIDs. In a recent study investigators studied the efficacy of two SSRI medications, fluoxetine (Prozac) and sertraline (Zoloft), in treating depressed women who were HIV positive (Ferrando, Rabkin, de Moore, & Rabkin, 1999). Thirty women were enrolled in an eight-week open trial. The mean age of the women was 35 and most of their HIV risk was related to intravenous drug use (53%) or heterosexual contact (40%). Eighteen women actually completed the study, and the most frequently reported adverse effect was anxiety, overstimulation, and insomnia.

Studies such as this one help to establish that HIV-seropositive women who are depressed can benefit from taking medications. Attention should not be diverted, however, from the need for aggressive outreach, education, and attention to the essential issues these women will have to face as a consequence of the illness. A diagnosis of HIV or AIDS can be overwhelming, and there are many aspects of the client's life that will need to be addressed. The importance of individual assessment, counseling, and education cannot be overestimated. In addition, clients should be made aware that the two major side effects of anxiety and insomnia may further jeopardize a woman's emotional and physical health. Through counseling and education, and medication use if warranted, social workers can facilitate client problem-solving with a variety of treatments that can address each client's individual psychosocial needs.

ALTERNATIVE AND SUPPORTIVE INTERVENTIONS

ELECTROCONVULSIVE THERAPY

The electroconvulsive therapy performed in the past is a far cry from the process used today in the treatment of major depressive disorder. In ECT a generalized central-nervous-system seizure is induced by means of an electric current. The objective is to achieve the full seizure threshold until the full therapeutic gains can be established. The exact process by which ECT works is unknown; however, the shock results in an increase in different neurotransmitter responses at the cell membrane. Four to twelve treatments are generally given until therapeutic results are noted (Sachs, 1996).

ECT is considered one of the most effective treatments (70% to 85%) for severe depression (Tierney et al., 1997). Comparative controlled studies using ECT instead of chemotherapy have shown that ECT is considered more effective (Tierney et al., 1997). ECT is often used to treat individuals who suffer from major depression, especially those who cannot take medications due to underlying medical conditions or when a nonresponse to traditional antidepressant medication therapy is noted.

Electrical stimulation is more reliable, simpler to use, and more cost-effective than chemical convulsants, a major advantage that has caused many professionals to believe it has tremendous potential as a treatment for depression. This procedure allows clients to be treated and released, whereas treatment with the newer antidepressants has been reported to have a relapse rate as high as 50% if the medication is discontinued in less than six months (Maxmen & Ward, 1995). In many states, psychiatrists are performing ECT on an outpatient basis, which greatly reduces inpatient hospital stays and the prolonged monthly expense incurred with traditional antidepressant medications. Although ECT clearly can prompt a remission of symptoms, there is no guarantee that relapse will not occur; at times maintenance ECT may be recommended to provide ongoing stability.

One of the major side effects of ECT is memory disturbance and headaches. Memory loss is related to two factors: the number of treatments and the oxygenation provided during the treatment experience (Tierney et al., 1997). Unfortunately, some memory loss may be permanent but most memory does return within several weeks of termination of the treatments. Social work professionals working with individuals who receive ECT must be supportive of the client during the treatment process, especially when verbal therapy is provided and the issue of memory loss is discussed. During this process, the client may feel the conflict between the expectation that he or she continue verbal interventions when normal cognitive functioning is compromised. To avoid unwanted pressure and strain on the client, it may prove useful to encourage the client to decline verbal therapy until the ECT treatments are discontinued. Despite the prominent gains evidenced by the practice of ECT as a treatment modality, the most significant drawback remains the general lack of acceptance for the technique based on the public's ignorance and skepticism about the procedure (Maxmen & Ward, 1995; Tierney et al., 1997).

SELF-INITIATED TREATMENTS FOR DEPRESSION

In today's evolving health care climate, many clients are taking an active role in their own physical and mental health treatment. Currently there are more than 600 over-the-counter preparations available that can be purchased without any expert guidance (*Physicians' Desk Reference*, 1997). These medications are usually dispensed in less potent dosages but can easily interact, diminish, or augment the treatment effects of prescribed medications. In addition, there are numerous alternative medicines and treatment strategies designed specifically to treat depression that are gaining in popularity. Social workers are exposed to clients who want to rely less on traditional medications and more on alternative or holistic means (Dziegielewski, 1998). These alternate approaches can include anything from acupuncture and exercise to nutrition and herbal medicines (Lee & Carlin, 1997).

Saint-John's-wort is one example of a natural herbal remedy for depression that has recently gained in popularity and prevalence across the United States. In Europe, it is reportedly outselling the prescription medication Prozac. Saint-John's-wort (*Hypericum perforatum*) is a lush green herb with bright yellow flowers that has traditionally been used to heal wounds and as a tea to soothe nerves and relieve melancholy. The natural antidepressant effect that results enhances the neurochemical serotonin, norepinephrine, and dopamine with few side effects (Lemonick, 1997).

The herb is native to Europe, western Asia, and northern Africa and is available at many health stores in the states without a prescription. It costs much less than prescription antidepressant medications.

Although studies have been carried out in Europe that support the efficacy of this product, pharmacologists in the United States caution use because of the scarcity of clinical trials on maintenance and long-term use of the product. There are no studies with regard to the herb's effectiveness in the treatment of severe depression or the ideal dosage levels. One side effect noted with the herb is a tendency to be more vulnerable to sunburn.

Although the FDA can monitor many of the claims made for traditional medicines, the ability of clients to gain easy access to alternative forms of medicine and to self-medicate is a practice reality (Lee & Carlin, 1997). Interest and continued use of alternative medicine and treatment strategy for depression is increasing (Ullman, 1993). The attitude within the medical community is changing, and physicians and other health care professionals are becoming more aware of alternative medicine strategies (Lee & Carlin, 1997); and in the future it may be more common practice to include these strategies as part of the client's health and mental health treatment regimen (Dziegielewski, 1998). But until then, social workers should be aware that clients may conceal their use of herbal medications for fear that it will be viewed in a negative and disapproving manner. Discussion about herbal preparations should take place in an open, supportive, and nonjudgmental way (Fugh-Bergman, 2000).

DIRECT SOCIAL WORK INTERVENTION

Traditionally social workers have used a biopsychosocial approach (Hepworth & Larsen, 1993) to understand the difficulties experienced by clients and to empower them to take charge of their lives and strive for new and improved levels of health and mental health satisfaction and functioning (Dziegielewski, 1998). Today's practice environment and the acceptance of using medications to treat depression have made social workers aware that medications have become an essential component in health and mental health treatment. As medications continue to be used as a primary form of therapeutic intervention for depression, the role that the social work professional assumes in understanding and monitoring medication treatment regimens must be proactive. Social workers often treat clients who are on medication and act as physician's assistant, professional consultant, collaborator, educator, researcher, client advocate, and broker (Dziegie-lewski, 1997, 1998). This means that they must be able to recommend, address, interpret, and help monitor medication regimens and medication-related treatment issues with their clients.

Particularly in more serious cases, medications are often used to supplement the treatment regimen, because they allow the client to do the necessary therapeutic work (Schatzberg & Cole, 1991). This is especially important when such great strides have been reported in the use of cognitive-behavioral treatments to treat symptoms of depression and anxiety. Because many of these interventions relate to depression and anxiety, more in-depth information on cognitive-behavioral interventions is covered in chapter 6 on anxiety disorders.

Medications are often used as a first line of treatment in depression, and social workers treating clients with these symptoms must be knowledgeable about basic medication information and about how these drugs can affect the counseling environment.

In health and mental health, social workers often serve as part of an interdisciplinary team and spend the most quality time with their clients. In all likelihood the social worker will be one of the first team members to become aware of regimen problems, possible side effects, or medication reactions. Social workers need to understand the antidepressant medications their clients are taking and assist with compliance issues, pharmacy shopping, side-effect profiles, and medication insurance coverage, as well as providing education information and support.

DOCUMENTATION AND TREATMENT PLANNING

In order to complete the advocacy and broker functions that are basic to social work, an accurate assessment and referral process must be performed in regard to medication usage. Professional social workers must consider the various types of medications a client is taking and include treatment planning with documentation that incorporates the medication regimen in treatment goals and objectives. They must stay abreast of side-effect profiles and dosage routines in order to assist clients in obtaining and maintaining the most therapeutically productive treatment possible. In addition, they must be able to recognize and document potential problem areas in order to refer the client for reevaluation.

In the case study of Jean presented at the beginning of this chapter, the social worker's primary task was to complete an appropriate discharge plan. She discovered that the client was depressed, as reflected by the client's stating that she considered death preferable to the feelings of separation and loneliness she was experiencing. The social worker decided that client safety was the major consideration in this case, and knowledge of antidepressant medications was necessary for a proper evaluation to ensure the client's safety after discharge. Given the complexities of the managed-care environment, it is common to begin the course of treatment for depression with medication therapy. Facilitating discharge must involve promoting client well-being and safety, and social workers must also clearly document goals and objectives for the client.

When a client reports feelings of depression, the social worker should first assess the frequency, intensity, and duration of the symptoms: how often the symptoms are being experienced, how severe they are and what impairment to daily functioning, and how long the symptoms have lasted. In the case study, Jean stated that she had experienced periods of depression most of her life, and after the death of her husband these incidents increased in frequency, intensity, and duration. When looking at these factors a direct link should be made to how these symptoms affect the activities of daily living with regard to impairment of social and occupational functioning. The client may report eating problems and difficulty sleeping (sleeplessness or insomnia, and sleeping too much or hypersomnia). All behaviors in functioning as well as other symptoms relevant to the depressive mood need to be clearly documented. In the case of a client's reporting eating difficulties, the social worker should document circumstances and the nature of the appetite loss or increase. Specific information with regard to recent weight gain or loss should be noted. Other signs and symptoms that need to be assessed and documented include: diminished interest and enjoyment in activities, lack of energy, indecisiveness, social withdrawal, feelings of hopelessness, worthlessness, or inappropriate guilt, low self-esteem, unresolved grief issues, mood-related hallucinations and delusions, and history of antidepressant medication use. Include a clear history of substance abuse and potential for medication addiction or misuse. Specific information on the potential for abuse and addiction can help the treatment team to decide which medications might be best for clients at risk. Information on the client's history should include previous hospitalizations and treatments for depression and whether they were successful.

An integral part of social work intervention with depressed clients is the inclusion of outcome measures that provide empirical data on changes in the reported symptoms and treatment effectiveness. Gathering empirical, objective data allows the social worker to evaluate the course of treatment, make changes in the treatment, and evaluate overall practice effectiveness (Dziegielewski & Leon, 1998). Assessment instruments that provide baseline data and subsequent changes provide consistency for the entire interdisciplinary team.

In self-reported measures, the client rates his or her own symptoms. One common self-report measurement instrument is the Beck Depression Inventory (BDI) (Beck, 1967). Used in a wide range of clinical and nonclinical samples, the BDI is a scale of 21 items that assess the existence and severity of affective, cognitive, motivational, vegetative, and psychomotor components of depression. Using a 3-point scale, the client rates the severity of each symptom that he or she is feeling. Scales like this one are standardized to the degree of reliability (measure the same thing repeatedly) and validity (measure the concept identified) and are easy for the social worker to administer and score. Another instrument for assessing depression is the Brief Depression Rating Scale (BDRS) (Kellner, 1986). This 8-item rating can help the social worker clearly identify and measure depressive mood, feelings of despair, somatic symptoms, lack of interest, initiative, activity, sleep disturbance, anxiety, worry and tension, appearance, depressive beliefs, and suicidal thoughts or behavior. A third standardized measure is the Center for Epidemiologic Studies–Depressed Mood Scale (CES-D) (Radloff, 1977). This scale of 20 items was first developed to measure depression in the general population for epidemiological research and was later adapted for use in psychiatric settings. The Generalized Contentment Scale (Hudson, 1992) is a self-report scale that was developed by a social worker to measure the degree, severity, or magnitude of nonpsychotic depression. Unlike other measures of depression, the GCS elicits client's feelings about various behaviors, attitudes, and events related to depression.

These scales provide objective clinical data on the existence of and changes in a client's depression. Social workers should become familiar in the use of such instruments and utilize them as pretests during the assessment phase and as posttests during different treatment intervals.

Whenever a client shows depressive symptoms, it is critical that a thorough assessment for suicidal ideation and intent be made. Direct questions should always be asked to determine the client's potential for suicide, and any current or past suicidal gestures should be documented. Because a depressed client is more likely to harm himself or herself when the depression lifts and energy returns, the documentation of potential suicidal behavior is particularly important with the use of the newer antidepressant drugs (SSRIs and SSNRIs) that help to lift depression quickly.

Sample Long-Term Goals for Depression

1. Develop the ability to recognize, accept, and cope with feelings of depression
2. Alleviate or decrease depressed mood enough to return to previous level of functioning
3. Develop cognitive patterns and beliefs about self that will lead to control or alleviation of depressive symptoms
4. Clearly assess for suicidal thoughts and feelings and ensure that a plan for action is available to the client if anything should arise

Short-term objectives	Plan or intervention	Time frame*
1. Take medications responsibly as prescribed by the physician and report any side effects from the medications	• Assess needs for antidepressant medications and arrange for prescription if needed • Monitor and evaluate medication compliance and plan or intervention effectiveness with medications in regard to level of functioning	
2. Verbally identify the source of the depressed mood	• Client to make a list of what he/she is depressed about (complete in session with social worker)	

Short-term objectives	Plan or intervention	Time frame*
	• Encourage client to share feelings of depression in order to clarify them and gain insight	
	• Assign participation in recreational activities and reinforce social activities and verbalizations	
	• Write at least one positive affirmative statement each day	
3. Identify cognitive self-talk that is used to support depression	• Educate about the condition of depression	
	• Assist in developing awareness of cognitive messages that reinforce messages of hopelessness and helplessness	
4. Complete assessments of functioning (scales, GAF, GARF, SOFAS, etc.) to determine level of depression or suicide precaution	• Arrange or complete administration of the tests.	
	• Assess and monitor suicide intervention.	
5. Client will learn more about medications	• Client will take medications responsibly.	
	• Client will be made aware and report side effects of medications.	
	• Client will agree to routine blood work and monitoring.	

*The time frame is to be completed as part of the intervention plan formulation.

Be sure when designing a treatment plan that a time frame is specified in terms of objective progress and expected completion.

SUMMARY AND CONCLUSIONS

The last 30 years have seen tremendous progress in the treatment of depression beginning with the discovery of the neurochemicals norepinephrine, serotonin and dopamine, and the medications that utilize them (tricyclics, MAOs and later the SSRIs and the SSNRIs). No one, however, could have predicted the changes and treatment gains over the last 10 years. The phenomenal advances made possible by the discovery of the SSRIs and SSNRIs have revolutionized traditional treatments for the depressed client (Moller, 2000). This new emphasis on mental health treatment is directly linked to pharmacological strides that make the knowledge of medications a practice necessity.

Social workers who treat a depressed client must understand the importance of identifying and treating exogenous factors and emphasize the importance of these factors to all members of the health care team. Medications alone may be a simple and easy course of action, but medications alone may not be enough to bring about positive results. It has been estimated that 70% to 80% of all visits made to primary health-care providers are made by individuals suffering from psychophysiological or mind–body illness (Corbin, Hanson, Happ, & Whitby, 1988). The importance of the interdependent relationship between the sociopsychological aspects of an illness and those that are physical, medical, or biological should not be underestimated; and though antidepressant medications often can have a profound effect on cognition, mood, and behaviors, they do not change the underlying disease process (Gitlin, 1996; Schatzberg & Cole, 1991). It is clear that every individual who suffers from any type of mental disorder is influenced by internal and external stresses, and medications alone do not address the social, environmental, and family factors that surround the depressed individual.

Social workers must remain keenly aware and educate clients so that they do not develop a false sense of security with regard to the "curative" nature of a pill for treating depression (Marano, 1999). The allure of a quick fix is strong when compared to engaging in supportive counseling that often takes substantial time, emotional energy, and effort. The mistaken belief that antidepressants can cure creates unrealistic expectations for the client. To facilitate intervention for clients who suffer from severe types of depression the following guidelines are suggested. First, be aware of the different types of antidepressant medications that can be used to treat the symptoms the client is experiencing. Second, learn what can be expected in terms of behavioral change in clients who take medication and how the medication can affect the counseling relationship. Third, monitor these medications for compliance and make recommendations when it appears that changes or adjustments are needed. Fourth, help to gather and interpret information and educate clients and their families with regard to medication and potential side effects. Fifth, assist the client to express needs and concerns about using medication in the treatment context. Last, ensure that a social-environmental assessment is completed that will identify the factors and support systems that can facilitate medication compliance and ensure treatment efficacy. In the treatment of depression, professional social workers are important to the interdisciplinary team and assist with improved communication and coordination and referral among primary health, mental health, and community-based programs (Van Hook, 1996).

This chapter cannot address all the medication concerns that social workers will encounter in the treatment of depression. It is written in the hope that it will provide basic information for social work practitioners and encourage them to broaden their knowledge in this area (Rowan & Dziegielewski, 1996). Social workers must be up-to-date on how antidepressant medications affect the depressed client's biopsychosocial functioning and how it influences the course of counseling.

REFERENCES

American Psychiatric Association. (1994). *Diagnostic and statistical manual of mental disorders* (4th ed.). Washington, DC: Author.

Austrian, S. G. (1995). *Mental disorders, medications and clinical social work.* New York: Columbia University Press.

Baldwin, D. S. (2000). Pharmacological provocation and prevention of suicidal behavior. *International Review of Psychiatry, 12*(1), 54–68.

Beck, A. T. (1967). *Depression: Clinical, Experimental and Theoretical Aspects.* New York: Harper & Row.

Bently, K. J. (1997). Should clinical social workers seek psychotropic medication prescription privileges?: No. In B. A. Thyer (Ed.), *Controversial issues in social work practice* (pp. 152–165). Boston: Allen & Bacon.

Brophy, J. J. (1991). Psychiatric disorders. In S. A. Schroeder, M. A. Krupp, L. M. Tierney, & S. J. McPhee (Eds.), *Current medical diagnosis and treatment* (pp. 731–786). Norwalk, CT: Appleton & Lange.

Corbin, L., Hanson, R., Happ, S., & Whitby, A. (1988). Somatoform disorders. *Journal of Psychosocial Nursing, 26,* 31–34.

Cowley, G. (1994, February 7). The culture of Prozac. *Newsweek, 123*(6), 41–42.

Craig, C. (1995). Teaching food-drug interactions. *Journal of Psychological Nursing, 33,* 44–46.

deVane, C. L. (1994). Pharmacogenetics and drug metabolism of the newer antidepressant agents. *Journal of Clinical Psychiatry, 55,* 12, 38–45.

Dziegielewski, S. F. (1996). Managed care principles: The need for social work in the health care environment. *Crisis Intervention, 3,* 97–111.

Dziegielewski, S. F. (1997). Should clinical social workers seek psychotropic medication prescription privileges?: Yes. In B. A. Thyer (Ed.), *Controversial issues in social work practice* (pp. 152–165). Boston: Allen & Bacon.

Dziegielewski, S. F. (1998). *The changing face of health care social work: An empirical approach to practice.* New York: Springer.

Dziegielewski, S. F., & Leon, A. M. (1998). Psychopharmacological treatment of major depression. *Research on Social Work Practice, 8*(4), 475–490.

Ferrando, S. J., Rabkin, J. G., de Moore, G. M., & Rabkin, R. (1999). Antidepressant treatment of depression in HIV-seropositive women. *Journal of Clinical Psychiatry, 60,* 741–746.

Fugh-Bergman, A. (2000). Herbs-drug interactions. *Lancet, 355,* 9918, 134–135.

Gitlin, M. J. (1996). *The psychotherapist's guide to psychopharmacology* (2nd ed.). New York: Free Press.

Hamilton, M. S., & Opler, L. A. (1992). Akathisia, suicidality, and fluoxetine. *Journal of Clinical Psychiatry, 53,* 401–406.

Hepworth, D. H., & Larsen, J. A. (1993). *Direct social work practice: Theory and skills.* Pacific Grove, CA: Brooks/Cole.

Higgins, E. (1994). A review of unrecognized mental illness in primary care: Prevalence, natural history, and efforts to change the course. *Archives of Family Medicine, 3,* 899–907.

Hudson, W. W. (1992). *The WALMYR Assessment Scales Scoring Manual.* Tempe, AZ: WALMYR Publishing.

Hussar, D. A. (2000). New drugs of 1999. *Journal of the American Pharmaceutical Association, 40,* 2, 181–221.

Jann, M. W., Jenike, M. A., & Liberman, J. A. (1994, January 30). The new psychopharmaceuticals. *Patient Care.*

Kaplan, H. I., & Sadock, B. J. (1990). *Pocket handbook of clinical psychiatry.* Baltimore, MD: Williams & Wilkins.

Kapur, S., Mieczkowski, T., & Mann, J. J. (1992, December). Antidepressant medications and the relative risk of suicide attempt and suicide. *Journal of the American Medical Association, 268,* 3441–3445.

Keller, M. B., Hanks, D. L., & Klein, D. N. (1996). Summary of the mood disorders field trial and issue and overview. *Psychiatric Clinics of North America, 19*(1), 1–28.

Keller, M. B., Klein, D., Hirschfield, R. M., Kocsis, J. H., McCullough, J. P., Miller, I., First, M. B., Holzer, I. C., Keitner, G. I., Marin, D. B., & Shea, T. (1995). Results of the *DSM-IV* mood disorders field trial. *American Journal of Psychiatry, 152*, 843–849.

Kellner, R. (1986). The brief depression rating scale. In N. Sartorius & T. A. Ban (Eds.), *Assessment of depression* (pp. 179–183). New York: Springer-Verlag.

Kent, J. M. (2000). SNaRIs, NaSSas, and NaRIs: New agents for the treatment of depression. *Lancet, 355*, 911–918.

Labbate, L. (1999). Sex and serotonin reuptake inhibitor antidepressants. *Psychiatric Annals, 29*, 571–579.

Larkin, M. (1993, March). Types of antidepressants. *FDA Consumer*, pp. 21–22.

Lee, K., & Carlin, P. (1997, January/February). Should you try mind–body medicine? *Health*, 77–78.

Lehne, R. A., & Scott, D. (1996). *Psychopharmacology*. In V. B. Carson & E. N. Arnold (Eds.), *Mental health nursing: The nurse patient journey* (pp. 523–570). Philadelphia: W. B. Saunders.

Lemonick, M. D. (1997). The mood molecule. *Time, 150*(13), 74–82.

Lemonick, M. D. (1999). Beyond depression: What do these "mood drugs" really do? *Time, 153*(19), 74.

Mann, J. J., & Kapur, S. (1991). The emergence of suicidal ideation and behavior during antidepressant pharmacotherapy. *Archives of General Psychiatry, 48*, 1027–1033.

Marano, E. H. (1999, March/April). Depression: Beyond serotonin. *Psychology Today, 32*, 30–36, 72–75.

Maxmen, J. S., & Ward, N. G. (1995). *Essential psychopathology and its treatment*. New York: W. W. Norton.

Merck Research Laboratories. (1992). *The Merck manual of diagnosis and therapy* (16th ed.). Rahway, NJ: Merck Research Laboratories.

Moller, H. (2000). Are all antidepressants the same? *The Journal of Clinical Psychiatry, 61*(6), 24–28.

Morris, M. R. (1999). Antidepressants and drug interactions: Prescriber beware. *Journal of American College Health, 47*(4), 191.

Physicians' Desk Reference. (2000). *Physicians' desk reference* (54th ed.). Montvale, NJ: Medical Economics.

Physicians' Desk Reference. (1997). *Physicians' desk reference: For nonprescription drugs* (18th ed.). Montvale, NJ: Medical Economics.

Psychopharmacology Update. (2000, January). Sildenafil may be effective for antidepressant-associated sexual dysfunction in women. *Psychopharmacology, 11*(1), 1.

Radloff, L. S. (1977). *Applied Psychological Measurement, 1,* 385–401.

Resnick, W. M., & Carson, V. B. (1996). The journey colored by mood disorders. In V. B. Carson & E. N. Arnold (Eds.), *Mental health nursing: The nurse patient journey* (pp. 759–792). Philadelphia: W. B. Saunders.

Rowan, D., & Dziegielewski, S. F. (1996, October). *Inclusion of psychopharmacological content in BSW curricula.* Paper presented at the 14th Annual BPD Conference, Portland, OR.

Rush, J. (1993, June). Depression in primary care: Detection, diagnosis and treatment. *American Family Physician, 47,* 1766–1788.

Rushton, J. L., Clark, S. J., & Freed, G. L. (2000). Primary care role in the management of childhood depression: A comparison of pediatricians and family physicians. *Pediatrics, 105,* 957–964.

Sachs, G. S. (1996). Bipolar mood disorder: Practical strategies for acute and maintenance phase treatment. *Journal of Clinical Neuropsychiatry, 16*(2)Suppl. 1, 32–47.

Schatzberg, A. F., & Cole, J. O. (1991). *Manual of clinical psychopharmacology* (2nd ed.). Washington, DC: American Psychiatric Press.

Shindul-Rothschild, J. A., & Rothschild, A. J. (1998). Psychotropics in primary care. In L. A. Eisenbauer & M. A. Murphy (Eds.), *Pharmacotherapeutics & advanced nursing practice* (pp. 37–51). New York: McGraw-Hill.

Stowe, Z. N., Cohen, L. S., Hostetter, A., Ritchie, J. C., Owens, M. J., & Nemeroff, C. B. (Feb. 2000). Paroxentine in human breast milk and nursing infants. *American Journal of Psychiatry, 157,* 185–189.

Teicher, M. H., Glod, C., & Cole, J. O. (1990). Emergence of intense suicidal preoccupation during fluoxetine treatment. *American Journal of Psychiatry, 147,* 207–210.

Tierney, L. M., McPhee, S. J., & Papadakis, M. A. (Eds.). (1997). *Current medical diagnosis and treatment* (36th ed.). Stamford, CT: Appleton & Lange.

Tollefson, G. D., Ramphey, A. H., Beasley, C. M., Enas, C. G., & Potvin, J. H. (1994). Absence of a relationship between adverse events and suicidality during pharmacotherapy for depression. *Journal of Clinical Psychopharmacology, 14,* 163–169.

Ullman, D. (1993, November/December). Renegade remedies? The medical establishment is turning a blind—and biased eye—to the alternative-medicine boom. *Utne Reader, 60,* 42–44.

Van Hook, M. P. (1996). Challenges to identifying and treating women with depression in rural primary care. *Social Work in Health Care, 23*(3), 73–92.

CHAPTER 5

Bipolar Disorders: Social Work Intervention

T he bipolar disorders, commonly known as *manic depression* or *bipolar affective disorder*, as the second grouping of diagnoses in the mood disorders, are included in the *Diagnostic and Statistical Manual of Mental Disorders* (*DSM-IV*; American Psychiatric Association, 1994) and are characterized by extreme fluctuations in mood. While approximately 9.5% of the population suffers from a type of mood disorder, between 1% and 5% of the population is diagnosed with bipolar disorder, and about 2% struggle with cyclothymic disorder (Regier, Narrow, Rae, Manderscheid, Locke, & Goodwin, 1993). Bipolar disorder appears to affect both men and women, with neither group showing more prevalence than the other. These disorders can be diagnosed as early as adolescence or later in adulthood through the age of 50 (Austrian, 1995). An example of an adult with bipolar disorder is the actress Margot Kidder who received attention when she was found homeless and exhibiting symptoms commonly seen in this illness. Although the *DSM-IV* (American Psychiatric Association, 1994) does not indicate separate criteria for diagnosing bipolar disorder in children and adolescents, it considers developmental parameters when using the adult criteria of the disorder in children (Kronenberger & Meyer, 1996; Netherton, Holmes, & Walker, 1999). For example, Kronenberger and Meyer (1996, p. 156) state that "mixed episodes occur when a child meets the criteria for a manic episode and a major depressive episode 'nearly every day' for 1 week or more, with marked impairment in functioning." Generally, it is more common for adolescents over the age of 13 to be diagnosed with bipolar disorders (Kronenberger & Meyer, 1996; Keller & Wunder, 1990), and the median age of onset has been documented as approximately 18 years of age (Burke,

Burke, Reiger, & Rae, 1990). Social work practitioners are cautioned when applying the diagnosis of bipolar disorder to children or adolescents, because other more common disorders of childhood such as attention deficit disorder or conduct disorder present similar symptoms (Carlson, 1998; Netherton et al., 1999; Weller, 1995). Social workers should ensure that a diagnosis is not reached too quickly or that it is based solely on behaviors exhibited in isolation.

Bipolar disorder is a challenging condition for clients and difficult to assess and treat. The bipolar disorders present with a variety of symptoms that often cause major functioning problems in clients and that lead to frustration for their family and support systems. Clients with this disorder are often overwhelmed by the symptoms and by despair over the fluctuating moods, which are difficult to monitor. The client who suffers from bipolar disorder is faced with the challenge of understanding and tracking two separate sets of symptoms within one illness—those that arise during a manic state and those reflected in the depressive phase.

It is also common for these clients to become resistant to seeking and maintaining treatment especially those who are in the manic or elevated high states of the illness. Clients in this "up" phase of the illness often avoid or refuse support during these periods. When social workers understand the differences that can occur in mood states and the specific criteria that characterize each of the bipolar disorders, they are in a better position to assist clients and their families in accepting, monitoring, and treating this form of mental illness. Understanding and managing this symptomlogy medically can be difficult for clients, their relatives, and other support systems as well. As with other mental illnesses, family members frequently experience a sense of shame and disgrace, because they do not understand that people with bipolar disorders do not willfully elect to display the extreme fluctuations and behavioral problems that accompany the illness. It is imperative, therefore, that social work practitioners educate and support family members about the diverse facets of bipolar disorder, because clients with this disorder inevitably experience problems in mood regulation that can result in alternating states that have both manic and depressive features (Kaplan & Saddock, 1996).

Mood swings can lead to serious problems such as suicide attempts and suicide. Symptoms that often plague clients with bipolar disorders include: suicidal ideation, violent behaviors leading to child abuse and domestic violence, major difficulties in functioning on the job, erratic behaviors, severe fluctuations in mood, psychomotor agitation, increased grandiosity, risk-taking behavior, pressured speech, problems with concentration, and periodic antisocial behaviors (Maxmen & Ward, 1995).

In clinical situations, clients will often describe the course of these symptoms and their severity as a roller-coaster ride not knowing when to expect the next drop (Hilty, Brady, & Hales, 1999). Unlike earlier perceptions, bipolar disorder is now understood as an illness with overlapping states of mood and accompanying symptoms. Mental health professionals also recognize that clients with bipolar disorders can suffer concurrently from other forms of mental illness such as alcoholism, drug use, and anxiety disorders (Cassano, Pini, Saettoni, & Dell'Osso, 1999). Regardless of how clients experience this disorder, it is important for social work practitioners to become knowledgeable about the types of medications successfully used in its treatment and the psychosocial treatments that can help.

CASE EXAMPLE: MICHAEL

Michael is a 24-year-old Hispanic male who was admitted to the psychiatric unit after a bizarre episode that lasted for several hours and was reported to the police by his roommate. When he arrived at the hospital, he reported feeling great and talked rapidly about his unique insight into God's ways. He reported that he alone had been chosen to understand what God's purpose was and how God would destroy the earth. In between the preaching, Michael would run to the nearby water fountain, drink water, and turn to the female social worker and state, "I am a child of God, because I am a man" and "You wouldn't understand because you are a woman." He understood everything that was going on with the world and "felt mighty good about it." He repeated his frantic trips to the water fountain at least four times, breaking into his sermon each time and stating that he was thirsty.

It seems that Michael had moved in with this roommate 10 months before and had started attending college again. He was also employed as a part-time sales clerk in a local department store, and his history indicated no previous psychiatric, substance abuse, or behavioral problems of any kind. He appeared to have a good grasp of reality throughout the interview. When addressing his current mental status he was oriented to person (he knew his name and gave history about himself and his family), place (he knew where he was), and time. The police report gave some information provided by his 20-year-old roommate who was quite surprised by Michael's behavior. The roommate reported Michael began acting strangely following a visit from his girlfriend and remained this way for several hours until the police arrived. The roommate said that in hindsight he noticed that Michael had had at least two previous episodes over the past months, when he appeared depressed, wasn't eating or sleeping sufficiently, and lost weight. When the roommate inquired about his depressed mood, Michael refused to talk about it and would only say that he felt things would never change and that he just needed to get over it. On at least one occasion, the roommate noticed that Michael sounded paranoid, saying that he knew his father had paid people in the neighborhood, at work, and at school to keep an eye on him. The roommate reported that Michael had locked himself in his room for several hours on a couple of occasions. When the roommate finally convinced Michael to open the door, he found Michael sitting on the bed, a pair of scissors beside him, muttering that he was "contemplating the meaning of life." After speaking to Michael for about an hour, the roommate was convinced that Michael would not harm himself and he persuaded Michael to spend some time with him in the living room watching television. To the roommate's knowledge it was the second time he had seen Michael so down and out. Michael's quick recovery from these depressive states left the roommate feeling that perhaps they were caused by the changes of young adulthood and Michael's adjustment to a new apartment and a new roommate.

This thinking was reinforced further soon after the depressive episodes when Michael began exhibiting great energy, began obsessively lifting weights, seemed to be quick in his thinking and also engaged in painting on canvas—an activity that he had not shown any interest in earlier. The roommate commented that his paintings were fabulous, and that it was nice to see how much energy Michael had. He was convinced that Michael was feeling better when Michael began engaging in major shopping sprees. Michael seemed to buy a lot of clothes and went out to dinner every night with his girlfriend. The roommate later found a bill in the apartment that showed Michael had maxed out two major credit cards, and the companies wanted immediate payment on overdue balances. According to the roommate, that period of energy was very much like the one that precipitated Michael's current hospitalization. The roommate also informed the intake worker that Michael had spent a lot of time pacing the apartment prior to being brought to the hospital and telling his roommate that he was chosen by God because he could write backwards very fast. Disbelieving, the roommate asked to see the writing, and to his surprise, Michael had written coherent sentences about his religious beliefs, and they were written backwards. The roommate asked him to write something else, and Michael stated very proudly, "It is a gift you know that only I am capable of."

The roommate reports that Michael's speech was pressured and very rapid and that the thoughts, many of which sounded coherent, shot "like missiles out of his mouth," while he continuously moved around the apartment talking about how great he felt.

Not knowing what to do at first the roommate asked another friend to watch Michael while he took a short drive to Michael's father's house to alert him about his son's condition. This second friend was reluctant to stay with Michael telling the roommate that Michael was a strange person who sometimes appeared to be an easygoing, happy, normal guy and at other times appeared irritable and manipulative and made people feel that he was better than everyone else. After understanding the severity of Michael's problem, the friend agreed to stay with him until his roommate returned.

The roommate describes that he was enthusiastically welcomed at Michael's father's home by a man in his underwear who, in a grandiose manner, began a dissertation on European history. It was difficult for the roommate to interrupt Michael's father, but he managed to inform him that his son was not doing well. Without showing much interest in the current situation, Michael's father continued discussing European history passionately and occasionally commented that Michael would be fine. Throughout his visit the roommate was aware of Michael's mother's presence in the kitchen. Not once did the woman stop her cooking to inquire on the nature of the visitor's call. The roommate left determined to call the police in order to get help for Michael.

At the hospital, Michael continued his quickened thoughts, still focused on his unique relationship with God. When asked other questions, he was able to respond with pressured speech, but his responses were coherent. Michael confirmed that he had not been sleeping much and actually was getting along well with only 2 hours of sleep a night for the past 3 days. His eating had decreased as well, though he made it clear that he really didn't need to eat much and that he felt better physically when he didn't "stuff his face." He quickly added, "I have more energy to do the things I need to do, and I can get a lot of good stuff done."

After an assessment at the hospital it was decided that Michael required hospitalization so that his bipolar disorder could be further assessed and treated. He did not want to be hospitalized, because he felt that there was nothing wrong with him. He commented to the intake worker, "What's wrong with having energy and being able to think so clearly about things— everything is right with my life."

This case illustrates the significant impairments that bipolar disorders can cause, especially for young clients. Someone like Michael, exhibiting a manic episode with a history of depressive episodes, is a good candidate for immediate assessment, hospitalization, and stabilization of symptoms. It is important in cases like this to assess the client's potential for suicide, especially once he begins to show depressive signs. It is also a good idea to explore the family history for evidence of bipolar disorder or depression, since it appears that in Michael's case his father exhibited similar symptoms. The case also illustrates that bipolar clients are not always the best informants since they tend to minimize or dismiss their symptoms and their effects. In Michael's case, important information was gathered from the roommate's report and the second friend and from the roommate's visit with Michael's father.

Michael agreed to stay in the hospital for a 72-hour evaluation only because he was informed that his father was aware of his difficulty. Michael did not wish to see his father or be "lectured" again on his getting into trouble. During the 72-hour evaluation, Michael agreed to go on medication, specifically Lithium. After the initial evaluation period Michael made friends with one of the other male patients and decided that he would stay in the hospital as long as necessary. He remained there for 12 days, long enough to experience the positive effects of the Lithium. During the hospital stay, Michael's parents were invited for a family therapy session. Though agitated at first about seeing his father, Michael agreed to the session and did quite well communicating with his parents. His mother recommended that Michael return home "to be taken care of," but Michael's father insisted that "Michael had to get a life" and that he "was an exceptional young man who could make it on his own." A compromise was reached with a discharge plan that included Michael's moving into an independent living program that assisted young clients with psychiatric problems. It was arranged that Michael would stay there for six months and then decide what he wanted to do. The discharge plan also included continuation of his medication and weekly sessions with a social worker. A six-month followup indicated that Michael had normalized his mood for about three months, and later his social worker identified the beginnings of another manic phase. However, early identification resulted in adjustments in Michael's medication, recognition of the need for increased therapeutic support, a recommendation for an extended stay at the independent living facility, and continued participation in a day treatment program.

BIPOLAR DISORDERS: FORMING THE DIAGNOSTIC IMPRESSION

This chapter will introduce the reader to the signs and symptoms of mood episodes and to the most common types of bipolar disorder. The four primary diagnostic categories in the *DSM-IV* that will be the focus of this chapter include: bipolar I disorder, bipolar II disorder, cyclothymic disorder, and bipolar disorder not otherwise specified (American Psychiatric Association, 1994). As shown in Table 5.1, the following criteria summarize each of the disorders that fall into this area.

MOOD EPISODES

Before discussing the different types of bipolar disorders, it is important to introduce the reader to what is commonly meant by a mood episode. These mood episodes are generally not diagnosed separately; they are considered building blocks for the disorders that follow. The types of mood episodes that clients who suffer from the bipolar disorders may manifest are manic, hypomanic, major depressive, or mixed episodes (American Psychiatric Association, 1994).

In the first type of mood episode, referred to formally as the manic episode, the client's mood is persistently elevated. Along with elevated mood, the client must also exhibit at least three of the following symptoms: increased psychomotor agitation, distractibility, flight of ideas, decreased need for sleep, and grandiosity. These symptoms should last for at least a week, or the symptoms can last less than a week if symptoms are severe enough to require hospitalization (American Psychiatric Association, 1994).

In a hypomanic episode the symptoms may initially appear similar to the manic episode of persistently elevated, expansive, or irritable mood. The time frame for this mood episode is approximately four days, and it should be clear that the individual exhibits signs that are uncharacteristic

TABLE 5.1   Description of Mood Disorders

Bipolar disorders: Mixed, manic, and depressed

Bipolar I disorder: One or more manic episodes, usually with a history of depressive episodes

Bipolar II disorder: One or more depressive with at least one hypomanic episode

Cyclothymic disorder: Persistent mood disturbance lasting at least two years, must not be without for two months, less severe than bipolar

Bipolar disorder NOS: This disorder does not meet the criteria for any specific mood disorder and has symptoms of depressive disorder NOS

Mental health diagnostic categories are from the *DSM-IV* classification system (American Psychiatric Association, 1994).

of previous levels of functioning. Individuals experiencing a hypomanic mood episode rarely need to be hospitalized; although symptoms may impair functioning, marked impairment is not noted. These individuals do not show evidence of psychotic features even though others are aware that the behaviors they are exhibiting are uncharacteristic (American Psychiatric Association, 1994).

Although the *DSM-IV* provides technical definitions of what constitutes the manic and the hypomanic episodes, it is helpful for the practitioner to know the kinds of symptoms that clients often present. In order to confirm the presence of a manic or hypomanic episode during the assessment process, the social worker should ask questions that will elicit information about the following areas:

- Changes in sleeping and eating habits/patterns
- Changes in energy levels
- Increased restlessness
- Increase in activities, especially those that are considered risk-taking or destructive
- Problems concentrating, easily distracted
- Extreme feelings of happiness
- Laughing inappropriately, usually accompanied by agitation
- Increased talking
- Talking takes on a pressured quality
- Thoughts are racing; the client may report he/she cannot keep up with the influx of thoughts
- Impaired judgment
- Grandiose thinking
- Inflated self-esteem
- Increased irritability and impatience with others
- Easily excitable
- Indications of violent behavior
- Disorientation
- Incoherent speech
- Bizarre hallucinations
- Lack of interest in personal relationship

The third type of mood episode involves the major depressive episode and it generally involves at least five or more characteristic signs. Oftentimes the individual will report appetite disturbances on an almost daily basis. At times these eating patterns will result in weight gain (5% of the body weight in one month) or weight loss.

Another common symptom is sleeping too much (hypersomnia) or an inability to sleep or disturbance in sleep (insomnia). Other signs and symptoms include daily bouts of depressed mood, markedly diminished interest or pleasure in activities that usually are pleasurable, psychomotor agitation or retardation nearly every day, fatigue or loss of energy. It is not uncommon for individuals experiencing these symptoms to consider suicide, and as discussed in chapter 4, a thorough assessment for suicide potential is always indicated. The symptoms must also be significant enough to impair occupational and social functioning and last for a period of at least two weeks and involve either depressed mood or loss of interest or pleasure (American Psychiatric Association, 1994).

The last type of mood episode is referred to as the mixed episode. This episode is referred to as mixed because it generally meets the criteria for the manic and the depressive episode. The major difference is that it does not last for two weeks; rather, it only lasts for approximately one week. In this type of episode the individual often experiences rapidly alternating moods with feelings of sadness, irritability, and euphoria.

In order for an individual to fall in the mood disorder category, he or she must experience one or a combination of these episodes. The reader may find it interesting to compare the information provided in this chapter with the previous chapter on the depressive disorders. Many of the symptoms, medications, and treatments that are described in the earlier chapter relate directly to this chapter and vice versa.

When completing an assessment of clients who suffer from the bipolar disorders, special attention needs to be given to identifying the mood episodes. The variability of the client's symptoms can complicate the determination of the type of episode, and these overlapping symptoms can be confusing to the beginning professional. For example, a client may appear either euphoric (elated or happy) or dysphoric (dissatisfied or angry) during either the manic or hypomanic episode (Cassidy, Murry, Forest, & Carroll, 1998). When the client presents as euphoric, he or she feels an abundance of energy, talks very rapidly, reports that thoughts are racing, has grandiose thoughts, and is in love with the world. In dysphoria, however, the client experiences a "high" state, but his or her thoughts and activities reflect agitation, rage, anxiety, panic, and destruction. During a dysphoric state, a client also can present with rapid and pressured speech and quickened thoughts. Dysphoria can also accompany depression and this combination can easily meet the criteria for the mixed episode, which places the client at greater risk for suicide.

For the client suffering from hypomanic episodes, a milder version of manic symptoms is reported. That is, the symptoms of mania can still exist within a hypomanic episode, but because they are not as severe and obvious as those during a manic state, those close to the individual can easily ignore them. The primary difference between the manic and the hypomanic episode is that during a hypomanic episode, the client should not report delusions or hallucinations (American Psychiatric Association, 1994). Early identification of the symptoms characteristic of the type of mood episode can help practitioners to complete more accurate diagnostic impressions, facilitating the assessment and treatment of psychiatric clients.

BIPOLAR I, BIPOLAR II, CYCLOTHYMIA, AND BIPOLAR NOS

When specifically addressing bipolar I disorders, the *DSM-IV* identifies six subgroups. The first subgroup includes criteria to determine if a client is experiencing a single manic episode, and the other five describe the most recent episode. In addition, there are specifiers that social work practitioners can use to describe the episode recurrence. Badger and Rand (1998) identify these specifiers as "rapid cycling, which indicates at least four episodes in a year; the presence or absence of interepisode recovery; and the emergence of a seasonal pattern in the depressed episodes" (p. 83).

The six subgroups included in the *DSM-IV* are as follows:

Bipolar I disorder single manic episode–296.0x

• Presence of only one manic episode and no past major depressive episodes

Bipolar I disorder, most recent episode hypomanic–296.40

• Currently (or most recently) in a hypomanic episode
• There has previously been at least one manic episode or mixed episode

Bipolar I disorder, most recent episode manic–296.4x

• Currently (or most recently) in a manic episode

• There has previously been at least one major depressive episode

Bipolar I disorder most recent episode mixed–296.6x

• Currently (or most recently) in a mixed episode
• There has previously been at least one major depressive episode

Bipolar I disorder, most recent episode depressed–296.5x

• Currently (or most recently) in a major depressive episode
• There has previously been at least one manic episode or mixed episode

Bipolar I disorder, most recent episode unspecified–296.7

• Criteria, except for duration, are currently (or most recently) met for a manic, a hypomanic or a major depressive episode
• There has previously been at least one manic episode or mixed episode (Adapted from *DSM-IV*, American Psychiatric Press, 1994).

When working with the bipolar I disorders it appears that either depressive episodes, manic episodes, or mixed episodes can be involved (Maxmen & Ward, 1995). Practitioners should keep in mind that clients with bipolar I disorders will often report depressive episodes as well as the agitation and hyperactivity that often are associated with it. In this condition a full depressive episode is also reported, and 20% to 30% of clients may continue to have mood fluctuations (lability) between episodes that are significant enough to disturb interpersonal or occupational relations. In some cases the development of psychotic features may occur, and when this happens subsequent manic episodes are more likely to also have psychotic features (American Psychiatric Association, 1994).

In the bipolar II disorders, there have been one or more major depressive episodes and no history of either a manic or mixed episode. Bipolar II disorders are best described as alternating episodes of major depression and periods of hypomania (Maxman & Ward, 1995). These hypomanic symptoms include increased levels of energy and mood that are not as intense as manic episodes, and clients with bipolar II disorder do not become delusional or require acute hospitalization (American Psychiatric Association, 1994).

In both bipolar I and bipolar II disorders, symptoms of persistent depressed mood, loss of interest in activities, poor concentration, feelings of hopelessness, and changes in eating and sleeping patterns characterize the depressive phase. In contrast, the hypomanic client usually exhibits increased levels of energy, irritability, changes in sleeping and eating patterns, increases in activities (including spending) and an increase in pressured verbalization (American Psychiatric Press, 1994). Because of the increase in energy and activities, many individuals become quite creative during these spurts and later experience the depressive trend. Bipolar II individuals are at higher risk for suicide and usually have a strong family history of bipolar or depressive disorders (McElroy, Strakowski, West, & Keck, 1997).

According to the *DSM-IV*, clients with a diagnosis of cyclothymic disorder have milder experiences than those who suffer from bipolar disorders although the symptoms are more consistent and last for approximately two years. In order to be diagnosed with cyclothymic disorder, the client's history must indicate that he or she has not been without hypomanic and depressive symptoms for a period of two months (American Psychiatric Association, 1994); a client with a major depressive episode only should not be diagnosed as cyclothymia.

Although it is a milder form of mood disorder, cyclothymia is considered chronic. Clients may experience less severe mood swings, but they are not free of symptoms for more than two months over a two-year period (Austrian, 1995). For many clients with bipolar disorders, the challenge is learning how to determine whether their cheery disposition or depressed states are within normal limits or indicative of a manic swing or a depressive downtrend. The client may not be able to depend on his or her own assessment to detect the changes in mood, but relatives and friends can be very helpful in identifying the mild mood fluctuations and changes that appear to represent an unusual state for the client. A thorough assessment that leads to an accurate diagnosis is only the beginning phase of the intervention. It is often very difficult to convince a client with a bipolar disorder that he or she is in fact experiencing serious changes in their mood states and that help is necessary.

Caution should always be exercised when diagnosing bipolar disorder not otherwise specified (NOS), because of the variety of symptoms that can be included. In clinical practice this diagnosis is generally used with clients who do not meet all of the criteria described for the bipolar disorders, yet still exhibit some of the basic symptoms evident in manic, major depressive, or mixed episodes (American Psychiatric Association, 1994).

Regardless of the type of bipolar disorder, it is important during assessment to remember that variability in the client's behavior and actions is indicative of this mental disorder. These changes in behavior and energy level can occur gradually or quite suddenly. One of the factors to consider during the assessment phase is whether the client is experiencing "rapid cycling." This refers to four or more complete mood cycles within a year's time, within days, or in some cases within hours (Badger & Rand, 1998). A confusing aspect of the diagnosis for the client, family, and practitioner is that a client with bipolar disorder may be in a mixed state, which indicates that their mood reflects concurrent depressive, manic or hypomanic symptoms.

If a social work practitioner suspects that any client, regardless of age, suffers from bipolar disorder, it is critical to confirm this diagnosis using the *DSM-IV* criteria (American Psychiatric Press, 1994; Meeks, 1999). This requires determining whether the client meets the criteria for depressive, manic, hypomanic, or mixed episodes. In addition, every practitioner should also assess for critical symptoms reflective of other mental health problems (Cassano et al., 1999).

Social work practitioners in clinical practice quickly learn that as with many other mental illnesses, the psychiatric problems clients present are complex and multifaceted. It is not unusual that clients with bipolar disorders often have other psychiatric problems that require attention and treatment. For example, many clients with bipolar disorder also have alcohol or drug-related problems (Carlson, Bromet, & Jandorf, 1998). Identifying other disorders is important during the assessment phase and continues to be so throughout the treatment phase. Clients with a history of alcohol and drug use will require special considerations when it comes to prescribing medications for the bipolar disorder. Failure to obtain this information at the point of assessment can put a client in harm if the client uses medications while taking these substances.

Once the diagnosis has been confirmed, thorough assessments should be made of critical issues such as suicide potential, history and risk of violence, psychotic symptoms, and risk-taking behaviors that can include sexual acting out, as well as assessing for substance and alcohol abuse (Gitlin, 1996). Since research has demonstrated that depressive episodes usually follow manic phases (American Psychiatric Association, 1995), watching for this trend can lessen the high risk of suicidal thoughts and attempts at suicide. Clients who already rely on alcohol and drugs have easy access to substances that can be used in a suicide attempt.

Social work practitioners must understand the intricate nature of bipolar disorders as they teach clients and their families about the disorder and help the client accept intervention efforts. It is beneficial to assist the client in understanding that bipolar disorder is not an all-or-nothing mental health condition, that is, that they are either depressed or not. In fact, clients need to be helped in gaining greater understanding of the overlapping and cyclical nature of the mood states that will be experienced as well as the subsequent course of the illness.

Practitioners should also engage in a thorough assessment of the client's present state of mind and history with regard to suicide potential, violence, and alcohol and drug use, especially if a client is in a depressive episode (Marlatt, 1998). The immediate plan for the bipolar client who exhibits acute symptoms in any of these areas should be to assess rapidly what appears to be occurring, to protect the client from harm, to begin a medication regimen, and to stabilize the dangerous symptoms. Hospitalization is usually recommended because it can ensure an environment where these objectives can be met and where the client can continue the therapeutic work. Furthermore, allowing time to adjust medications in a supervised setting may help contribute to continued medication compliance and management upon discharge to a less restrictive environment. The period of hospitalization can also serve as a time when clients and family members become educated about the nature of the illness and the treatment alternatives. Having family understanding and support can help to facilitate discharge.

INTERVENTIONS WITH CLIENTS WHO HAVE BIPOLAR DISORDERS

In the previous section we discussed the importance of accurately assessing and diagnosing bipolar disorders and fully distinguishing between the different mood states that these clients can experience. In this section the emphasis will be on the types of treatment interventions that are available and often used successfully to manage bipolar symptoms.

Although bipolar disorders are long-term illnesses that require monitoring and treatment measures, they can, in fact, be managed with psychosocial as well as psychopharmacological means (Brotter, Clarkin, & Carpenter, 1998). The most comprehensive assessment process, however, should include the client and his or her family as a crucial part of formulating an effective treatment plan. The major goals of treatment are to provide the necessary interventions when the client is in an acute state and to prevent further episodes from developing. As with other mental illnesses, prevention requires that the client and his or her support systems be educated about the cyclical nature of the illness and that the client agrees to utilize the necessary interventions to manage the illness. Educating someone about bipolar disorder is an ongoing endeavor that will require many attempts by the social work practitioner to dispel the stigma of the illness and to empower the client with new information about this disorder. During the education process, the family should be made aware of the differences in levels of motivation that affect the client's desire to seek help. For example, it is not unusual for clients during a manic episode to feel that they are on top of the world and that they don't require any assistance. During manic states, clients often accuse family members and helping professionals of being overprotective or worrying needlessly when they attempt to prepare the client for the depressive phase that follows. Many hospitals, agencies, and mental health organizations provide educational pamphlets on bipolar disorders for clients and their families. Information from these sources can be integrated into the therapeutic discussions with both the client and family members. Whenever possible, the authors suggest that the cyclical nature of the illness be graphically illustrated in therapeutic sessions to enable clients to grasp the complexities of the disorder.

As with all clients, the social work practitioner should establish a therapeutic relationship that will allow the client to seek the practitioner out over the course of the illness. This disorder results in a long-term relationship where ideally the client will follow a specific treatment protocol to avoid future mood episodes. Throughout this therapeutic relationship, the client should also feel comfortable in seeking the necessary assistance when the symptoms become acute. A trusting relationship with the social worker will encourage the client to seek help early in the process, enabling the client to receive help as soon as indications of a new episode arise.

It is important for social work practitioners to remember that clients with bipolar disorders follow a predictable course of manic episodes followed by depressive states. It is during the depressive episode that the client will need to be assessed for potential suicidal thoughts and behaviors

(Austrian, 1995; Maxmen & Ward, 1995). A working therapeutic relationship also ensures that the client is actively involved in his or her treatment process and that the client is taking responsibility for monitoring a complex mental illness.

Frequent relapse is a reality for individuals with bipolar disorders, especially for those who do not comply with the treatment regimen and stop medication abruptly and without consultation (Perry, Tarrier, Morriss, McCarthy, & Limb, 1999). When all is going well it is especially difficult for clients to grasp fully the chronic, cyclical, long-lasting nature of their illness. Although mania leads to a depressive episode, the exhilaration experienced during the manic phase may be appealing and not something the client wants to give up. Clients with any mental illness often feel that if they take medication and seek psychosocial treatment, they are validating the existence of a problem that may carry a stigma and result in alienation from others. One can point out past patterns and consequences of medication noncompliance, but social work practitioners will find that bipolar clients have minimal insight into their behaviors and also have a tendency to blame others (Nassir, Boiman, & Goodwin, 2000).

It is extremely important to engage family members and other support systems to help clients maintain compliance with medications. In many instances, practitioners can develop journal logs and other tracking mechanisms that will help clients and their families monitor the symptoms and identify the triggers that precipitate changes in symptoms and moods. Tracking mood changes can also be beneficial when clients are trying to determine the amount of structure necessary in their lives to control those mood fluctuations. For example, if a client can identify through journaling that a certain amount of sleep and rest will prevent mood changes, then client and practitioner can agree that this is a desirable activity. Clients can assess other personal activities and factors, including relationships, that may alter their moods significantly and identify ways to avoid situations or decrease those activities that have a negative effect (Ellicott, Hammen, Gitlin, & Brown, 1990). Once these precipitants have been identified, the social work practitioner can also help the client work through the interpersonal dynamics that arise when the client either confronts or avoids these stressors (Swendsen, Hammen, Heller, & Gitlin, 1995).

The general objectives of treating acute episodes, preventing future episodes, and restoring the client's functioning become the primary focus of treatment with clients who present with bipolar disorder symptoms. Use of medication becomes the front line of intervention with bipolar clients who need to eliminate symptoms that often worsen and that affect all areas of functioning.

MEDICATION INTERVENTION

Because bipolar disorders are recurring illnesses, clients will often require an ongoing regimen of medication. There are various categories of psychotropic medications that are used in the treatment of bipolar disorders. This includes the SSRIs (discussed in chapter 4), which are generally used to treat depression and some types of anxiety, and the most recent addition Zyprexa (olanzapine), which is one of the newer antipsychotic medications (Portyansky, 2000). Of all of the medications that can be used, however, the most common are generally termed mood stabilizers (Dulcan, 1999) and include Lithium or other medications that fall within the anticonvulsant category.

Regardless of the type of mood stabilizing medication that is used, it is critical to remember that clients who suffer from a bipolar disorder will experience varying moods. When they are feeling good as they do in the manic and hypomanic phases, they may want to stop taking their medications. This is especially true during manic episodes, when the feeling of exhilaration can be influential in stopping medication. When clients stop taking their medication, this is particularly problematic for clients who are on the mood stabilizers. When a manic mood has receded, the medication should be continued in order to help prevent cyclic recurrences (Boerlin, Gitlin, Zoellner, & Hammen, 1998).

LITHIUM

Treatment of bipolar disorder during the 1950s through the 1970s consisted primarily of Lithium as the medication of choice. Lithium salts are used to treat manic episodes of bipolar disorder when a person's mood swings fluctuate severely from normal to elated to depressed. The recent use of Lithium with all age groups including children and adolescents is notable (Botteron & Geller, 1995; Kafantaris, 1995). For children and adolescents with bipolar disorder, Lithium can be prescribed for up to 2 years (Dulcan, 1999), and over the last few years it has been used in children and adolescents to control behavioral outbursts or rage. When it is used for this purpose, the medication will generally be prescribed until more appropriate ways to control the anger can be found (Dulcan 1999). In children, this medication can offer control of rage with the intention that more effective problem-solving and coping skills will replace its use or another safer medication will be substituted.

Lithium can assist in providing symptomatic control of both the manic and depressive phases of the illness, and in long-term prophylaxis against condition recurrence (Karper & Krystal, 1996; Lehne & Scott, 1996). The use of Lithium should diminish manic symptoms in 5 to 14 days, but it may take months before the condition is fully controlled (Dulcan, 1999). Lithium has a short half-life because it is rapidly excreted, but the drug is highly toxic and must be monitored regularly. Because the medication is excreted through the kidneys, clients with any type of renal impairment should avoid this medication (Lehne & Scott, 1996). With its high toxicity and excretion rate, Lithium can be particularly problematic in older people (*PDR*, 2000) who should only take it if they have normal sodium intake and normal heart and kidney function.

The therapeutic range for Lithium is a limited one and there is a fine line between the therapeutic dose and a toxic one. Its use requires routine Lithium levels, and at a minimum an established baseline between other recommended tests (white blood cell, calcium, kidney function, thyroid function, etc.). A Lithium level is always obtained at the beginning of treatment to determine the best level for the client. Once stable, Lithium levels should be checked every few months, especially since they may vary over time (Dulcan, 1999).

Lithium has been known to cause an enlarged or overactive thyroid gland, which is why the client on lithium is always monitored for thyroid functioning (*PDR*, 2000). Many times a thyroid hormone will be prescribed along with Lithium to restore normal functioning.

Initially clients may report drowsiness, weakness, nausea and vomiting, fatigue and hand tremor. These side effects usually subside quickly, although the hand tremor may remain. Other side effects include:

- weight gain
- muscle weakness
- increased thirst
- increased urination
- diarrhea

There are some very serious toxic effects that can be associated with too much Lithium. According to Dulcan (1999) the client and his or her family should be encouraged to go to a physician's office or the emergency room immediately if these symptoms occur:

- irregular heartbeat
- fainting
- staggering
- blurred vision
- ringing or buzzing in the ears
- inability to urinate
- muscle twitches
- high fever
- seizures (fits or convulsions)
- unconsciousness

Given the serious side effects and other potential complications, social work practitioners treating clients on Lithium should ensure that prior to taking the medication the client has a thorough medical examination and blood work, that a complete medical history is taken, and that other factors such as potential thyroid, renal problems, and possible pregnancy be assessed. In addition, there should be frequent monitoring of potential problems every 2 to 3 months while the client is on the medication. Overdosing with Lithium can be fatal (*PDR*, 2000), and the seriousness of properly educating clients and family members to the dangers of using this medication cannot be overemphasized.

ATYPICAL MEDICATIONS

The medications known as anticonvulsants are often used as front-line treatment of the bipolar disorders. The most common of these medications include: Tegretol (carbamazepine), Depakene or Depakote (valproate or valproic acid), and Klonopin (clonazepam), and they are used under the following circumstances: (a) inadequate response or intolerance to antipsychotics or lithium; (b) manic symptoms; (c) rapid cycling of the condition; (d) EEG abnormalities; and (e) head trauma (Kaplan & Sadock, 1996). In practice, these medications seem particularly effective for clients who suffer from schizoaffective disorders or agitated depression of a cyclic nature. They are considered the medication of choice if an individual has a history of brain damage or of severe or rapid mood swings (Dulcan, 1999). Furthermore, if an individual has atypical features of the mental disorder (an unusual mixture of mania and depression symptoms), or rapid cycling (more than four cycles a year), these medications are often considered a first choice (Brotter et al., 1998). Because of the toxicity associated with Lithium it is not uncommon for these atypical medications to be used with children who have been diagnosed with bipolar disorder (Dulcan, 1999). They can also be given to individuals who do not appear to respond well to Lithium or who have developed a nonresponse pattern (Bezchlibnyk-Butler & Jeffries, 1999). When these medications are used, they are generally prescribed one at a time as physicians worry about interactions and about overtaxing the hepatic system (Brotter et al., 1998). To avoid problems of this nature, blood tests are often done to ensure suitability before starting carbamazepine and valproic acid. These tests are continued every month or so afterward to be sure the dosing is correct and that side effects are not overwhelming. Blood tests are not generally needed with clonazepam (Dulcan, 1999). When these medications are used to treat bipolar disorders it is likely that they will be continued for many years. If they are used to treat impulse-control disorders, however, the course of the medication is much shorter and is discontinued when behavioral approaches appear to be helping (Dulcan, 1999).

Medications Used to Treat Bipolar Disorders

Brand name	Generic name
Tegretol	carbamazepine
Depakene or Depakote	valproate or valproic acid
Klonopin	clonazepam

One of the most important roles of the social worker is to help monitor for side effects. Common side effects for Tegretol (carbamazepine) that often occur when the medication is first started include double or blurred vision, sleepiness, dizziness, clumsiness or decreased coordination, mild nausea and stomach upset (if this occurs advise the client to take the medication after a light meal or a snack), hair loss, increased risk of sunburn, and skin rash (*PDR*, 2000). Some of the behavioral or emotional side effects for social workers to be aware of are anxiety and nervousness, agitation and mania, impulsive behavior, irritability, increased aggression, hallucinations, and motor and vocal tics (Dulcan, 1999). Serious but rare side effects listed in the *PDR* (2000) include a decrease in the number of blood cells, lung irritation, worsening of seizures, yellowing of the skin, loss of appetite, increased or decreased urination, dark urine or pale bowel movements, sore throat or fever, mouth ulcers, vomiting, and severe behavior problems.

The side-effect profile for Depakene or Depakote (valproate or valproic acid) generally appears early in the course of treatment and includes upset stomach, increased appetite, thinning hair, tremor, drowsiness, and weight gain (*PDR*, 2000). The two biggest behavioral or emotional side effects involve increased aggression and irritability (Dulcan, 1999). Serious but rare side effects are very similar to Tegretol (carbamazepine) except valproic acid has not been noted to decrease the number of blood cells or lead to lung irritation. It is important to warn clients that if the medication is stopped suddenly, uncomfortable withdrawal symptoms may occur, and a planned course for discontinuance of this medication should always be implemented (Bezchlibnyk-Butler & Jeffries, 1999).

With Klonopin (clonazepam), the most common side effects are difficulty with balance and drowsiness (*PDR*, 2000). Social workers need to be aware that there may be behavioral and emotional side effects that include irritability, excitement, increased anger and aggression, trouble sleeping or nightmares, and memory loss (Dulcan, 1999). These side effects can be very disturbing to the client as well as to family members, and it is critical that families be educated about the problems that can occur and how to handle them. The most serious side effect with Klonopin is probably the interaction if this medication is combined with alcohol or other drugs, which can result in sleepiness, unconsciousness, and death (*PDR*, 2000).

PSYCHOPHARMACOTHERAPY IN THE TREATMENT OF BIPOLAR DISORDERS

When working with the medications used to treat bipolar disorders, the most important factor to remember probably is the high potential for interacting with other drugs (Larkin, 1993). Many times the use of atypical drugs is discouraged when clients are taking other types of medications (Bezchlibnyk-Butler & Jeffries, 1999), and it is always a good idea to check for interaction effects that can occur rather than underestimate this problem. For example, carbamazepine can interact with several types of mental health medications including some of the antidepressants, antipsychotics, benzodiazepines (often used to treat anxiety), and Lithium. When in doubt it is always best to look up these medications rather than to risk an uncomfortable and dangerous interaction effect (Bezchlibnyk-Butler & Jeffries, 1999).

In addition to medication, social work practitioners use various psychosocial interventions such as individual and group therapy in the treatment of the bipolar disorders. Of equal importance as treatment modalities are specialized addiction groups designed to also treat coexisting disorders such as substance abuse that clients with bipolar disorders experience (Weiss, Griffin, Greenfield, Najavits, Wyner, Soto, & Hennen, 2000).

DOCUMENTATION AND TREATMENT PLANNING

Treatment interventions for bipolar clients should be structured clearly and mapped out in a plan that delineates strategies for handling the problems associated with bipolar symptoms. Social work practitioners will often encounter resistance from clients with bipolar disorders, especially those experiencing a manic episode where energy, creativity, and feelings are at an all-time high. Regardless of the resistance, it is the practitioner's responsibility to help the client and family members formulate, implement, and monitor the interventions necessary to eliminate the bipolar symptoms.

In developing the treatment plan, special attention must be given first to any critical and harmful symptoms presented by the client. The problems that often constitute a crisis include suicidal ideation, violent behavior, substance abuse, and risk-taking behaviors. As with any mental illness, the accurate assessment and treatment of these significant problems will enable the practitioner to help the client and the family focus on the basic noncrisis-oriented symptoms that cause overall impairment of functioning in the client. The goal in addressing the critical problems presented by clients is to eliminate those immediate, acutely harmful symptoms to ensure the client's safety and eventual return to a more productive level of functioning.

Throughout the treatment planning process, social work practitioners must involve the client and the family in identifying problem areas and viable strategies to address them. Involving family members and other significant support systems will be important during the times when the bipolar client experiences hypomanic symptoms or manic states and is not able to identify the fluctuations in mood. Because hypomanic symptoms present in less severe ways, the client will need to rely on those in the support system who interact with the client on a regular basis and who can distinguish normal moods from those mood states that characterize hypomania or mania. During a manic episode, family members and others who can identify the extreme "highs" will be very important, because the client doesn't feel uncomfortable during these times and will therefore not usually seek help for the symptoms.

Once problems are identified, it is important to document them in concrete and measurable terms that will allow the practitioner, client, and family members to assess whether objectives and outcomes have been successfully met. Identifying problems leads to prioritizing of goals to be worked on by the client and the practitioner. Each of these broad goals is then addressed through a series of objectives, and each objective indicates the target behavior to be changed, who will work on the change, the measurable outcome desired, specific dates by which the change will be visible, and the measures or instruments that will show the objective has been met. Accompanying the objectives are action tasks that are the specific steps the client and family members will take in order to ensure that the objective is met.

Examples of identified problem behaviors often include the following:

- Depressed feelings that can lead to suicidal ideation
- Difficulty managing feelings of anger, which can include irritability, hostility, explosive outbursts, and violent behaviors
- Feelings of low self-esteem evident in fear of rejection, feeling that people dislike oneself, and blaming oneself
- Manic or hypomanic symptoms, which include pressured speech, grandiosity, changes in sleeping or eating patterns, inability to concentrate, increased agitation and impulsive behaviors
- Evidence of psychotic thought processes

Identification of these problems should lead to a targeting of appropriate objectives and action steps that will decrease or eliminate the behaviors. For example, if the treatment-plan goal is to decrease manic or hypomanic symptoms, one of the objectives would be to have the client sleep a specific number of hours per night (Jongsma & Peterson, 1995). Effective treatment planning must include a medication regimen that enables the client to follow through on objectives. The objective of ensuring a specific amount of sleep, for instance, should indicate the time frame for accomplishing this goal and the specific way that the client will monitor the activity (perhaps by keeping a sleep log). It should also specify how (e.g., with a glass of warm milk), when, and where (e.g., going to bed at 10:00 pm) the target behavior would be changed.

It is essential that social work practitioners help their clients develop treatment plans that are tailored and realistic for the individual client. Involving the client in what he or she can accomplish and setting realistic time frames helps to ensure success in treatment planning.

SUPPORTIVE INTERVENTIONS WITH BIPOLAR DISORDERS

The literature reports the necessity of providing medication therapy to clients with bipolar disorders before or concurrently with any psychosocial interventions that are used (Brotter et al., 1998). Biologically controlling the various symptoms presented by these clients enables them to proceed with psychosocial strategies that will complement the medication regimen. Bipolar clients cannot be helped until the medication component of their overall treatment is identified, assessed, and implemented as the correct regimen for the individual client. Even when medication is first tried, it may be necessary to make changes in the drug choice or dosage until an appropriate regimen is established.

Treatment planning is not only a sound way to coordinate all the services needed by clients, but is also a required component of health care policies. Social work practitioners should be ready to integrate a case management function in their therapeutic work with bipolar clients and in some instances be available to coordinate with an outside case manager. Because bipolar clients present with symptoms that affect all aspects of their functioning, they will require different mental health and health services to ensure that they return to a productive level of functioning and stay there. Some of these services include medical exams, ongoing lab testing to monitor effects of medication, vocational counseling, securing possible disability benefits, and identification of specialized support groups in the community.

Clients with bipolar disorders can present with other existing problems that may exacerbate manic, hypomanic, or depressive symptoms. Some of these include anxiety disorders, substance abuse and dependence, and alcoholism. Since many bipolar clients demonstrate patterns of cyclic behavior (i.e., a biological rhythm) that can be somewhat predictable, mapping out high-risk times or events can be helpful. In cases where another mental illness coexists with the bipolar disorder symptoms, clients may benefit from referrals to specialized groups that focus on the other problems (Weiss, Najavits, & Greenfield, 1999). Caution should be used when making these referrals, because clients whose bipolar illness is stabilized can make more effective use of specialized support groups.

As with all mental illnesses, involving family members in the treatment of bipolar disorder is an important and useful strategy. Family members often can be of support to the client and help monitor the fluctuations in mood episodes, and it is essential that family members be educated about the nature and course of the illness and be given an opportunity to express their own feelings of frustration and anger (Brennan, 1995). Clients and family members alike can feel the strain of changes in the interpersonal relationships when clients begin to demonstrate active symptoms of the bipolar disorder. If they are not helped to understand how the illness and subsequent changes in the client affect all parties involved, the strain between client and support systems continues to increase. In particular, family members need to understand that clients with this disorder will behave strangely and will often act intensely and inappropriately.

Throughout the therapeutic relationship, the social work practitioner is continuously working with the client via case management, family therapy, and individual therapy. The focus of individual therapy is centered on helping the client monitor the mood changes and, more important, in helping the client identify ways that he or she can meet the treatment plan objectives. This means that the social work practitioner needs to be acutely aware of the subtle changes in the client's moods and that early identification will prompt the social worker to assess and change the current course of treatment. Sometimes this will require a change of medication or evaluating medication compliance. The social work practitioner sees the client more frequently than the prescribing psychiatrist and is in a position to provide vital information to the doctor (Dziegielewski & Leon, 1998).

SUMMARY AND CONCLUSIONS

Dealing with any form of mental illness is a major challenge for clients, practitioners, and family members. Bipolar disorders with their varying mood episodes present a unique challenge because symptoms may not be addressed until clients reach an acute episode of mania. In addition, the client with this disorder often presents with coexisting psychiatric disorders that require concurrent attention.

The assessment process in diagnosing bipolar disorder is an essential component of the treatment process for this illness. Assessing the client for critical, harmful problems such as suicidal ideation during a depressive episode may require addressing these problems first as a way of securing the client's safety. Assessment also includes the appropriate use of the criteria provided by the *DSM-IV* manual and the inclusion of medication as the first priority in treatment planning.

Clients with bipolar disorders cannot be helped until they have been thoroughly assessed for appropriate medication. Once the need for medication is determined, the goal is to identify the appropriate medication and dosage. Clients with bipolar disorder, and for that matter any client with a serious psychiatric illness, should not be prescribed medication as the sole treatment intervention. Although major advances have been made in the field of psychotropic medication, clinical practice and the literature have always emphasized the multifaceted approach for multidimensional problems. It is important to remember that all mental illnesses impact on the biological, social, and psychological spheres of a client's life and functioning (Walsh, 1989).

Psychosocial interventions have their appropriate place in treatment planning once the client's acute symptoms have been stabilized by medication. In the case of bipolar disorders, psychosocial interventions will address the individual client and the family system. Families are encouraged to ventilate their frustration and anger at the client's behaviors (Simoneau, Miklowitz, Richards, Saleem, & George, 1999). This is done through the use of case management to obtain and coordinate the necessary health and mental health services needed by the client and through family education and family sessions, where members learn to understand the illness. In addition, the individual client is assisted in the tracking and monitoring of bipolar symptoms. Clients are assisted with basic living functions that will enable them to relate to people appropriately, obtain and hold employment, and improve their overall social skills.

Social workers developing treatment plans with bipolar clients must recognize and understand the role of medication in the treatment of this disorder. Because medication will always be prescribed for clients with bipolar disorders, it is essential that social work practitioners be aware of the different types of medications, their dosages, side effects, and the potential health problems that they may present in some clients. Social workers are also in a position to provide important information about the client's functioning to those health care professionals who prescribe and changed a client's medication regimen. Therefore, the social work professional should have a working knowledge of medications and of the rapid changes in the field of psychopharmacology.

REFERENCES

American Psychiatric Association. (1994). *Diagnostic and statistical manual of mental disorders* (4th ed.). Washington, DC: American Psychiatric Press.

Austrian, S. G. (1995). *Mental disorders, medications and clinical social work.* New York: Columbia University Press.

Badger, L. W., & Rand, E. H. (1998). Mood disorders. In J. B. W. Williams & K. Ell (Eds.), *Mental health research: Implications for practice* (pp. 49–117). Washington, DC: NASW Press.

Bezchlibnyk-Butler, K. Z., & Jeffries, J. (1999). *Clinical handbook of psychotropic drugs.* Seattle, WA: Hogrefe & Huber.

Boerlin, H. L., Gitlin, M. J., Zoellner, L. A., & Hammen, C. L. (1998). Bipolar depression and antidepressant-induced mania: A naturalistic study. *Journal of Clinical Psychiatry, 59,* 374–379.

Botteron, K. N., & Geller, B. (1995). Pharmacologic treatment of childhood and adolescent mania. *Child and Adolescent Psychiatric Clinics of North America: Pediatric Psychopharmacology II,* 283–302.

Brennan, J. W. (1995). A short-term psychoeducational multiple-family group for bipolar patients and their families. *Social Work, 40,* 737–744.

Brotter, B., Clarkin, J. F., & Carpenter, D. (1998). Bipolar disorder. In B. Thyer & J. Wodarski (Eds.), *Handbook of empirical social work practice: Mental Disorders Vol. 1* (pp. 287–308). New York: Wiley.

Burke, C. K., Burke, J. D., Reiger, D. A., & Rae, D. (1990). Age at onset of selected mental disorders in five community populations. *Archives of General Psychiatry, 47,* 511–518.

Carlson, G. A. (1998). Mania and ADHD: Comorbidity or confusion. Journal of Affective Disorders. *Journal of Affective Disorders, 51,* 177–187.

Carlson, G. A., Bromet, E. J., & Jandorf, L. (1998). Conduct disorder and mania: What does it mean in adults? *Journal of Affective Disorders, 48,* 199–205.

Cassano, G. B., Pini, S., Saettoni, M., & Dell'Osso, L. (1999). Multiple anxiety disorder comorbidity in patients with mood spectrum disorders with psychotic features. *American Journal of Psychiatry, 156,* 474–476.

Cassidy, F., Murry, E., Forest, K., & Carroll, B. J. (1998). Signs and symptoms of mania in pure and mixed episodes. *Journal of Affective Disorders, 50,* 187–201.

Dulcan, M. K. (1999). *Helping parents, youths, and teachers understand medications for behavioral and emotional problems: A resource book of medication information handouts.* Washington, DC: American Psychiatric Press.

Dziegielewski, S. F., & Leon, A. M. (1998, Winter). Psychopharmacology knowledge and use with social work professionals: A continuing education evaluation. *International Journal of Continuing Education, 1*(3), 31–40.

Ellicott, A., Hammen, C., Gitlin, M., & Brown, G. (1990). Life events and the course of bipolar disorder. *American Journal of Psychiatry, 147,* 1194–1198.

Gitlin, M. J. (1996). *The psychotherapist's guide to psychopharmacology* (2nd ed.). New York: Free Press.

Hilty, D. M., Brady, K. T., & Hales, R. E. (1999). A review of bipolar disorder among adults. *Psychiatric Services, 50,* 201–213.

Jongsma, A. E., & Peterson, L. M. (1995). *The complete psychotherapy treatment planner.* New York: Wiley.

Kafantaris, V. (1995). Treatment of bipolar disorder in children and adolescents. *Journal of the American Academy of Child and Adolescent Psychiatry, 34,* 732–741.

Kaplan, H. I., & Sadock, B. J. (1996). *Pocket handbook of primary care psychiatry.* Baltimore: Williams & Wilkins.

Karper, L. P., & Krystal, J. H. (1996). Augmenting antipsychotic efficacy. In A. Breier (Ed.), *The new pharmacotherapy of schizophrenia.* Washington, DC: American Psychiatric Press.

Keller, M. B., & Wunder, J. (1990). Bipolar disorder in childhood. In M. Hersen & C. G. Last (Eds.), *Handbook of child and adult psychopathology* (pp. 69–81). New York: Pergamon Press.

Kronenberger, W. G., & Meyer, R. G. (1996). *The child clinician's handbook.* Needham Heights, MA: Allyn & Bacon.

Larkin, M. (1993, March). Types of antidepressants. *FDA Consumer,* pp. 21–22.

Lehne, R. A., & Scott, D. (1996). Psychopharmacology. In V. B. Carson & E. N. Arnold (Eds.), *Mental health nursing: The nurse–patient journey.* Philadelphia: W. B. Saunders.

Marlatt, G. A. (Ed.). (1998). *Harm reduction: Pragmatic strategies for managing high-risk behaviors.* New York: Guilford Press.

Maxmen, J. S., & Ward, N. G. (1995). *Essential psychopathology and its treatment* (2nd ed.). New York: Norton.

McElroy, S. L., Strakowski, S. M., West, S. A., & Keck, P. E. (1997). Phenomenology of adolescent and adult mania in hospitalized patients with Bipolar disorder. *American Journal of Psychiatry, 154*(1), 44–49.

Meeks, S. (1999). Bipolar disorder in the latter half of life: Symptom presentation, global functioning, and age of onset. *Journal of Affective Disorders, 52,* 161–167.

Nassir, G. S., Boiman, E., & Goodwin, F. K. (2000). Insight and outcome in bipolar, unipolar, and anxiety disorders. *Comprehensive Psychiatry, 41,* 167–171.

Netherton, S. D., Holmes, D., & Walker, C. E. (1999). *Child and adolescent psychological disorders: A comprehensive textbook.* New York: Oxford University Press.

Perry, A., Tarrier, N., Morriss, R., McCarthy, E., & Limb, K. (1999, January). Randomized controlled trial of efficacy of teaching patients with bipolar disorder to identify early symptoms of relapse and obtain treatment. *British Medical Journal, 318,* 149–157.

Physicians' Desk Reference. (2000). *Physicians' desk reference* (54th ed.). Montvale, NJ: Medical Economics.

Portyansky, B. E. (2000, May 1). Antipsychotic drug receives indication for bipolar disorder. *Drug Topics,* p. 29.

Regier, D. A., Narrow, W. E., Rae, D. S., Manderscheid, R. W., Locke, B. Z., & Goodwin, F. K. (1993). The De Facto U.S. Mental and Addictive Disorders Service System. *Archives of General Psychiatry, 50,* 85–92.

Simoneau, T. L., Miklowitz, D. J., Richards, J. A., Saleem, R., & George, E. L. (1999). Bipolar disorder and family communication: Effects of a psychoeducational treatment program. *Journal of Abnormal Psychology, 108*(4), 588–568.

Swendsen, J., Hammen, C., Heller, T., & Gitlin, M. (1995). Correlates of stress reactivity in patients with bipolar disorder. *American Journal of Psychiatry, 152,* 795–797.

Walsh, J. (1989). Treatment of the bipolar client: Clinical social work contributions. *Clinical Social Work Journal, 17,* 367–382.

Weiss, R. D., Najavits, L. M., & Greenfield, S. F. (1999). A relapse prevention group for patients with bipolar and substance use disorders. *Journal of Substance Abuse Treatment, 16,* 47–55.

Weller, E. B. (1995). Bipolar disorder in children: Misdiagnosis, underdiagnosis, and future directions. *Journal of the American Academy of Child and Adolescent Psychiatry, 34,* 709–715.

CHAPTER 6

Treatment of Anxiety Disorders

A nxiety is a subjective emotional and physical state experienced by all at some point. Anxiety becomes problematic when it cannot be controlled and begins to interfere with an individual's ability to work, sleep, or concentrate. More than one-third of all clients who seek mental health treatment present with some type of anxiety-related problem, yet due primarily to diagnostic error only one in four people with anxiety disorders receive adequate intervention (Hales, 1995). It is alarming that so many individuals who suffer from anxiety are incorrectly diagnosed or inadequately treated, because most anxiety disorders respond to intervention with short-term success rates as high as 70% (Roth & Fonagy, 1996).

It is essential for social workers to recognize that there are several different types of anxiety disorders and that the medications used to treat these disorders are usually taken regularly because symptoms can occur with random frequency (Koerner, 1999; Nordenberg, 1999). Furthermore, the severe dietary restrictions and the withdrawal and dependency issues related to the use of these medications need to be monitored closely, especially with regard to their continuing use (Stein, 1998). Psychotherapy that focuses on changing maladaptive thoughts and behaviors is also considered essential when assisting those who suffer from anxiety (Stein, 1998). To highlight the use of such techniques, recent reviews of literature support the usefulness of brief treatment models that can help diminish anxiety (Barlow, Esler, & Vitali, 1998; Roth & Fonagy, 1996). Using a psychopharmacological intervention alone does not appear to provide sustainable relief for those suffering from these disorders. Researchers are finding that a short-term approach, either alone or in concert with medications, seems to provide the most effective form of intervention. Although great improvements may be reported when treating clients with severe anxiety, however, most interventions are not curative. This means that clients are likely to need additional help and monitoring in the form of reassessment or booster sessions. It is important to recognize when medication alone may not be enough and including psychosocial interventions can assist the client in gaining control over anxious feelings. Most professionals would agree that a combined approach is required to reduce or eliminate an anxiety disorder, using medications as well as cognitive behavioral techniques such as exposure and systematic desensitization. In this chapter the authors emphasize the importance of being familiar with the medications and the supplemental psychosocial interventions that can be effective in treating these disorders.

CASE EXAMPLE: OBSESSIVE-COMPULSIVE DISORDER

Ron, a practicing forensic pathologist, was well respected in his field and was recognized within the professional community as a conscientious practitioner and scientist. Originally seen by a psychiatrist principally for compulsive symptoms that were increasingly interfering with his practice and social life, Ron decided to see a social worker about changing some of his behavior patterns.

The client's history consisted of distressing and intrusive thoughts (referred to as obsessions) that led to anxiety-reducing behaviors (compulsions), which appeared to be fairly consistent throughout his life. In the last 6 months, however, these behaviors had worsened to the point that they were significantly impairing his occupational and social functioning. When describing himself, Ron stated that he was always a systematic and somewhat rigid person who believed in establishing concrete plans and in designating a proper place for every thing he owned. His obsessive-compulsive tendencies had served him well in medical school as he channeled his anxiety into disciplined study habits. He did admit that there were times he resented missing out on having fun with his friends because he was so worried about passing a test, even though he almost always scored at the top of his class. He reported that his "perfectionist nature" proved expensive in college because it forced him to move out of the dormitory and into his own apartment. He could not stand to live in the dormitory because of his lack of control over the disorganization there.

When discussing his childhood, Ron stated that he was an only child who was rewarded for keeping his room clean. He described his mother as a "neat freak" and his father as frequently absent from home. He always maintained a clean and tidy bedroom because he knew that neatness would gain his mother's approval and praise. One of his greatest fears was that he would catch diseases or germs from the people he came in contact with, especially women. When questioned about this, Ron stated that he believed women were dirty and needed to be monitored routinely for cleanliness. His way of guaranteeing and monitoring their cleanliness was to require the women he dated to maintain certain hygiene habits. He always asked the women to wear cotton because it could be cleaned with bleach and disinfected. When asked whether men also were basically dirty, Ron agreed that they could be, but not in the same way as women. Ron reported an earlier incident in which he realized how dirty women could be and how their outward appearance could be deceiving. He described something that had occurred approximately 10 years earlier while he was in the military and stationed in Hong Kong. He had started dating a very beautiful woman whom he considered marrying but was devastated to learn that he had contracted a venereal disease from her. Soon after dating her, he began to have a discharge from his penis and immediately sought medical treatment. There were no complications from the treatment for the venereal disease, but he considered this event a significant turning point in his life. He stated he had learned that although women looked clean, they could still harbor and transmit diseases. At this time he decided to stop dating unless he could ensure that the woman he dated could be trusted. He began purchasing women's cotton clothing. From that point on when he would invite a female over to his apartment, he would ask her to remove her street clothes and wear the cotton clothing he had purchased. He would change into comfortable cotton clothing as well. According to Ron, the majority of the women he dated were not offended and actually liked the pampering they received when donning the cotton robe and slippers. He also cooked dinner and served it, because he did not trust that outside sources would be sanitary. He also wanted to monitor what went into the food he ate to be sure it contained no potentially toxic substances. He stated that this arrangement generally worked well but that recently things had gotten worse, and he described several stresses in his life that intensified his rituals and routines. First, his previous girlfriend had decided she was not going to wear the cotton clothing anymore and refused to see him again if he continued to insist on it. He felt that his girlfriend was just trying to punish him because she had brought over take-out food, and he immediately threw it in the trash and accused her of trying to poison him. He also became extremely upset when his colleagues teased him about being infected after conducting an autopsy on an HIV-positive client. Later he verified that the client was not HIV positive, but he was infuriated that his colleagues would even consider teasing him about such a thing when they knew of his intense desire to remain free of germs and disease.

Since the autopsy his cleaning behaviors had intensified. Each day when he returned home he would spend hours bathing to ensure that he was clean. His skin was beginning to show the effects and appeared to be peeling and scaling over. Ron was so concerned about cleanliness that he frequently went back into the bathroom to make sure that the water had drained from the tub, reducing the danger of standing water. He also found himself performing many ritualistic behaviors over and over again particularly at work where he would spend hours checking and rechecking the storage of chemicals and supplies.

Several weeks earlier, Ron had gone to see a physician who was a friend of his and began taking Paxil, an antidepressant medication (SSRI) approved by the FDA for obsessive-compulsive disorder. The physician felt that Ron was depressed and that Paxil might help with the behaviors he was exhibiting. Since taking the medication Ron reported that he felt relief, but at certain times he felt his anxiety heighten. When this happened it would take him a few minutes to compose himself and control his feelings of anxiousness and agitation. Ron asked the social worker her opinion of the medication and asked if there was anything she could suggest from a behavioral perspective that would control the compulsive behaviors that were still distressing him.

Upon assessment it was evident to the social worker that Ron's symptoms were consistent with individuals who suffer from a type of anxiety disorder known as obsessive-compulsive disorder (OCD). The person who suffers from obsessive-compulsive disorder frequently has reoccurring obsessions (thoughts that interfere with action) and compulsions (behaviors that help ease current anxiety levels) that are related to the traumatic event. In OCD, the fourth most common psychiatric disorder in the United States, there appears to be a wide spectrum of symptoms (Cohen & Steketee, 1998). These symptoms can range from mild to severe, yet if left untreated can impair an individual's previous level of functioning at work, school, or at home (De Silva & Rachman, 1998).

Social workers should be aware of the diagnostic symptoms of clients who suffer from this type of anxiety disorder, as the symptoms can leave the client feeling insecure and frightened. Unfortunately, no matter how educated a client is, feeling uncomfortable and unsure about how to best address and handle what is happening frequently occurs. Being driven by a pattern of repetitive thoughts that lead to anxiety-reducing behaviors can appear senseless and distressing to clients like Ron. At the same time, they are significantly difficult to overcome. In addition, many individuals in the client's support system may not understand the condition or the behaviors demonstrated by the client. This can result in the client's becoming the object of jokes or teasing that inevitably leave the client more anxious and unsure. Therefore, before any psychopharmacological intervention is implemented, a comprehensive assessment and intervention plan are needed that clearly identify the client's behaviors as well as the environment's reactions to the behaviors.

ANXIETY DISORDERS: FORMING THE DIAGNOSTIC IMPRESSION

It is important to recognize that anxiety is generally a normal reaction to stress and that there will always be situations that create stress and discomfort (Newman & Newman, 1995). These unavoidable situations create feelings of anxiety that represent appropriate reactions to the stressor. Generally speaking, anxiety characterizes a response to threat and alerts the individual to danger, preparing him or her for the challenges that will need to be met. Anxiety can create feelings of uneasiness and tension as well as a sense of immediate danger or conflict. The symptoms indicative of anxiety can involve a combination of cognitive, behavioral, and somatic responses that include nervousness, sweating, irritability, sleeplessness, fear, muscular tension, obsessive thoughts, poor concentration, compulsive actions, feelings of depression, and other types of general discomfort (American Psychiatric Association, 1994).

Anxiety: An unpleasant state characterized by subjective feelings of worry, apprehension, **(cognitive)** difficulties concentrating, **(behavioral)** restlessness, irritability, insomnia, **(somatic)** sweat, shortness of breath, etc. Everyone experiences anxiety; it only becomes pathological when the magnitude and/or duration exceed normal limits (taking into account the preceding event).

(American Psychiatric Association, 1994)

In adults, some degree of anxiety is considered normal and in some cases may act to mobilize individuals into creative action or problem-solving modes; however, when these feelings impair occupational or social functioning, some degree of attention and concern is warranted. Anxiety only becomes pathological when it interferes with an individual's daily, social, interpersonal, or emotional functioning (American Psychiatric Association, 1994). For example, checking to see if the stove has been left on is generally a good safety measure. It becomes dysfunctional when the client is so concerned about the stove, for instance, that he or she checks repeatedly or makes numerous telephone calls to ensure that no one has accidentally left it turned on. This type of obsessive behavior is clearly disruptive to an individual's daily functioning.

Clients can be exposed to uncertainty and are expected to address many problems that include health and wellness issues, finances, recent and multiple medical problems, or the death of loved ones. Defined simply, fear is the body's response to a real threat, and anxiety is an exaggerated response to something that is unrealistic or unknown.

Human beings all have experiences that result in either pleasure or pain. As they develop, most seek to restore a homeostatic balance where pleasure dominates and pain is avoided at all costs (Newman & Newman, 1995). For many the avoidance of pain is critical, and early theorists such as Erikson (1963) identified the tension that is created when an individual has to resolve the conflict between individual needs and those of the environment. Erikson made it clear in his theory that a certain amount of tension, conflict, and anxiety is sometimes necessary to precipitate human growth and development.

Although anxiety is considered a normal part of development, it can cause very uncomfortable feelings that prompt individuals to seek relief or alternative ways of avoiding it (Nordenberg, 1999). Although psychotropic medications can provide relief from symptoms produced by anxiety, they do not address the underlying problems nor do they provide the coping skills needed to prevent future anxiety (Stein, 1998). Therefore, the most effective treatments for anxiety disorders involve medication therapy in conjunction with psychosocial interventions that are usually of a cognitive-behavioral nature.

THE PRESENTATION OF ANXIOUS CLIENTS

- Anxious clients usually present to the primary care physician before seeing a mental health professional.
- Few clients say that the actual problem is related to anxiety or nervousness; they often attribute what they are feeling to other factors.
- Many individuals present with physical or mental symptoms (tremors, dyspnea, dizziness, sweating, irritability, restlessness, hyperventilation, pain, heartburn, etc.).

TABLE 6.1   Anxiety Disorders and Related Conditions

Panic disorder with or without agoraphobia: Attacks involving intense anxiety and apprehension lasting several minutes, with or without agoraphobia

Agoraphobia with history of panic disorder: Fear of being in places where escape may be difficult

Social phobia: Persistent fear of one or more social situations

Specific phobia (formerly simple phobia): Fear of an object or stimulus, not generalized fear

Obsessive-Compulsive disorder: Recurring obsessions (thoughts) and compulsions (behaviors) severe enough to affect social/occupational functioning

Post-traumatic stress disorder: Symptoms must last at least one month; if more that six months after event should specify delayed onset, must be outside range of usual experience; individuals frequently report that they relive the situation

Acute stress disorder: (a new category in *DSM-IV* to address acute reactions to extreme stress) Occurs within four weeks of the stressor and last from two days to four weeks; may help predict the development of PTSD

Generalized anxiety disorder: Undue persistent worry about two or more life circumstances for at least 6 months (overanxious disorder of childhood was placed in this category in *DSM-IV*)

The definitions for these categories are adapted from the *DSM-IV* (American Psychiatric Association, 1994).

- Somatic symptoms of anxiety are similar to those of organic disease; generally, however, the symptoms seem unrelated or involve two or more organ symptoms (e.g., headache and back pain).

All social workers should be familiar with the *DSM-IV* diagnostic criteria that distinguishes when anxiety has become problematic enough to impair functioning in vital areas of the client's life (American Psychiatric Press, 1994). Anxiety becomes problematic when (a) the client begins to feel powerless to address what is happening to him or her; (b) the feelings of anxiety force the client to develop alternative physiological or cognitive strategies to prepare for or avoid a threat or danger that is not realistic (Nordenberg, 1999); (c) the person becomes physically or psychologically exhausted by constantly preparing to face his or her fears; and (d) self-attention or self-absorption consume the client, preventing him or her from responding appropriately to situations.

Table 6.1 provides a list of the mental health diagnoses that can manifest in anxiety-like symptoms. Rather than describe each of these disorders in detail, we present general information and the treatment strategy related to most of these disorders.

PANIC DISORDER

Although there are numerous specific types of anxiety disorders, most clients who experience anxious feelings will also develop symptoms of panic. When these symptoms are severe enough panic disorder (PD) may develop. This disorder is characterized by the spontaneous, unexpected occurrence of panic attacks. A panic attack is a brief episode characterized by an intense sense of dread and doom and physical symptoms such as a racing heart, sweating, and hyperventilation. These attacks begin suddenly, and the symptoms peak quickly (American Psychiatric Association, 1994, p. 395). It appears that the actual panic attack is not truly spontaneous (Wilhelm & Margraf, 1997), but is related to a combination of physical sensations and fearful cognition that give rise to thoughts of danger and anxiety. These attacks are differentiated from the experience of genuine fear because the cause for the anxiety may not be externally precipitated or known. Feeling panic is considered a disorder in itself, and when a person experiences repeated attacks together with anticipatory concern or fear about impending attacks, a diagnosis of panic disorder is suggested (American Psychiatric Association, 1994, p. 397).

Furthermore, when these panic symptoms are combined with agoraphobia, this can result in a genuine and intense concern that escape, although necessary, is unobtainable. According to the *Diagnostic and Statistical Manual of Mental Disorders,* panic disorder and agoraphobia are not considered codeable mental health disorders when experienced alone (APA, 1994). Therefore, when panic and agoraphobia symptoms exist in some combination, it is noted as panic disorder with or without agoraphobia or with a history of agoraphobia (American Psychiatric Association, 1994).

In agoraphobia with or without panic or with a history of panic disorder, there is a desperate habitual attempt to avoid the specific anxiety-producing stimulus (Nordenberg, 1999). Many times these attempts at avoidance include characteristic patterns and cluster around situations such as being outside the home, in a crowd, in an automobile or other mode of transportation, or being on a bridge (American Psychiatric Press, 1994).

When completing an assessment for panic or the symptoms of agoraphobia, it is essential to include information on the frequency, intensity, and

duration of the attacks (Barlow, O'Brien, & Last, 1984). Symptom variation occurs especially among individuals who have multiple attacks during
a single day and those who have only a few attacks a year. Regardless
of how panic or agoraphobia is experienced, a common characteristic of
all anxiety disorders is the client's misinterpretation of symptoms that
result in unrealistic fears or dread of common situations. The diagnostic
criteria as outlined in the *DSM-IV* delineate the different types of symptoms
present and can enable the mental health professional in developing differential treatment interventions (American Psychiatric Association, 1994).
Symptoms that frequently exist are palpitations or pounding of the heart,
sweating, trembling, shaking, a sensation of choking, nausea or abdominal
distress, feeling faint, and derealization (the feeling that what is occurring
is not real).

The symptoms of panic tend to be chronic in nature (Mattick, Peters, &
Clark, 1989), and the severity reported during the pretreatment phase
should always be considered. In addition, measuring the pretreatment
level of anxiety, which yields baseline information, is critical. In today's
practice environment there is a growing emphasis on measuring intervention success by using outcome indicators such as degree of improvement
(Jacobson, Wilson, & Tupper, 1988). The prognosis is guarded for individuals who suffer from panic disorder with agoraphobia, and some studies
report that fewer than half the clients treated achieve symptom-free status
(Burns, Thorpe, & Cavallaro, 1986; Cohen, Monteiro, & Marks, 1984;
Munby & Johnston, 1980). It is expected that approximately 50% of all
individuals treated for panic disorder will respond positively to intervention, so it is important to. anticipate and plan for the possible recurrence
of anxiety symptoms (Jacobson et al., 1988).

PHOBIC DISORDERS

In general, a phobia can be best defined as an intense, unrealistic fear of
an object, event, or feeling (Plaud & Vavrovsky, 1998). It is estimated
that 18% of the American adult population suffers from some type of
phobia (Hall, 1997). Yet exactly how phobias develop and what triggers
and sustains the phobic response remains elusive. There are three primary
types of phobias: (a) agoraphobia, the fear of being unable to escape when
leaving a safe place); (b) social phobia, the fear, embarrassment, and
avoidance of social situations; and (c) specific or simple phobia, the fear
of an object or other than social situations.

According to the *DSM-IV*, when an individual suffering from a phobia is exposed to an anxiety-provoking stimulus, an immediate anxiety-response develops. The reactions are far beyond the nervousness associated with being in a stressful situation. The fear is intense and generally prevents the individual's engaging in many of the usual activities (Nordenberg, 1999). Similar to one who suffers from panic, phobic individuals will also adopt avoidance behavior in a desperate attempt to escape the feared stimulus (Stein, 1998). They will try to rearrange their lives in order to sidestep what they believe to be the personal triggers that lead to frightening panicked reactions. If the situation cannot be avoided, it is endured with discomfort and dread. In order to be diagnosed with a phobic disorder, the fear or anxiety must be severe enough to interfere with an individual's daily functioning and routine or social and occupational functioning (American Psychiatric Association, 1994; Hall, 1997).

It is essential for social workers to ensure that a functional behavioral assessment is completed. According to Plaud and Vavrovsky (1998) some of the critical clinical information to be gathered includes: (a) all the problems the client is experiencing; (b) how regularly the problem is occurring and what occurs before and after the anxiety provoking situation; (c) the client's preexisting strengths and coping skills for handling the anxiety-provoking situations; (d) previous treatment and the nature of such treatment; and (e) resources for help.

POSTTRAUMATIC AND ACUTE STRESS DISORDER

In posttraumatic stress disorder (PTSD), the person generally has directly experienced or witnessed a traumatic event, and the symptoms must last more than a month. The reported discomfort frequently persists, creating difficulty in falling asleep and temper-control problems as reflected in irritability or angry outbursts. Individuals who suffer from this condition frequently want to avoid thoughts, feelings, or conversations associated with the stressful event (American Psychiatric Association, 1994).

In the *DSM-IV*, there is a new category similar to PTSD called acute stress disorder (ASD), which was added to address acute reactions to extreme stress. The onset of the stress reaction is expected to occur within four weeks of exposure to the stressor, and the experience will generally last from two days to four weeks. Many professionals believe that this condition may later lead to heightened symptoms present in the development of PTSD.

There is limited empirical evidence to support relying on one type of treatment alone in PTSD or ADS (Meichenbaum, 1994). Therefore, most social workers combine techniques and can encourage the use of medication to supplement treatment (Vonk & Yegidis, 1998). In assessment social workers need to assist clients in the following ways: (a) help the client monitor and identify side effects of the medications that are being taken to reduce symptoms; (b) help the client gain a cognitive understanding of the trauma, thereby reducing feelings of guilt and self-blame; (c) educate the client by increasing understanding of the condition of PTSD; (d) identify client strengths and increase coping skills; and (e) take into account factors relevant to the client's environment that may lead to problems at work or home.

GENERALIZED ANXIETY DISORDER

The type of anxiety disorder known as generalized anxiety disorder (GAD) involves undue persistent worry about two or more life circumstances that occurs for at least six months (American Psychiatric Association, 1994). Many professionals believe that GAD is extremely difficult to treat because clients frequently report marked fluctuations in symptoms that last most of the adult life (McLellarn & Rosenzweig, 1998). Since the course of the illness is so long, some professionals believe it would be better termed as a personality disorder (Beck & Emery, 1985).

In assisting clients who suffer from this type of anxiety, the first task is to assess whether the symptoms the client reports are serious enough to disrupt daily functioning. If so, the intensity, pervasiveness, and persistence of the symptoms should be carefully documented (McLellarn & Rosenzweig, 1998). Once the symptoms are identified, careful attention should be given to establishing a clear plan to address and alleviate them. Second, in most of the anxiety disorders and especially GAD, it is critical to determine whether the client is exhibiting the primary symptoms of anxiety or depression. According to Barlow et al. (1998), the fewer coping mechanisms a client has when faced with an extreme stressor, the more likely the client is to develop depression along with the anxiety. This interrelationship between anxiety and depression explains why many of the medications used to treat anxiety can also be used as antidepressants (Marshall, 1994). When addressing GAD, the symptoms the client experiences can be so varied they can directly affect managing daily affairs, from work-related issues to family relationships. Furthermore, McLellarn and Rosenzweig (1998) warn that the problems these individuals encounter may become more chronic with poor treatment outcomes. If managed health care requirements delay access to services, clients can be denied needed treatment. Because current approaches to treating GAD need to remain individualistic and be based on the symptoms reported, relying solely on medications for the sake of convenience is problematic. Avoiding other types of intervention such as cognitive-behavioral, family, and environmental assessments can lead to incomplete or inadequate intervention.

INTERVENTIONS FOR CLIENTS WHO HAVE ANXIETY

There are several different types of medication that are shown to be effective in reducing levels of anxiety and panic symptoms in individuals who suffer from anxiety. Positive results have not been as promising when working with the phobias, including agoraphobia (Marshall, 1994). Regardless of the type of anxiety a client is experiencing, prescribed psychopharmacologic agents appear to be most effective when the intervention is accompanied by some type of psychosocial intervention (Cohen & Steketee, 1998). For example, agoraphobia is often treated with a psychotherapeutic technique that includes real-life exposure to the stimulus that triggers the panic or anxiety (Ost, Salkovskis, & Hellstrom, 1991). This method could also be used for other anxiety conditions with a combination of cognitive-behavioral interventions, deep breathing, and stress reduction techniques.

MEDICATION

The increased use of medications in the treatment of anxiety has led many professionals to question why these medications appear to work so well. Based on information gained in studying medications and the neurochemical responses that are enhanced, it appears that anxiety is an integral part of human physiology (Marshall, 1994). For some reason the normal biological process that helps an individual control levels of anxiety becomes disturbed, and the client's anxiety becomes so intense it upsets the usual patterns of coping. Therefore, it is common for those who plan to implement psychosocial strategies to consider initially starting a course of medication therapy (Marshall, 1994). Once the medication is started, the social worker should always encourage the client to use additional psychosocial strategies to address problem behaviors.

More in-depth information on the medications most frequently used to treat anxiety will be discussed later, but the primary categories include the benzodiazepines, which address the symptoms of anxiety and panic; the atypical medications such as BuSpar that do not fall in the benzodiazepine category; and the other types of medications that are used for these symptoms such as the antidepressants (including SSRIs such as Paxil) (Nordenberg, 1999). When working with clients who have been prescribed medications to treat anxiety, social workers providing clinical services should keep the following in mind regardless of the medications used.

First, many of these medications have the potential to be addictive and clients may believe that taking a pill for a "quick fix" is the recommended course of treatment. Social workers must establish quickly the understanding that supplementing medications with other types of cognitive or behavioral interventions can prove most effective (Cohen & Steketee, 1998). For this reason, a behavioral-based contract should be initiated early in the intervention process, preferably before the medication is prescribed. By contracting prior to the medication, the client remains keenly aware that the pill is only one facet of a multidimensional approach to the treatment of anxiety disorders.

Second, the intervention should be related directly to the identified stressor (Himle & Fischer, 1998). This means that some agreement must be reached between the client and the practitioner as to the cause of the anxiety and how best it can be addressed.

Third, clearly defined contracts with goals and specific objectives can help both the social worker and the client stay on task (Plaud & Vavrovsky, 1998). This will help the client know what to expect from treatment and can also serve as a road map for the intervention.

Fourth, it is best in the contracting phase to identify and plan for addressing exogenous or external factors, rather than endogenous or internal ones. This requires identifying the stresses in the client's environmental and family system that can be changed. In the case example of Ron, intervention would involve helping Ron identify his obsessive-compulsive rituals and how to change them, rather than rooting around for the cause of the behavior. Although it is important for clients to develop some insight into their behaviors, approaches that focus actively on changing the symptoms behaviorally may provide the client with a sense of hope and accomplishment (Marshall, 1994). This is not intended in any way to diminish the value of helping the client develop an understanding into the causes of his or her behavior, but rather to suggest that this type of insight may come later in the course of treatment.

The last probably most important consideration is the potential for addiction when using these medications, especially the benzodiazepines (Stein, 1998). The addictive reliance and false sense of security these types of medications can produce may create a false sense of security that discourages the client from exploring other therapies designed to address the exogenous factors. It is important to recognize the potential for reliance and addiction with these medications because many times they are prescribed at the beginning of any intervention process. When treating the anxiety disorders, it is also important to stress to the client that relying on medication as the sole treatment modality has not been proven as effective as combining it with other psychosocial interventions (Cohen & Steketee, 1998; Plaud & Vavrovsky, 1998; Stein, 1998).

These drugs are potentially addictive and therefore should be used for anxiety related to an identified stressor and not as a permanent solution. Address the anxiety that can prevent someone's functioning and dealing with the problem, and encourage the client to seek supplemental psychosocial interventions.

(Dziegielewski, 1998)

TYPICAL ANTIANXIETY MEDICATIONS

One of the most common types of medication used in the treatment of the anxiety disorders has traditionally been the benzodiazepines (see Table 6.2). These medications can work quickly to address the anxiety symptoms that frequently lead to panic. These antianxiety medications work by helping to calm the parts of the brain that have become overly excited in anxious individuals (Dulcan, 1999). Furthermore, using a medication in this category can help in getting the client to agree to psychosocial intervention efforts.

A second major consideration for social workers when a client is taking benzodiazepines is the potential for addiction and abuse. In addition to the potential abuse, the benzodiazepines are central nervous system depressants that when combined with another depressant such as alcohol can result in significant depression or have a lethal effect (Dulcan, 1999;

TABLE 6.2   Benzodiazepines (Usually Used to Treat Anxiety, Panic, and Night Terrors)

Brand name	Chemical or generic name
Ativan	lorazepam
Klonopin	clonazepam
Librium	chlordiazepoxide
Valium	diazepam
Xanax	alprazolam
Dalmane*	flurazepam

*This medication is usually used to treat sleep problems.

Medication listing information was taken from Dulcan (1999); *Physicians' Desk Reference*, 2000.

Kaplan & Sadock, 1990). It has been estimated that in 70% to 90% of all suicides these are the drugs of choice, particularly Valium (diazepam), which is used by 51% of individuals who attempt suicide. For this reason it is essential that the clinical social worker be aware of and advise other professionals against prescribing this medication to clients who have a history of substance abuse. These clients, especially those 18 to 25 years old, have a greater tendency to attempt suicide using these drugs. Because of the potential for abuse, it is illegal for anyone to give or sell these medications to someone for whom the medication has not been prescribed (Dulcan, 1999).

BUSPAR (BUSPIRONE)

BuSpar is a popular medication used to treat anxiety. If a history of drug seeking or drug abuse is suspected, this drug may be a better drug of choice than the benzodiazepines. BuSpar has a chemical composition different from the benzodiazepines and does not have the same hypnotic, muscle relaxant, and anticonvulsant actions (Dulcan, 1999). BuSpar is different from benzodiazepines in three ways: (a) it does not cause sedation, (b) it has no abuse potential, so it is not regulated by the Controlled Substance Act; and (c) it does not potentiate other central nervous system depressants (Kaplan & Sadock, 1990). Side effects with BuSpar include dizziness, nausea, headache, and nervousness, lightheadedness, and excitement (Kaplan & Sadock, 1990). This medication is not considered to have a high potential for abuse; however, the full effect may not be felt for three to four weeks (Dulcan, 1999).

CATAPRES (CLONIDINE HYDROCHLORIDE USP) AND TENEX (GUANFACINE HYDROCHLORIDE)

Two medications that have recently become more popular for the treatment of posttraumatic stress disorder (PTSD) and the symptoms of anxiety as well as panic and other conditions are Catapres (clonidine) and Tenex (guanfacine) (Dulcan, 1999). These medications were first used to treat high blood pressure but now have been explored as a potential treatment for a variety of disorders. Generally both of these medicines can help decrease symptoms of hyperactivity, impulsivity, anxiety, irritability, temper tantrums, explosive anger, conduct problems, and tics (Dulcan, 1999). When used with adults, there appears to be support that these medications can help improve self-control as well as increase cooperation with treatment regimens.

According to Dulcan (1999), common side effects that occur when the medications is first prescribed include a slow pulse rate, trouble sleeping (which may be due to the medicine's wearing off), ringing in the ears, and redness and itching when using Catapres skin patch. Other side effects as the dose increases include sleepiness, fatigue, low blood pressure, headache, mild dizziness or lightheadedness, and stomachache. Some of the most common side effects that should be reported immediately to physicians are fainting, irregular heartbeat, trouble breathing, and increased frequency of nighttime urination, itching, rapid puffy swelling of the feet, and sudden headaches with nausea and vomiting.

Before prescribing these medications, a physician may decide to order blood tests or an electrocardiogram (ECG), which measures heart rhythm. As a general rule, a thorough physical exam is always recommended regardless of the medication a client is taking for anxiety. This type of exam may help ease the client's feelings of anxiousness by providing reassurance that they are physically stable enough to begin the medication and subsequent treatments.

ANTIDEPRESSANTS IN THE TREATMENT OF ANXIETY

As discussed in the chapter on depression, antidepressants are used in the treatment of anxiety, particularly the ones known as the selective serotonin uptake inhibitors (SSRIs). These medications are frequently considered because they help block the signs of panic experienced by clients who suffer from anxiety (Internal Medicine Review, 1999). Many antidepressants have demonstrated antianxiety properties independent of their antidepressant properties. In fact, SSRI antidepressants have been considered the drug of choice for panic disorder (Ballenger, Lydiard, & Turner, 1995), in part because the side effects of tricyclic and MAO antidepressants are more pronounced. For OCD, the SSRIs that are frequently prescribed include Prozac (fluoxetine), Zoloft (sertaline), Paxil (paraoxetine), and Luvox (fluvoxamine) (Cohen & Steketee, 1998). Luvox has also been approved for treating OCD in children. Unfortunately, many of these medications usually take up to six weeks to have significant antianxiety effects (Reid, 1997), so quicker-acting benzodiazepine anxiolytics (antianxiety agents) are still commonly prescribed. Furthermore, Pato, Zohar-Kadouch, Zohar, and Murphy (1988) warn that when these medications are withdrawn previous symptoms may return, thereby requiring clients to remain on these medications for longer periods. When used specifically to control the symptoms of anxiety these medications can help many individuals to move beyond these symptoms (Cohen & Steketee, 1998). In cases where the anxiety symptoms are so severe, starting a course of these medications before beginning psychological treatment can help the client focus and control anxiety. For many clinicians, however, using medications to control symptoms of anxiety can be a two-edged sword.

The authors strongly suggest that the intent and plan for supplementing the medication with psychosocial intervention be clearly outlined before a client is put on a medication. Decisions on how the medications are to be taken need to be clearly outlined particularly if they are to be taken on an as-needed basis or in a routine fashion. It is always important to remind clients that these medications should never just be stopped abruptly, and that consultation should be sought when planning to discontinue a medication (Dulcan, 1999). Tapering off these medications will almost always be indicated. Furthermore, recent research supports that relapse rates as high as 90% have been indicated when withdrawing clients from some of the SSRIs used to treat anxiety (Pato et al., 1988).

When medications are used as a sole treatment modality, researchers have questioned their effectiveness. For example, several researchers contend that low-potency benzodiazepines show no greater efficacy than placebos (success rates are reported to range from 30% to 45%) (Craske & Waikar, 1994; Roth & Fonagy, 1996). In addition, Clum, Clum, and Surls

(1993) found behavioral interventions to be comparable to antidepressants including the use of high-potency benzodiazepines. When looking specifically at psychosocial interventions Clark et al. (1994) found that cognitive therapy techniques were significantly more effective than using imipramine (a tricyclic antidepressant). To further complicate the use of medications as a supplement to intervention, Wardle (1990) found that using antianxiety medications (particularly benzodiazepines) in the treatment of anxiety could actually interfere with the psychosocial intervention process. This has led to further exploration of how medication as an adjunct to psychosocial intervention can affect the cognitive-behavioral interventions employed. Since many of the medications prescribed for anxiety lessen the physical symptoms, behavioral interventions that emphasize exposure to fear-provoking stimuli may be compromised. Therefore, client gains resulting from behavior-based attempts at overcoming fears may be falsely attributed to the effect of medications. This detracts from the primary purpose of implementing psychosocial interventions, which is to help empower clients to develop the confidence to overcome their fears. Falsely attributing changes to the medication fosters the belief that they are solely responsible for major changes in symptom decrease. The client may start to question the validity of psychological interventions, leading to an unnecessary dependence on the medication in order to prevent the return of anxiety symptoms that limit functioning ability.

PSYCHOLOGICAL INTERVENTIONS

There are several factors that should be considered when providing psychosocial interventions for the client who suffers from anxiety. First, unless it is excessive anxiety is considered a natural part of life. If a client is diagnosed with a medical condition, some degree of anxiety is expected as well as beneficial in creating an discomfort that can help prepare the client for action or acceptance. Therefore, psychosocial interventions may be suggested but generally are not considered essential unless the anxiety is so pronounced that it affects occupational and social functioning.

Second, when dealing with individuals who suffer from anxiety, the first course of action is to refer the client for a complete physical exam. The symptoms of anxiety are multifaceted (cognitive, behavioral, and somatic), and it is important that the client have a proper medical assessment to rule out physical causes for the anxiety or medical complications that may be caused by the disorder.

Third, although the social worker does not prescribe medications, an accurate medication history is needed to assist the prescriber in determining the need for medications and duration. This history should include prescribed medications, over-the-counter medications, and alternate therapies such as herbal preparations that may be used to control the anxiety (American Neuropsychiatric Association Committee on Research, 2000).

Social workers should also screen the client with regard to any history of previous substance abuse. If substance abuse has occurred or is present, it may be more effective to recommend a medication like BuSpar that does not have the same addiction profile.

Fourth, the social worker should also gather information on medications that the client is currently taking and explore whether any potential for substance abuse might occur. For example, the client may be using another stimulant such as caffeine and not realize the effect that it can have.

The last point with regard to assisting clients who suffer from anxiety is probably the most frustrating for social workers who implement verbal therapies. Many times when clients are placed on a benzodiazepine, they start to feel better fairly quickly. This feeling can create a resistance that sometimes leads clients to believe that they no longer need any intervention for the exogenous factors that are troubling them. That is, the clients may attribute feeling better to the medicine alone. To help avoid discontinuance of the intervention efforts, some attempt should be made to formalize and contract for the continuation of psychosocial counseling. Psychosocial counseling and problem-solving, skill-building interventions can help a person recognize and prepare for future anxiety-provoking situations. Current social work treatments in this area include cognitive-behavioral interventions and exposure intervention such as systematic desensitization.

Cognitive-behavioral interventions are considered a primary supportive intervention for those who suffer from anxiety-related conditions (Reid, 1997). In fact, a 1991 consensus statement from the National Institutes of Health recommended referrals to cognitive-behavioral or medication treatments if changes are not observed within the first 6 to 8 weeks of alternative treatment (including hypnotherapy or psychoanalytic therapy). Typically, cognitive-behavioral treatment for anxiety symptoms can include cognitive restructuring, breathing retraining, and in vivo exposure components (Craske & Waikar, 1994). While variation exists in the implementation of these technique, combining these techniques into a "treatment package" proves useful in clinical settings (Reid, 1997).

Cognitive restructuring targets the misinterpreting and misjudging bodily sensations as threatening, based on the concept that cognitions precede (or trigger) anxiety and panic. Thus identifying aberrant cognitive structures and challenging misinterpretations and biases through reasoning and experience can eliminate the anxiety. As part of the cognitive behavioral intervention relaxation training can be an important component of most interventions with clients that are troubled by anxiety. We know that people suffering from anxiety spend a great deal of time worrying about life or bodily sensations that accompany the early symptoms of their attacks. Teaching clients how to relax successfully can lead to their learning how to direct their energy in a more productive way, thereby reducing anxiety levels (Ost, Salkovskis, & Hellstrom, 1991). Learning to identify the indicators and reduce the physiological manifestations of stress is as an important precursor to exposing the clients to the source of their anxiety. Breathing retraining is of particular interest for those treating panic disorder because nearly 50% of these clients report hyperventilation symptoms (Craske & Waikar, 1994).

Teaching applied relaxation requires that the client learn to use progressive relaxation skills and apply these in times of anxiety and apprehension. This method requires the application of relaxing thoughts to stressful situations. Basically a client is helped to identify stressful cues and to address them while in a relaxed state. To start, the individual is instructed to assume a restful position. It is important to educate the client about diaphragmatic breathing and to encourage deep slow breaths. Many times clients prefer to use a mantra or saying as they breathe in and out. For example, each time the client inhales he or she is instructed to say that he or she is breathing in relaxing energy and exhaling tension. Other restful suggestions are made once the client had entered a relaxed state by breathing deeply. These suggestions help the client to become aware of the following bodily sensations: a feeling of heaviness, a feeling of warmth and tingling, a calmness of the heart, a calmness of breathing. Generally a minute or so is spent allowing the individual to notice each sensation. The individual is then asked to focus on the overall feeling of being relaxed. When the social worker has a sense that the client is truly relaxed, a statement is initiated to anchor this state of mind such as, "My body is calm," or, "I am relaxed" (Feltman, 1996; Gottlieb, 1995). This relaxing phrase will be used continually to anchor further relaxation training.

The client is instructed to repeat the diaphragmatic breathing and relaxing phrases at home, and clients usually contract to "exercise" five times a day (Dziegielewski & MacNeil, 1999). Because clients sometimes weaken the effectiveness of the autogenic phrase by engaging in negative self-talk, purchasing a stress-reduction tape can supplement the exercises. Learning this technique and practicing it is essential, because the client uses it at each stage of the systematic desensitization and the cognitive restructuring process. Initiating the relaxation sequence in this order helps clients learn the process quickly and realize the importance of adhering to the tasks of treatment.

EXPOSURE INTERVENTIONS AND SYSTEMATIC DESENSITIZATION

Systematic desensitization and exposure techniques are used to assist those who suffer from anxiety symptoms; however, this technique is generally regarded as the treatment of choice for specific phobias (Plaud & Vavrovsky, 1998). Using this in combination with in vivo techniques (real-life experiences) appears to have an even greater effect than that produced by simulating an experience in the office setting only (Marshall, 1988). Utilizing behavioral therapy that involves exposure and response prevention can be particularly effective in reducing panic symptoms (O'Sullivan & Marks, 1990). Where systematic desensitization has been used some clients find it particularly helpful when exposure to the anxiety-producing stimuli has been long enough to allow the anxiety to be markedly reduced (Marshall, 1996). Similarly, exposure to the feared stimulus is thought to be most effective when internal and external distractions from the phobic object or situation are minimized (Foa & Kozak, 1986). Treatment of this type requires that the client be systematically exposed to the object or situation that provokes the fear and the subsequent avoidance.

There are many variations of in vivo exposure treatment, and no single model has emerged as superior to others; however, long sessions are generally thought to be more successful than shorter or interrupted sessions (Chaplin & Levine, 1981; Marshall, 1985). Establishing a plan where sessions or exercises are conducted on a daily basis is considered by many to be superior to spacing the sessions out on a weekly schedule (Foa, Jameson, Turner, & Payne, 1980). Although Feigenbaum (1988) found a high-intensity (flooding) method effective, most practitioners favor the progressive model. Research suggests that exposure-based interventions can be administered by the social worker or by the client (Dziegielewski & MacNeil, 1999; Al-Kubaisy, Marks, Logsdail, & Marks, 1992), and there are clear cost benefits to having the client self-direct the intervention.

In this type of systematic desensitization three phases are suggested: (a) relaxation training, (b) the visualization of increasingly stressful anxiety-producing scenes while maintaining good relaxation, and (c) actually confronting and coping with the anxiety-arousing situation. Triggering events can be based on either internal or external physical sensations, which the client identifies as being associated with his or her panic attacks. In systematic desensitization, the client and the social worker develop a hierarchy of anxiety-producing situations relating to the panic symptoms. Usually the social worker tries to help the client find 5 to 10 situations that represent progressively more exposure to the source of the anxiety. These situations are ranked by the client from the least anxiety producing response to the greatest and can range from seeing the target, to touching, or handling it. These situations form the hierarchical steps by which the client will overcome the phobic reaction (Beck, Stanley, Baldwin, & Deagle, 1994). Relaxation training and cognitive restructuring components of treatment address the internal sensations.

To facilitate this process it is possible to develop a summative rating, which identifies the degree of fear each of the situations elicits. Scales usually range from 1 (no fear) to 7 (extreme, paralyzing fear). It is not unusual for clients to indicate that the least severe situation causes extreme fear. When this happens, it is best not to rate the other situations but to begin work on the least severe one. Having established the situations of interest and a means of evaluating how anxious the client feels about each objective, a plan for gradual exposure to the feared stimulus is developed. Based on the scale the client is asked how much anxiety he or she would be willing to tolerate in the hierarchy progression. Generally clients are willing to endure anxiety ratings of 3–5 (Dziegielewski & MacNeil, 1999). When this level has been obtained, establish a contract with the client stipulating that he or she will rate his or her anxiety five times each day. The contract clearly establishes anxiety levels for continued participation. For example, if a client has indicated that he or she is willing to endure anxiety at a level of 4, it is expected that the least severe situation that produces that level of anxiety will be selected. If the current task produces more anxiety than that, he or she is given permission to return to the previous situation. When anxiety levels diminish to a manageable level (according to self-rated scoring), the client is ready to proceed to the next graduated task.

For consistency and ease of treatment, five repetitions can be used to sequence all behavioral events (e.g., five times in a row, five times a day). After completing each set of five repetitive tasks, the client is asked to rank the anxiety level. Once the level of anxiety is self-scored at 3, the client moves to the next step, and in a graduated sequence previous steps are repeated as part of the new behavior sequence. Clients sometimes indicate that they feel silly with all the repetition, but they also note that repetition reinforces their progress and provides confidence for continuation with the treatment protocol. Clients report their scores in weekly sessions and are encouraged to elaborate on the patterns that evolved. They are praised for their courage and the significant progress that they make.

Based on client readiness to proceed to more difficult situations, the social worker continues the steps in the hierarchy. Each successive step is addressed until the client is able to complete the task at or below the contracted level of anxiety. The entire sequence of events is completed primarily through homework exercise and is typically completed in six to eight individual sessions.

INTERVENTION AND TREATMENT PLANNING

When dealing with individuals who suffer from the anxiety-related conditions, a physical exam is essential. A physical exam is needed to determine and address the multifaceted symptoms that often coexist in individuals who suffer from the anxiety disorders. For example, it can be difficult to differentiate symptoms related to anxiety from those related to medical conditions such as heart difficulties, asthma, and hypertension. Clear identification of these symptoms is important because these medical conditions can produce anxiety-like symptoms that confuse both the client and the health care professional. Professionals agree that a thorough medical examination is needed to rule out potential physiological difficulties and to assist in preparing for the psychosocial strategies that will follow.

Many people experience anxious events in their lives, and dealing with these types of situations can be very difficult. Therefore, when medication alone is used to address these stressful situations it may not be enough. Psychosocial intervention strategies such as those described in this chapter could clearly assist individuals who are having difficulties adjusting to stress and coping with anxiety. The importance of suggesting that the client utilize such strategies in addition to medication intervention is apparent.

The social worker can assist the intervention team by taking an accurate history of prescribed and over-the-counter medications, alternate therapies, and herbal preparations, which should then be shared with the prescribing professional.

Because many of the medications used to treat anxiety are addictive, it is essential to screen the client for potential substance abuse. It should come as no surprise to social workers that many people who suffer from anxiety often seek relief by using drugs or alcohol. Similar to the medications used to treat anxiety, alcohol and some of the recreational street drugs can stimulate the release of certain neurochemicals in the brain that inhibit anxiety. Subjectively, the result of this biochemical process is social ease, experienced as pleasure, that seduces the users of chemical intoxicants to continue despite the side effects: slurred speech, slowed thoughts, memory failure, poor motor control, and the possibility of addiction (Marshall, 1994, p. 152). If a history of substance abuse or a tendency to abuse prescription medication is noted, it is important to flag this potential problem.

Lastly, for clients who suffer from anxiety the medications that are used to assist with anxious feelings can also lead to the development of a false sense of security (Marshall, 1994). When clients feel better quickly, they may not want to commit the time and energy that is generally required to approach relaxation or cognitive therapy interventions. To help with treatment compliance, it is suggested that whenever possible a client agree to continue psychosocial treatment even after the medication has been started. It is ideal to ask the client to contract prior to taking the medications. If premedication contracting is not possible, ask the prescriber to remind the client of the importance of continued psychosocial interventions in order to identify current and future psychosocial stressors that can disturb functioning. Despite the time-limited nature of psychosocial counseling intervention as a supplement to medication, it can help a person recognize and prepare for anxiety-provoking situations.

ESTABLISHING THE TREATMENT PLAN

Because anxiety involves cognitive, behavioral, and somatic responses, documenting what is being experienced in these areas is essential. Good record-keeping needs to be problem-oriented and as specific as possible.

From a cognitive perspective, does the client seem to worry excessively about certain circumstances in his or her life? If so, what specific things? It is important to be specific and to give examples of how these anxious thoughts lead to the exhibited behaviors. Making a connection between the thought and the resulting behavior is critical, and later the thoughts as evidenced through the behaviors can be addressed in the contract and the intervention plan. In addition to the cognitive-behavioral responses, a connection to the bodily or somatic responses should also be made. The social worker should document concrete examples of symptoms of motor tension (restlessness, tiredness, shakiness, or muscle tension), autonomic hyperactivity (palpitations, shortness of breath, dry mouth, trouble swallowing, nausea or diarrhea), or symptoms of hypervigilance.

As in the case example, Ron was constantly worried and unsure about whether the chemicals had been put away and because of this dread he felt an uncontrollable desire to check and recheck them. Once this behavior is identified and outlined clearly, a plan can be established to address it. In this case, cognitive restructuring can be used to assure Ron that rechecking is not necessary. When he feels he is becoming anxious, he can begin deep-breathing exercises to initiate relaxation. Because the behavior is so prevalent, a preplanned contract can be made that will provide a plan of action when the anxiety increases. For example, after checking two times he must breathe deeply and reassure himself that it is done. Once this is completed he can contract to walk away and immediately begin another project. Although this may sound simple, in reality changing a behavior that has been ritualized into a habit is anything but simple for an obsessive client. It is never easy and will take a sincere effort to institute another more constructive pattern of behavior in its place. In addition, anxious individuals, like those who are depressed, may have trouble with eating and sleeping. They may have no appetite or they may have trouble falling asleep because of excessive worry. These behaviors should be documented and identified as part of the treatment component. Table 6.3 offers a sample treatment plan.

All medications taken should be documented and monitored. Do the medications appear to be helping the client to relax and address treatment issues? When dealing with the anxiety disorders and the medications prescribed to treat them, note previous anxiety treatments as well as medications taken in the past and any history of substance abuse. Since addiction and suicide potential are high with many of these medications, assessing for suicidal ideation and intent is a must. Document any history

TABLE 6.3   Sample Treatment Plan for Anxiety

Long-term goals

1. Stabilize anxiety level while increasing ability to complete own activities of daily living
2. Assist to reduce overall frequency, intensity and duration of anxiety symptoms

Short-term objectives	Plan or intervention	Time frame*
1. Take medications responsibly as prescribed by the physician and report any side effects from the medications.	Assess needs for antianxiety medications and arrange for prescription if needed. Monitor and evaluate medication compliance and the effectiveness of the medications in regard to level of functioning. Carefully monitor for potential abuse or suicidal tendencies. Contract at beginning of medication treatment to continue treatment regimen while taking medication.	(to be assessed)
2. Verbally identify the source of the anxiety.	Client to make a list of what he/she is anxious about in past and present (complete in session with worker). Encourage client to share feelings of anxiety and develop healthy self-talk as a means of handling anxiety. Assign participation in recreational activities and reinforce social activities and verbalizations. Train in guided imagery and biofeedback as means of stress reduction. Write at least one positive affirmative statement each day. Identify at least one irrational thought and one way to address it.	
3. Identify cognitive self-talk that supports irrational thoughts.	Educate client about the condition of anxiety. Assist in developing awareness of cognitive messages and fears that reinforce control, and address of irrational fears.	
4. Complete assessments of functioning (scales, GAF, GARF, SOFAS, etc.).	Arrange or complete administration of the tests. Assess and monitor suicide intervention; determine level of anxiety or suicide precaution.	

*Note In treatment planning an individualized time frame should be established for each client.

of current suicidal thoughts or gestures, which is particularly important for the client who has a history of such gestures.

SUMMARY AND CONCLUSIONS

All social workers should know the different anxiety conditions and remain familiar with current treatment strategies. Since many social workers have clients who are taking at least one or more psychotropic medications in conjunction with other prescribed medications, it is essential to understand how these medications work and how they affect treatment regimens. There is a tremendous amount of information available on these conditions, and it may be difficult for clients to determine the best medication for their problem. Social workers can assist in sorting through this material.

Social work professionals can provide important services to those who suffer from anxiety conditions including assessment and diagnostic and treatment services. They can also assist clients by creating an environment for improved communication and coordination between the client and other health care professionals. Social workers can also facilitate communication and services with other treatment team professionals and primary health care providers as well as mental health and community-based programs. In terms of direct intervention efforts, many of the techniques described in this chapter to assist with anxiety can also be used to help clients suffering from depression because the symptoms of anxiety and depression frequently overlap.

When using medication as an adjunct to therapy, it is important to realize that usage includes more than the prescription drugs. With more than 600 over-the-counter preparations and numerous alternative medicines available, a proper assessment must clearly address their use (American Neuropsychiatric Association Committee on Research, 2000). Mental health counselors should never underestimate the simple fact that clients can self-medicate with legal or illegal preparations. Knowing all the medications a client may be taking truly is a practice necessity today.

Regardless of the anxiety-related condition, social workers need to complete an accurate assessment and referral process for all clients served. This requires their taking an active role in advocating for their clients, particularly when medications are used to supplement intervention strategy. The confounding nature of the anxiety condition requires social workers to become aware of the psychological, sociological, and physiological practice implications when treating these disorders. This does not mean that they must become experts in all these areas; however, they must have some foundation of knowledge and information to assist clients in obtaining and maintaining the most therapeutically productive treatment possible. Social workers must be able to recognize potential problem areas related to medication usage and misuse and effective psychosocial interventions in order to recommend changes in the client's course of treatment.

This chapter presents an overview of the knowledge and skills necessary to treat clients with anxiety disorders, and it encourages social workers to seek additional information on these disorders and their treatments. Given the rapidly changing health and mental health practice environments, social workers must stay abreast of new trends and therapeutic strategies in the mental health field.

Therapy must limit the scope of the problem being targeted. In each case there will be numerous marital and family relationships and environmental factors that will not be addressed, especially when they do not relate directly to the targeted behavioral-based outcome. Because of the limited nature of the therapeutic encounter, referrals are warranted to encourage clients' help-seeking behavior. This is particularly important as social workers may be unable to provide the client with additional therapeutic sessions or intervention strategies.

Regardless of the type of therapy used to assist individuals suffering with anxiety and related disorders, the degree to which clients are "cured" remains questionable. Although the controlled studies described in these chapters have documented statistically significant improvements in these clients, these improvements may not be clinically significant or may not provide enduring effects. Literature suggests that while clients improve over the course of treatment, most remain below the mean of the general population on fear measures (Marks & Mathews, 1979; Mattick & Peters, 1988; Mattick & Newman, 1991). This requires professionals to accept that there are no guarantees clients will be cured regardless of treatment modality. The ultimate therapeutic outcome rests in helping clients regain previous levels of functioning. The hope is that all therapeutic efforts will produce lasting effects, yet social workers must be aware and help prepare their clients for the possibility of relapse. Relapse is always a possibility since most interventions of a psychological or medical nature are not curative. Physicians who provide concrete medical services are not distressed when clients return for additional services, and social workers must not be disturbed by clients returning for "checkups" or booster sessions. This type of follow-up should be expected.

REFERENCES

Al-Kubalsy, T., Marks, I. M., Logsdail, S., & Marks, M. P. (1992). Role of exposure homework in phobia reduction: A controlled study. *Behavior Therapy, 23*, 599–621.

American Neuropsychiatric Association Committee on Research. (2000). The use of herbal alternative medicines in neuropsychiatry. *Journal of Neuropsychiatry, 12*, 177–192.

American Psychiatric Association. (1994). *Diagnostic and statistical manual of mental disorders, 4th ed.* Washington, DC: American Psychiatric Press.

Ballenger, J. C., Lydiard, R. B., & Turner, S. M. (1995). Panic disorder and agoraphobia. In G. O. Gabbard (Ed.), *Treatments of psychiatric disorders* (2nd ed., pp. 162–192). Washington, DC: American Psychiatric Press.

Barlow, D. H., Esler, J. L., & Vitali, A. E. (1998). Psychosocial treatments for panic disorders, phobias, and generalized anxiety disorder. In P. E. Nathan & J. M. Gorman (Eds.), *A guide to treatments that work* (pp. 288–318). New York: Oxford University Press.

Barlow, D. H., O'Brien, G. T., & Last, C. G. (1984). Couples treatment of agoraphobia. *Behavior Therapy, 15*, 41–58.

Beck, A. T., & Emery, G. (1985). *Anxiety disorders and phobias: A cognitive perspective.* New York: Basic Books.

Beck, J. G., Stanley, M. A., & Baldwin, L. E., & Deagle, E. A. (1994). Comparison of cognitive therapy and relaxation training for panic disorder. *Journal of Consulting Clinical Psychology, 64*, 818–826.

Burns, L. E., Thorpe, G. L., & Cavallaro, L. A. (1986). Agoraphobia eight years after behavioral treatment: A follow-up study with interview, self-report, and behavioral data. *Behavior Therapy, 17*, 580–591.

Chaplin, E. W., & Levine, B. A. (1981). The effects of total exposure duration and interrupted versus continued exposure in flooding therapy. *Behavior Therapy, 12*, 360–368.

Clark, D. B., Salkovskis, P. M., Hackmann, A., Middleton, H., Anastasiades, P., & Gelder, M. (1994). A comparison of cognitive therapy, applied relaxation and imipramine in the treatment of panic disorder. *British Journal of Psychiatry, 164*, 759–769.

Clum, G. A., Clum, G. A., & Surls, R. (1993). A meta-analysis of treatments for panic disorder. *Journal of Consulting and Clinical Psychology, 61*, 317–326.

Cohen, S. D., Monteiro, W., & Marks, I. M. (1984). Two-year follow-up of agoraphobics after exposure and imipramine. *British Journal of Psychiatry, 144*, 276–281.

Cohen, I., & Steketee, G. (1998). Obsessive-Compulsive Disorder. In B. Thyer & J. Wodarski (Eds.), *Handbook of Empirical Social Work Practice: Mental Disorders* (Vol. 1, pp. 343–363). New York: Wiley.

Craske, M. G. (1996). An integrated treatment approach to panic disorder. *Bulletin of The Menninger Clinic, 60*(2) (Suppl. A), a87–a104.

Craske, M. G., Brown, T. A., & Barlow, D. H. (1991). Behavioral treatment of panic disorder: A two-year follow-up. *Behavior Therapy, 22*, 289–304.

Craske, M. G., & Waikar, S. V. (1994). Panic disorder. In M. Hersen & R. T. Ammerman (Eds.), *Handbook of prescriptive treatments for adults* (pp. 135–155). New York: Plenum Press.

De Silva, P., & Rachman, S. (1998). *Obsessive-compulsive disorder: The facts.* New York: Oxford University Press.

Dulcan, M. K. (1999). *Helping parents, youth, and teachers understand medications for behavioral and emotional problems: A resource book for medication information handouts.* Washington, DC: American Psychiatric Press.

Dziegielewski, S. F. (1996). Managed care principles: The need for social work in the health care environment. *Crisis Intervention and Time-Limited Treatment, 3*, 97–110.

Dziegielewski, S. F. (1998). *The changing face of health care social work: Professional practice in the era of managed care.* New York: Springer.

Dziegielewski, S. F., & MacNeil, G. (1999). Time-limited treatment considerations and strategy for specific phobic conditions. *Crisis Intervention, 5*, 133–150.

Erikson, E. (1963). *Childhood and society* (2nd ed.). New York: Norton.

Feigenbaum, W. (1988). Long-term efficacy of ungraded versus graded massed exposure in agoraphobics. In I. Hand & H. Wittchen (Eds.), *Panic and phobias: Treatments and variables affecting course and outcomes* (pp. 171–182). Berlin, Germany: Springer-Verlag.

Feltman, J. (1996). *The prevention how-to dictionary of healing remedies and techniques.* New York: Berkley Books.

Foa, E. B., Jameson, J. S., Turner, R. M., & Payne, L. L. (1980). Massed vs. spaced exposure sessions in the treatment of agoraphobia. *Behavior Research and Therapy, 18*, 333–338.

Foa, E. B., & Kozak, M. S. (1986). Emotional processing of fear: Exposure to corrective information. *Psychological Bulletin, 99*, 20–35.

Gottlieb, B. (1995). *New choices in natural healing.* Emmaus, PA: Rodale Press.

Hales, R. (1995). Anxiety disorders. In D. Hales & R. Hales (Eds.), *Caring for the mind* (pp. 119–153). New York: Bantam Books.

Hall, L. L. (1997). Fighting phobias: The things that go bump in the mind. *FDA Consumer, 31*(13), 13–15.

Hudson, W. W. (1990). *The WALMYR Assessment Scale Scoring Manual.* Tempe, AZ: WALMYR Publishing.

Internal Medicine Review. (1999, November). Antidepressants for general anxiety disorder. *Internal Medicine Alert, 21*(21), 164.

Jacobson, N. S., Wilson, L., & Tupper, C. (1988). The clinical significance of treatment gains resulting from exposure-based interventions for agoraphobia: A re-analysis of outcome data. *Behavior Therapy, 19,* 539–554.

Kaplan, H. I., & Sadock, B. J. (1990). *Pocket handbook of clinical psychiatry.* Baltimore: Williams & Wilkins.

Koerner, B. I. (1999, June 21). Coming to you direct (social anxiety disorder medication). *U.S. News & World Report, 126*(24), 54.

Marks, I. M., & Mathews, A. M. (1979). Brief standard self-rating for phobic patients. *Behaviour Research and Therapy, 17,* 263–267.

Marshall, J. R. (1994). *Social phobia: From stage fright to shyness.* New York: Basic Books.

Marshall, J. R. (1996). Comorbidity and its effects on panic disorder. *Bulletin of The Menninger Clinic, 60*(2) (Suppl. A), a39–a53.

Marshall, W. L. (1985). The effects of variable exposure in flooding therapy. *Behavior Therapy, 16,* 117–135.

Marshall, W. L. (1988). Behavioural indices of habituation and sensitization during exposure to phobic stimuli. *Behaviour Research and Therapy, 26,* 67–77.

Mattick, R. P., & Newman, C. R. (1991). Social phobia and avoidant personality disorder. *International Journal of Psychiatry, 3,* 163–173.

Mattick, R. P., & Peters, L. (1988). Treatment of severe social phobia: Effects of guided exposure with and without cognitive restructuring. *Journal of Consulting and Clinical Psychology, 56,* 251–260.

Mattick, R. P., Peters, L., & Clarke, J. C. (1989). Exposure and cognitive restructuring for social phobia: A controlled study. *Behavior Therapy, 20*(1) 3–23.

McLellarn, R. W., & Rosenzweig, J. (1998). Generalized anxiety disorder. In B. Thyer & J. Wodarski (Eds.), *Handbook of empirical social work practice: Mental disorders* (Vol. 1, pp. 385–397). New York: Wiley.

Meichenbaum, D. (1994). *A clinical handbook/practical therapist manual for assessing and treating adults with Post-Traumatic Stress Disorder.* Waterloo, Ontario, Canada: Institute Press.

Munby, J., & Johnston, D. W. (1980). Agoraphobia: The long-term follow-up of behavioural treatment. *British Journal of Psychiatry, 137,* 418–427.

Newman, B., & Newman, P. (1995). *Development through life: A psychosocial perspective.* Pacific, California: Brooks/Cole Publishing.

Nordenberg, T. (1999). Social phobias: Traumas and treatments. *FDA Consumer, 33*(6), 27–33.

Ost, L. A., & Westling, B. E. (1995). Applied relaxation vs. cognitive behavior therapy in the treatment of panic disorder. *Behavior Research and Therapy, 33,* 145–158.

Ost, L. G., Salkovskis, P., & Hellstrom, K. (1991). One session therapist directed exposure vs. self-exposure in the treatment of spider phobia. *Behavior Therapy, 22,* 407–422.

O'Sullivan, G., & Marks, I. M. (1990). Long-term outcome of phobic and obsessive-compulsive disorders after treatment. In R. Hoyes, M. Roth, & G. D. Burrows (Eds.), *Handbook of anxiety: Vol. 4 The treatment of anxiety.* Amsterdam: Elsevier.

Pato, M. T., Zohar-Kadouch, R., Zohar, J., & Murphy, D. L. (1988). Return of symptoms in patients with obsessive-compulsive disorder. *American Journal of Psychiatry, 145,* 1521–1525.

Plaud, J. J., & Vavrovsky, K. G. (1998). Specific and Social Phobias. In B. Thyer & J. Wodarski (Eds.), *Handbook of empirical social work practice: Mental disorders* (Vol. 1, pp. 326–341). New York: Wiley.

Physicians' Desk Reference. (2000). *Physicians' desk reference* (54th ed.). Montvale, NJ: Medical Economics.

Reid, W. H. (1997). Anxiety disorders. In W. H. Reid, G. U. Balis, & B. J. Sutton (Eds.), *The treatment of psychiatric disorders* (3rd ed., pp. 239–262). Bristol, PA: Brunner/Mazel.

Roth, A., & Fonagy, P. (1996). Anxiety disorders I: Phobias, generalized anxiety disorder, and panic disorder with and without agoraphobia. In A. Roth & P. Fonagy (Eds.), *What works for whom? A critical review of psychotherapy research* (pp. 113–144). New York: Guilford Press.

Salkovskis, P., Clark, D., & Hackmann, A. (1991). Treatment of panic attacks using cognitive therapy without exposure or breathing retraining. *Behavior Research and Therapy, 29,* 161–166.

Stein, M.D. (1998). Paroxetine treatment of generalized social phobia (social anxiety disorder). *The Journal of the American Medical Association, 280,* 8, 708(1).

Vonk, M. E., & Yegidis, B.L. (1998). Post-traumatic stress disorder. In B. Thyer & J. Wodarski (Eds.), *Handbook of empirical social work practice: Mental disorders* (Vol. 1, pp. 365–383). New York: Wiley.

Wardle, J. (1990). Behavior therapy and benzodiazepines: Allies or antagonists? *British Journal of Psychiatry, 156,* 163–168.

Wilhelm, F., & Margraf, J. (1997). A cognitive-behavioral treatment package for panic disorder with agoraphobia. In W. T. Roth (Ed.), *Treating anxiety disorders* (pp. 205–244). San Francisco: Jossey-Bass.

CHAPTER 7

Schizophrenia and the Psychotic Disorders

The conditions that are characteristic of psychotic disorders such as schizophrenia can be devastating due to the prevalence of symptoms such as hallucinations, delusions, and bizarre or inappropriate behaviors. This illness not only disrupts the individual's life and alienates the client from his or her family and support systems, but it can also create tremendous stress and frustration for families. Many social workers and other helping professionals are reluctant to work with these individuals because of their unpredictable and uncertain behavior. Complete or total remission is rare for most individuals who suffer from this disorder; instead a chronic yet variable course of illness is expected.

Of all the psychotic disorders, schizophrenia is often considered the most devastating (Breier, 1996) and to date no known prevention or cure exists (Carpenter, 1996). At a conference to update professionals on the newer antipsychotic medications several speakers who were psychiatrists stated that because of managed care and its handling of those clients few professionals would compete to serve psychotic disordered clients. The authors sadly concur with the truth of these statements, as there is indeed little interest in building practices that primarily assist clients who suffer from this type of mental illness.

Clients who suffer from psychosis vary greatly in their responses to medication and other forms of intervention. Therefore, most primary-care practitioners steer away from prescribing medicine for these individuals, although primary care and general medicine physicians often treat conditions such as depression. One major aspect of treatment expectations is that the client with a psychotic disorder is rarely given a prescription and sent home. After assessing the client, extensive monitoring and support is needed, which most primary-care physicians are not able, interested, or qualified to deliver. Professionals outside direct mental health practice are reluctant to seek out this population due to the unpredictable course of the illness, the varied responses to medication and treatment, and the severe level of impairment the client may experience.

CASE EXAMPLE: EVA

Eva is a 71-year-old female with a long and consistent history of psychotic episodes that have interfered with her functioning and have disturbed her entire life. Her first episode occurred when she was in her early 30's, after the birth of her fourth child. Eva was raised in the Catholic faith and believed that abortion was a sin. In describing her past, she states that she felt overwhelmed by the birth of each child and the care that was required to raise them. She describes her husband as an alcoholic who spent little time at home and even less time supporting her and helping to raise the children. She does say, however, that her husband was a good provider and often worked long hours in a blue-collar job. At age 30, Eva, who had no previous history of mental illness, was admitted for the first time to a state hospital for what she described as a complete and total "nervous breakdown." According to the medical records, Eva reported hearing voices that told her to harm her children and to kill her husband, and she believed her husband was trying to kill her. She is not sure why she did it, but Eva deliberately lit the gas oven in her home, exposing herself and her children to the deadly fumes. Fortunately, she and her children were saved when her husband returned from work early that evening. She was diagnosed with schizophrenia and was immediately admitted to the state hospital. According to her records, and when discussing the admission today, Eva continues to disagree with what was written in her medical record. She states that her husband was the one who lit the gas stove. During the current discussion, her affect was initially flat as evidenced by the lack of emotional expressiveness. Yet as she continued to talk about the event, her affect changed to agitation and irritability, which resulted in her refusing to discuss it any further. According to the record, she did not ask the interviewer about the condition of her children after the experience. After six months of minimal improvement and subsequent shock treatments, Eva was discharged and sent home. In the current interview, she reported that she remembered the shock treatments and thought that they were a horrible punishment for running away from her responsibilities. To date, she has had 25 admissions since her first one approximately 40 years ago. Many of these occurred in the same year.

With the advent of deinstitutionalization, Eva spent shorter intervals in the state hospitals that would accept her without insurance. She had a long history of repeatedly being admitted and within weeks being discharged to wherever she had been living prior to the admission. The most noted problem for Eva, according to previous hospitalization records, was that she often stopped and refused to continue taking her medicines. When she stopped taking her medications it usually lead to her readmission.

For approximately 40 years, Eva had been given the medication Thorazine. When taking this highly sedative medication she often complained of feeling tired and unable to function. During this time she had numerous episodes of violence related to feelings of paranoia, and frequently stopped taking her medicines and was often labeled as medication noncompliant. Eva was found wandering the streets in a state of disarray numerous times, and on at least one occasion she was the victim of a violent rape, resulting in her hospitalization. After 10 years Eva's husband told family and friends that he was overwhelmed by his wife's condition and the care of his four young children. After many additional violent episodes and repeated hospitalizations, he filed for divorce and took custody of the children. He refused to maintain contact with her after he remarried. Meanwhile, Eva's problems continued to escalate. She often refused to take her medicines and reported paranoid beliefs and ideas such as that her husband often followed her and threatened her life. Furthermore, she believed her children were crying for her because they were being neglected and needed care. This seemed highly unlikely, however, as her husband was reportedly living with her children in another state.

Eva described her life as horrible both before and after her divorce. She was unable to work since she could not concentrate on the task she was assigned. At one point she got a job in a department store but was quickly fired because she insisted that voices were coming over the public-address system saying that her youngest child was being abused. She never applied for disability, and had no income other than what she was able to borrow or beg on the streets. Eva moved frequently, and her living arrangements alternated between boarding homes, relatives, and boyfriends. She did not stay in one place very long as she often got into trouble for her erratic and unpredictable behaviors. Eva never received any case management or counseling services on a consistent basis because she often moved or refused to see anyone affiliated with the mental health system.

Most of her history was obtained from medical records from the repeated admissions to mental health facilities. Eva was considered an unreliable historian. When questioned directly, her explanation of dates, times, and events was not consistent with what was obtained from the records. Eva often felt that people persecuted her deliberately and that she often had to defend herself from family and neighbors. She stated that she had no friends and over the years had managed to alienate every family member she had. At one point, her son came to stay with her in a small one-bedroom apartment. He was later found guilty of taking her Cogentin (a medication prescribed to control the side effects of her antipsychotic medicines), and trying to sell it on the street. After her son was placed on court-ordered probation, he moved out and she was readmitted to the hospital for stabilization. Later she was discharged to a supervised group home sponsored by the community mental health center.

Today, however, new advances in pharmacotherapy offer Eva many opportunities for an improved quality of life. Much of her recent success can be attributed to the right combination of medicines. In 1994 Eva was placed on a new type of antipsychotic medicine called Risperdal (resperidone). At first the psychiatrist was considering Clozaril but decided against it because of Eva's resistance to medication and history of noncompliance with treatment requests. After a short trial period, the Risperidone had a significantly diminished side-effect profile when compared to Thorazine. Eva contracted with the social work case manager to take the medicine because it made her feel more alive. She was placed on a combination-effect medication often noted for its antidepressant and antianxiety properties called Wellbutrin and a mood stabilizing medication called Depakote. Upon assessment, the social worker who was assigned as her case manager suggested to the treatment team that Eva needed something to stabilize her mood. Although Eva was never diagnosed with bipolar disorder or schizoaffective disorder, she often had unpredictable mood swings in the supervised living facility, which triggered violent outbursts toward those around her. Based on this history and documented evidence of her mood swings, the mood stabilizing medication was added. This combination appears to be working for Eva.

Now when approached, she quickly describes her mood as "less dazed" and "more alive," and she no longer hears voices. Eva has not been rehospitalized since 1995 and has moved from the supervised living facility. She is currently living with her sister. Eva is also participating in a day-treatment program and sees her social work case manager once every six months. She is working on improving her problem-solving skills and increasing her skills at performing her daily tasks of living.

This case serves to demonstrate how tortured and alienated the schizophrenic client can feel. It also describes many of the behaviors that are characteristic of this condition and how they present a scenario that requires intervention and that cannot be ignored. The unpredictable nature of the condition and the reactions that Eva and other schizophrenic clients exhibit often make family support and tracking nearly impossible (Stomwall & Robinson, 1998). This case illustrates the importance of utilizing the new or atypical antipsychotic medications (Apfeldorf & Alexopoulos, 1998). These medications can offer many who suffer from chronic schizophrenia a chance at a new life that otherwise would be impossible to expect. Unfortunately, cases such as this one are all too common for clients with schizophrenia. Furthermore, the role of the social worker as a professional who assists these clients with adaptation and other case management needs is essential. Medication as part of the intervention regimen is critical but should not be used as the only mode of intervention. The newer antipsychotic medications that will be described in this chapter may bring a new ray of hope when supplemented by effective counseling and case management services. These newer medications clearly hold promise for helping these clients enhance their own quality of life.

SCHIZOPHRENIA: FORMING THE DIAGNOSTIC IMPRESSION

As we begin to discuss formulating a diagnostic impression for this disorder, two factors must be understood clearly. First, schizophrenia is probably not a single disorder as is so often assumed (Flaum, 1995; McGrath, 1999). In professional practice, clinicians realize quickly that there really is no such thing as the single-problem client. The clients we see often have multiple problems that require a multifaceted approach to intervention. The same can be said for the client with schizophrenia who has multiple mental health problems. Some of these problems can overlap with other mental health conditions such as the affective disorders (bipolar and depression) and the dementia or delirium-based disorders. Because the etiology of this tragic illness is not yet fully understood, the use of medications is essential to control what little we do understand. As understanding increases about the causes and origins of schizophrenia and the psychotic disorders, so will the ability to better address the illness. A study by Brzustowicz, Hodgkinson, Chow, Honer, and Bassett (2000) found that there is a susceptibility point on a particular gene for schizophrenia. This finding lends significance to the theory that schizophrenia is related to genetics and not solely to the environment.

The diagnosis of schizophrenia is often complicated by the fact that symptoms are likely to change during subsequent assessment. In understanding schizophrenia and the related conditions, it becomes obvious that the disorder itself is multifaceted and that there are many positive and negative symptoms to be considered (American Psychiatric Press, 1994). Basically a positive symptom involves the development of delusions, conceptual disorganization, hallucinatory behavior, excitement, grandiosity, suspiciousness, persecution, and hostility. These symptoms are often obvious and easy to detect in the assessment process. Negative symptoms, however, are often more common than the positive symptoms and harder to detect. These symptoms often involve avolition (lack of goal directed behavior), blunted affect, emotional withdrawal, poor rapport, passivity, apathy, social withdrawal, difficulty in abstract thinking, lack of spontaneity, and stereotyped thinking patterns. Malhotra, Pinsky, and Breier (1996) warn that the negative symptoms, which are often more subtle in the condition, can be real stumbling blocks for clients who are trying to lead fruitful and productive lives. These negative features overlap, and can include reduced appetite, lack of energy, lack of pleasure, and inattention in both schizophrenia and depression. Depression and its symptoms occur in 25% of the cases in which there is clear documentation of schizophrenia (Siris, 2000). In order to provide the best care, social workers must realize that negative symptoms can overlap and therefore can be easily confused with other mental health conditions such as depression.

To complicate diagnostic impressions of this disorder, the symptoms tend to be so arbitrary and susceptible to change that the course of the illness remains unpredictable. The social worker must not only be aware of current and past symptoms, but must also anticipate changes in symptoms that may develop during the intervention process and during the course of the illness. Understanding this becomes particularly important as we gain more knowledge about the disease process and the mechanisms that lead to development of difficulties (Flaum, 1995).

Many clients who receive both medication and counseling only experience limited relief, and often we refer to them as partial responders. Research supports that only about 70% of all schizophrenics treated with psychopharmacologic means ever reach a truly optimal response (Breier, 1996), so there are many individuals who are not substantially helped by the traditional courses of medication intervention. For those who partially respond to intervention, the prognosis appears even dimmer: only 15% will attain maximum or optimal symptom relief or functional restoration (Breier, 1996).

TABLE 7.1   Schizophrenia and Primary Psychotic Disorders

Five types of schizophrenia:
Disorganized type: marked incoherence, lack of systematized delusions, blunted, disturbed, or silly affect
Catatonic type: stupor, negativism, rigidity, bizarre posturing, and excessive motor activity
Paranoid type: one or more systematized delusions or auditory hallucinations with a similar theme
Undifferentiated type: contains aspects of the other prominent types
Residual type: symptoms of schizophrenia not currently displayed but have been in the past

Brief reactive psychosis: This condition has been historically called "three-day schizophrenia" because symptoms generally last at least a few hours but no longer than a month and sudden onset is generally linked to some type of psychosocial stressor.
Schizophreniform disorder: This is usually considered a provisional diagnosis. It is generally related to the first episode of psychosis. If and when the episode lasts longer than six months, the diagnosis should be changed to schizophrenia.
Schizoaffective disorder: Individuals who suffer from this disorder experience the signs and symptoms prevalent in both the schizophrenic disorder and the mood disorder.
Shared psychotic disorder aka induced psychotic disorder: This disorder is often found in rural areas and historically has been referred to as the *folie à deux.* In this disorder two people generally share the same delusional system.

Note. Definitions are based on the *Diagnostic and Statistical Manual for Mental Disorders* (APA, 1994).

SCHIZOPHRENIA AND THE PSYCHOTIC DISORDERS

Schizophrenia involves the exhibiting of psychotic symptoms. For many social workers trying to help, these clients can be difficult because the mental health conditions in this category usually include symptoms of delusions, hallucinations, uncooperativeness, and thought disorders (Kaplan & Sadock, 1990). The specific conditions that are treated with antipsychotic medications usually include schizophrenia, delusional disorders, depressive psychoses, mania, and drug-induced psychoses (Kaplan & Sadock, 1990). See Table 7.1 for a list and brief description of the schizophrenic or primary psychotic disorders.

A general understanding of the condition of schizophrenia and the resulting behaviors is necessary in order for social workers to accurately facilitate and complete the diagnostic impression. Generally most individuals who suffer from schizophrenia experience a characteristic deterioration in adaptive functioning that accompanies the psychotic symptoms. The first psychosis or break with reality usually occurs between the ages of 17 and 30 in males and between 20 and 40 in females (Carpenter, Conley, & Buchanan, 1998). The course and variation of this illness remain extremely variable, and some individuals may not become psychotic again after a first episode. The majority of others improve after the first episode but continue to manifest symptoms and future occurrences remain unpredictable. The active phase of the disorder generally lasts a minimum of 6 months with the symptoms lasting for at least one month (American Psychiatric Press, 1994).

In terms of addressing the symptoms, the four As determine and influence the intervention process. Associative disturbances are related directly to how the client interacts or associates within the environmental context. Very often these individuals are not sure how to relate with others. At times, a client may invade another's social or personal space. When saying good morning, for example, a client may get so close that your noses almost touch. On the other hand, he or she may withdraw from social contact. Taken together, these behaviors might seem disturbing to family and friends who are trying to express their concern. The associative disturbances that are characteristic of this disorder can clearly impede social functioning and may result in the client's being isolated within his or her environmental context.

Affective disturbances are a prevalent feature of the disorder and may be particularly unsettling to everyone involved because the client often exhibits unpredictable moods and emotions. Traditionally this has been referred to as a splitting of mood. Here the client with schizophrenia exhibits polarities in emotions, angry one minute and laughing the next. The lack of relevance to what is actually happening may be alarming to family and friends as well as to mental health professionals. It is hard for many to understand that the individual is suffering from something beyond his or her control because oftentimes they appear to be in control of their behaviors.

Autism was once referred to as childhood schizophrenia. Autism actually means that a separation or lack of responsiveness occurs. This makes it difficult to communicate with the client or to determine exactly how much the client is able to comprehend. It can be particularly difficult or frustrating for professionals and family because it limits the client's ability to follow an intervention program or participate in counseling.

Ambivalence is indecisive behavior that causes difficulty in making decisions or adhering to an intervention plan. Furthermore, how much of the plan the client is actually able to comprehend may be unclear. Clients may express willingness to do something but within moments change their minds and refuse to go somewhere or participate in an activity. Completing simple tasks such as dressing or deciding whether to go outside may become a daunting task for some clients.

The Four A's of Schizophrenia

Associative Disturbances affect how the client responds and relates to others.
Affective Disturbances are disturbances in the client's mood.
Autism involves the client's becoming isolated and questions of whether the client is able to communicate and understands his/ her environment.
Ambivalence symptom hampers the client's ability to make decisions or complete follow-up.

The secondary symptoms that may also be present must be considered as part of the diagnostic impression. The first and probably the most common secondary symptom is delusions. A delusion can be defined simply as a belief that a client holds despite evidence to the contrary. In schizophrenia there may be numerous beliefs so disturbing that functioning is impaired. Often these delusions are systematized and may involve family and friends. These may be difficult for loved ones to tolerate, because they cannot see any real or external basis for such behavior or understand why it is so difficult to control.

It is essential to differentiate between the *delusions of reference* so common in schizophrenic conditions and *ideas of reference* as experienced in some of the personality disorders. In schizotypal personality disorder, social withdrawal from family and friends is common, accompanied by ideas of reference. An idea of reference is much more individualized than a delusion of reference. An idea of reference often refers to a specific individual, event, or item that can encompass magical thinking or involve a certain degree of exaggerated importance. An example of this is the client who believes she is so useless and worthless that a physician would come into her home and offer to assist in ending her life. Other areas of her life are not affected by such beliefs. This is very different from the more extensive condition of schizophrenia where the client exhibits delusions of reference. An example would be the person's thinking that everyone who wears green is sending messages to take over the world. These delusions of reference are much more obvious and affect almost every aspect of the client's life.

Individuals who suffer from schizophrenia often experience hallucinations. This break with reality can be particularly problematic for the social worker to address. Most often, medications are used to help gain control of this aspect of the illness. It appears that auditory hallucinations are the most common, making up almost 70% of all reported hallucinatory symptoms such as hearing voices (Hoffman, 2000). This means that the schizophrenic client will often struggle to address these auditory hallucinations and how they relate to what the client is experiencing. Many clients who are hallucinating often report that they hear voices and may be commanded by these voices to engage in certain behaviors. Visual hallucinations are less common, and it is suspected that if they exist there may actually be some kind of organic brain damage present. Less common forms of hallucinations in schizophrenia include tactile (touch) and olfactory (taste and smell) sensations. These may also be indicative of an organic problem. In some cases, clients may report feeling that bugs crawling on them, a phenomenon often related to substance use and abuse. (It may help the social worker to remember that "bugs are often related to drugs.") The client should be referred immediately for a drug screen or physical examination to determine if the psychosis is related to substance abuse or another type of delirium.

When working with clients who have chronic types of schizophrenia, it is important to realize that many of these clients can experience disturbances in motor behavior such as bizarre posturing, catalepsy (a state of stupor), and waxy flexibility. In waxy flexibility, a client may appear somewhat rigid and may seem to get stuck in certain positions or stay frozen in these positions for a long period of time. Waxy flexibility and catalepsy are both characterized by a state of continual and unusual muscle tension (Moore & Jefferson, 1997), in which a client appears to be stuck, soldered in place, and unable to move. To the inexperienced social worker, family member, or friend, this type of behavior can be very frightening. The bizarre nature of the behavior can often result in posturing and an inability to respond, which may cause family members to withdraw their support of the client. Therefore, it is essential to educate the client, his

TABLE 7.2   Selective Adjunctive Medications in the Treatment of Schizophrenia

Brand name	Use in schizophrenia
Lithium	May be used for treatment-resistant schizophrenia
Mood stabilizers/Anticonvulsant Carbamazepine and Valproic acid	Anticonvulsant medications used primarily for treatment bipolar affective disorder with psychosis
Benzodiazepines	Used in treatment-resistant schizophrenia
Antidepressants	Used to address the depressive episodes often found in schizophrenia

*Note. Information summarized from Carpenter, Conley, and Buchanan (1998).

or her family, and professionals about the signs and symptoms of schizophrenia and the interventions that work best to address them.

Clients who have these disorders are usually thought to be out of touch with reality and to have an impaired ability to evaluate their environments. Oftentimes they are not receptive to the intervention that the social worker may try to provide even though they require help. Schizophrenia is a very complex disease that can manifest itself in numerous ways. Overall, the understanding of schizophrenia and the related psychotic disorders has improved; however, it still remains a significant challenge for those who try to provide therapeutic treatment. Many different types of medications in addition to antipsychotic drugs may be used to treat this disorder and to supplement treatment (see Table 7.2). These additional medicines include lithium, the mood stabilizers and anticonvulsants (e.g., valproic acid), beta-blockers, and benzodiazepines. When trying to address the disease, cognitive, behavioral and psychosocial symptoms are emphasized most often (Kane, 1996; Sensky, Turkington, Kingdon, Scott, Scott, Siddle, O'Carroll, & Barnes, 2000).

INTERVENTION WITH CLIENTS WHO HAVE SCHIZOPHRENIA

Intervention for clients with schizophrenia can be varied. When planning the intervention, the unique needs of each client should always be considered (Kane, 1996). There is no standard intervention strategy that fits all clients. Intervention generally involves the use of medication, medication management and monitoring, as well as supportive interventions such as training in daily living, problem-solving, and psychosocial skills, supportive counseling, family education, community treatment or case management and, when warranted, vocational rehabilitation (Farmer, Walsh, & Bently, 1998). Most professionals agree that of all the types of intervention available for those individuals with psychotic disorders, medication is often viewed as the most critical component, and medications are generally the first line of intervention regardless of the type of intervention strategy used (Kane, 1996). This requires social workers to be well versed in these medications and how they can affect the intervention process.

HISTORY AND DEVELOPMENT OF ANTIPSYCHOTIC MEDICATIONS

Medications for the treatment of schizophrenia date back to the early 1800s and include drugs such as opium, bromide derivatives, chloral hydrate, and barbiturates (Bently, 1998). Traditionally these drugs were used to calm down the violent or combative client, but they did little to control the symptoms that go along with the mental disorder. The calming effect was particularly important in state institutions or asylums because chemical restraints afforded staff the ability to exercise what seemed like a more humane form of intervention. Therefore, the use of these neuroleptic medications (another name for mental health drugs) prevented long-term institutionalization. The development of antipsychotic medications and the control they afforded actually encouraged deinstitutionalization and our current emphasis on community-based outpatient care (Breier & Buchanan, 1996; Empfield, 2000).

The science of medication is a fairly recent one. It was not until the early 1950s that the first medication was introduced to treat the hallucinations, delusions, and psychotic depression of schizophrenia. Chlorpromazine (the chemical name) or Thorazine (the brand name) was discovered serendipitously. It was believed originally that this medication might be able to lower body temperature and serve as a type of cold pack. (In the 1950s cold packs were thought to calm the agitated client.) It was believed that the potential sedative effect from the medication could also be beneficial in reducing agitation, and the results were quite surprising. Although it did not decrease the body temperature, it did appear to lessen many of the psychotic symptoms of schizophrenia, and it was marketed as a wonder drug for treatment of the condition (Berstein, 1995; Bently, 1998). Numerous other drugs followed (see table 10) and these typical antipsychotics became one of the five most common classifications of medication for treating mental health disorders.

Some researchers report that numerous studies now show that schizophrenia has an effect on the frontal lobes, temporal lobes, limbic system, and basal ganglia (Farmer & Pandurangi, 1997). Other researchers strive to define the etiology and to identify clearly the role of the neurochemical dopamine. The dopamine hypothesis has been prominent in the literature as a probable explanation for developing the disease (Buchanan, Brandes, & Breier, 1996; Karper & Krystal, 1996). According to this perspective, there is a functional excess of dopamine in the central nervous system, and it has been believed for many years that the traditional antipsychotic drugs achieve their beneficial action by blocking the dopamine receptors in the brain (Farmer & Pandurangi, 1997).

According to Carpenter, Conley, and Buchanan (1998), stimulants such as cocaine and amphetamines activate the dopaminergic system in the brain, which explains why the abuse of stimulants can induce a paranoid psychosis that mimics the positive symptoms representative of schizophrenia. In turn, if a person who is diagnosed with schizophrenia is given stimulants of this type, the psychosis may be exacerbated. It follows, therefore, that the typical antipsychotic medications act by blocking the dopamine receptors.

In addition, some researchers believe that involvement of the neurochemical dopamine alone is not comprehensive enough to explain the complex changes that occur in schizophrenia. Although dopamine does seem to be directly involved in the positive symptoms of the condition, it appears to have little effect on the negative symptoms of the disease (Carpenter, Conley, & Buchanan, 1998). Other neurotransmitters such as serotonin also need to be taken into account when dealing with schizophrenia (Karper & Krystal, 1996).

At present there are several medications that have been approved that involve the neurochemical serotonin. The first two medications are clozapine and risperidone; and the two newer medications are Seroquel and Zyprexa. To date, these medications have been termed the "atypical" antipsychotic medications, because they are effective in reducing symptoms of schizophrenia and are less likely to cause extrapyramidal side effects than the other antipsychotic medications (Karper & Krystal, 1996).

TRADITIONAL OR TYPICAL ANTIPSYCHOTIC MEDICATIONS

The traditional or typical antipsychotics are dopamine inhibitors that block other neurotransmitters such as acetylcholine, histamine, and norepinephrine. Extrapyramidal symptoms (EPS) are a common side effect with these medications, and the social worker must be able to recognize them. Dystonia is one of the movement problems that may occur, and acute dystonic reactions may present as grimacing, difficulty with speech or swallowing, oculogyric crisis (upward rotation of the eyeballs), muscle spasms of the neck and throat, and extensor rigidity of the back muscles (Carpenter, Conley, & Buchanan, 1998). Very often these parkinsonian reactions will occur within the first few days of treatment. It is not uncommon for the client to approach the social worker complaining of a thick or stiff tongue that impairs the ability to speak.

Akathisia is less obvious than dystonia although it is the most common form of EPS. Akathisia is an extreme form of motor restlessness and may be mistaken for agitation. The individual feels compelled to be in a constant state of movement, and many times clients will report an "inner restlessness" that is evidenced by a shaking leg or constant pacing across the floor. During assessment these clients cannot sit still and often appear to have restless legs or exhibit uncontrollable foot tapping. Although akathisia generally appears early in the course of treatment and can be related to other extrapyramidal symptoms it can also occur independently (Carpenter, Conley, & Buchanan, 1998).

Another form of EPS that involves involuntary movements of any group of muscles is tardive dyskinesia (TD). The most common involuntary movements involve the mouth and tongue. Awareness of this side effect is particularly important because it is generally reported as a negative consequence of taking long-term conventional antipsychotic medications, with intervention duration being the primary developmental factor (Carpenter, Conley, & Buchanan, 1998). One way to address this issue is to prescribe the medication in lower doses, but for chronic schizophrenia this may not be an option. The newer or atypical antipsychotics may offer a more hopeful course of treatment for patients with this disorder, because these medications seem to have fewer EPS side effects especially when given in low doses (Lambert, 1998). A rarer side effect associated with the more traditional antipsychotic medications is neuroleptic malignant syndrome. Although it occurs in only 0.1% of cases, 15% to 20% of those affected die (*PDR*, 2000; Torey, 1988). This condition typically occurs in men and within ten days of starting the medication. The symptoms include severe rigidity of the muscles, a high fever, confusion, pallor, sweating, and rapid heart rate. Because of the extreme severity of this condition, it is imperative that social workers with clients who have schizophrenia be aware of the symptoms and the potentially lethal consequences.

Medications are often prescribed to decrease or control movement-related side effects and are referred to as anti-parkinsonian medications. When a client is receiving a traditional or typical antipsychotic medicine it is essential to determine if something has been prescribed to counter the side effects that might result. The medications that are often used to address the side-effect profiles just described are listed. (See list that follows for typical antipsychotic and antiparkinsonian medications.)

Typical Antipsychotic Agents:*

chlorpromazine (Thorazine)
trifluoperazine (Stelazine)
haloperidol (Haldol)
thiothixene (Navane)

thioridazine (Mellaril)
fluphenazine (Prolixin)
loxapine (Loxitane)

*The first name is the chemical name of the drug; the name in parentheses is the brand name of the medication.

There are some factors to consider with the use of these anti-parkinsonian medications. It is especially important for the social worker to note whether a client has a history of substance abuse or who might be involved in trying to sell these drugs on the street. This is particularly true for the drugs Cogentin and Artane as clients state openly that many times these medicines make a person feel good, which increases the potential for abuse. When the potential for abuse is suspected it might be best for the social worker to share this information with the treatment team or with the prescriber and consider an over-the-counter medication such as Benadryl to help control the symptoms of EPS.

Antiparkinsonian Medications

Name	Dosage Range
Cogentin (benzotrpine)	0.5–6 mg a day
Akineton (biperiden)	2–8 mg a day

Benadryl (diphenhydramine)   50–300 mg a day
Artane (trihexyphenidyl)   1–15 mg a day

NEWER OR NONTRADITIONAL ANTIPSYCHOTIC MEDICATIONS

Atypical or nontraditional antipsychotic medications have fewer movement symptoms than the typical antipsychotics. Examples of these medications include (see Table 7.3): clozapine (Clozaril), risperidone (Risperdal),
sertindole (Serlect), olanzapine (Zyprexa) and quentiapine (Seroquel).
These medications have gained popularity because they appear to have
lower EPS profiles and they help individuals to think more clearly and
follow directions better, to learn new facts and master new skills, and to
interpret emotion more accurately (Lambert, 1998).

  Although we include clozapine as a newer atypical antipsychotic medication, it does have a long history and in some texts may be listed as a
traditional antipsychotic. Known by the brand name Clozaril, clozapine
was originally synthesized in 1957 and in 1960 was one of the first
antipsychotics released on the European market (Hippius, 1989). It was
believed to be more successful than the typical antipsychotics because it
did not seem to have the same negative side-effect profiles. Years later,
eight documented cases of death were attributed to infections secondary
to clozapine-induced agranulocytosis, and the product was withdrawn
from unrestricted use (Davis & Casper, 1977). Based on later studies that
supported the success of clozapine with strict monitoring for treatment-
resistant schizophrenia, the FDA approved it in 1990 (Barnes & McEvedy, 1996).

TABLE 7.3   Atypical Antipsychotic Medications

Generic name	Brand name	Adult daily dosage*
Clozapine	Clozaril	300–600 mg
Risperidone	Risperdal	4–6 mg
Sertindole	Serlect	12–24 mg
Olanzapine	Zyprexa	5–10 mg
Quetiapine	Seroquel	300–400 mg

*Note. Different sources may report slightly different dosages and dosage recommendations can
vary. These dosage recommendations are taken from the Physicians' Desk Reference (2000) except
for Serlect, which was obtained from product information.

Although there are several medications on the list that fall into this category, special attention is given to Clozaril because of the potential problems in monitoring its use. Social workers who have clients on Clozaril should consider two factors: This medication is usually dosed one week at a time to ensure client compliance with the medical regimen; and the clients must have a blood count every week to ensure that the potentially fatal condition called agranulocytosis does not develop. Agranulocytosis causes a severe reduction in the number of granulocytes, a particular type of white blood cell. Without these granulocytes, the body is unable to fight life-threatening infections. While the percentage of the population that this occurs in is small (1% to 2%) all clients taking this medication need to be monitored closely for complications. Once this side effect occurs, the drug must be promptly discontinued and is now precluded for future use. Because of its effectiveness and side-effect profile when monitored correctly Clozaril is a frequently prescribed drug. The expense and inconvenience for clients who take it, however, can be very limiting.

Based on the side-effect profile and the monitoring required, a trial of at least two other standard antipsychotic drugs is recommended prior to using Clozaril (McGrath, 1999; *PDR*, 2000). In addition, this is still a fairly new medication on the market, and the monitoring process will continue to be modified as the potential for developing agranulocytosis becomes more controlled. Sandoz Pharmaceuticals has suggested new guidelines requiring that weekly monitoring be done for the first 6 months and every 2 weeks thereafter if the white blood count remains stable (*PDR*, 2000).

Weekly monitoring can be very inconvenient for clients who cannot get to the medical provider, the pharmacy, or lab regularly, especially those who live in rural areas. Assistance may be needed to help the client gain weekly access to the drug. It is important to know that several individuals have died despite weekly hematological monitoring.

Some early signs of infection that need to be reported immediately to health care providers include fever, sore throat, fatigue, and mucous membrane ulcerations. The most common side effects of Clozaril are seizures, tonic and clonic convulsions, drowsiness, sedation, dizziness, and postural hypotension. Clozaril should never be used with drugs that can suppress bone marrow such as anticancer drugs (*PDR,* 2000).

Social workers need to be aware of the other atypical antipsychotic medications, such as risperidone, olanzipine and quentiapine. Risperidone (Risperdal) was introduced as the first official atypical antipsychotic medication in 1992 (Schulz, 2000). It is often used more widely than Clozaril and comprises more than one quarter of all prescriptions written for antipsychotic medications (Schulz, 2000). Studies on this medication have supported the reduction of positive and negative symptoms when compared with the older more traditional medications such as Haldol (Armenteros, 1997). Risperidone has been used with the schizotypal personality disorder to help decrease the psychotic-like or positive symptoms of the condition as well as negative symptoms such as cognitive impairment (Saklad, 2000). Another atypical antipsychotic, olanzipine (Zyprexa), was marketed after Risperdone because neither has been associated with the condition of agranulocytosis. Zyprexa appears to be well tolerated and readily accepted by clients, especially because of its low incidence of EPS and its ability to address the negative symptoms found in schizophrenia when given at higher doses (Harvard Mental Health Letter, 1999). Social workers should be aware, however, that Zyprexa may increase blood glucose levels in individuals with diabetes ("APA studies focus on side effects," 2000; *PDR*, 2000; Saklad, 2000). Quentiapine (Seroquel) is the most recently developed atypical antipsychotic medication, having been introduced in this country only two years ago. Quentiapine has fewer side effects, but does cause considerable sedation in the early stages of treatment (*PDR*, 2000; Schulz, 2000).

It is critical that social workers inform clients and their family members that taking these medicines will not result in a quick fix. Antipsychotic medications do not cure but only help to control the symptoms. Depending on the specific medication, peak concentrations in the system can vary as well as the time it takes before therapeutic effects can be detected. The side-effect profiles of these medications show a lower incidence of EPS, but there can be other disturbing side effects. Clients may experience disturbances in the menstrual cycle, which is particularly important for women of childbearing age who are taking these medications. In some cases these women may become pregnant and not know it because of an irregular menstrual cycle and therefore may not seek early prenatal care and professional advice about whether to continue their medication.

Pregnancy rates appear to be rising among women with schizophrenia, so it is best to avoid all medications during the first trimester of pregnancy (Empfield, 2000). When a woman knows she is pregnant, informed decisions can be made allowing her to choose to discontinue the medication if she wishes to avoid endangering the fetus. These women can benefit from counseling and assistance with regard to prenatal counseling to support healthy life-style patterns and choices. Unfortunately, the chance of clinical decompensation increases by two-thirds when the medication is discontinued (Empfield, 2000). Current literature indicates that it is possible to maintain a mother with schizophrenia on low doses of atypical medication, without causing harm to the fetus (Empfield, 2000). Immediate hospitalization is always advised if a client becomes acutely psychotic during pregnancy.

Drug interactions with this new classification of atypical medications are multiple. Therefore, it is essential to take a thorough medication history. Clozapine (Clozaril), risperidone (Risperdal), sertindole (Serlect), olanzapine (Zyprexa), and quentiapine (Seroquel) are fairly new and a long history of use in the practice setting has not been established. There are many side effects and possible interactions that have not been discovered yet. It is imperative that potential drug interactions be recorded and monitored closely for changes in efficacy, toxicity, and if applicable, drug concentration (Lam, 2000).

General side effects with all antipsychotic medications:

- drowsiness, rapid heart rate
- dizziness in changing position (orthostasis)
- anxiety
- somnolence (feeling sleepy and sluggish)
- constipation
- dyspepsia (indigestion, disorder of digestion with pain or discomfort in the lower chest area)
- urinary retention
- psychosexual dysfunction
- weight gain
- decreased sexual ability or interest
- problems with menstrual cycle
- more prone to sunburn or skin rashes

EPS side effects:

- Dystonia: acute contractions of the tongue (stiff or thick tongue)
- Akathisia: inner restlessness; most common form of EPS

DOCUMENTATION AND TREATMENT PLANNING

When working with the client who has schizophrenia or related psychotic disorder, treatment plan formulation and execution can be difficult as clients may resist or have difficulty participating in them. It is important that each treatment plan be individualized and reflect the general as well as the unique symptoms and needs of the client. The importance of a formal treatment plan cannot be overestimated as it will help to determine, structure, and provide focus for any type of social work intervention. A clearly established treatment plan can help deter any litigation by the client or by a concerned family member. When the treatment plan clearly delineates the intervention plan, families and friends of the client may feel more at ease and may actually agree to participate and assist in any behavioral interventions that will be applied.

In developing the treatment plan for the client with schizophrenia there are several critical steps that need to be taken (Jongsma & Peterson, 1995). First, the problem behaviors that are interfering with functioning must be identified. In social work it is considered essential that the client and his or her family participate and assist in this process as much as possible. The client needs to remain a part of the plan as much as he or she is able, particularly in identifying the issues that cause the most discomfort. It is essential to identify and emphasize those behaviors that impair independent living skills or that cause difficulty in completing tasks of daily living. Furthermore, facilitating educational and communicative interventions can enhance communication between the client and family members. This is especially helpful and productive because the bizarre nature of unpredictable symptoms and concerns for the client's physical and psychological safety may leave family members searching for the cause and cure for schizophrenia. As the client's symptoms worsen, family members find themselves in an environment characterized by increased tension, frustration, fear, blame, and helplessness. To address these issues family members can be made aware of the treatment plan goals and objectives that will be used. Family and friends can be encouraged to become involved and to participate in sharing valuable input and support in order to ensure intervention progress and success. By being involved families feel as if their input is important and essential for intervention progress.

Next, it is critical to state the identified problem behaviors in behavioral-based outcomes (Dziegielewski, 1998). In completing this process, the assessment data that lead to the diagnostic impression as well as the specific problems often experienced by the clients with schizophrenia need to be outlined. Once identified the client's problems are then prioritized so that goals, objectives, and action tasks can be developed. Then the goals of treatment, which constitute the basis of the plan of intervention, must be outlined and applied. These goals must be broken down clearly into specific objective statements that reflect the target behaviors that need to be changed and ways to measure the client's progress on each objective. Action tasks must be included that delineate the steps to be taken by the client and the worker to ensure successful completion of each objective.

Identified problem behaviors often include the following:

- Ambivalent feelings that impair general task completion related to independent living skills
- Affect disturbances such as feelings of depression or a difficulty in controlling anger
- Poor concentration
- Autism, in terms of feeling isolated or detached from others
- Associative disturbances, particularly in terms of being touched or approached by others
- Auditory hallucinations (hearing voices that berate, torture, or degrade the client)
- Paranoid ideation (the client's belief that someone is trying to harm him/her)
- Avolition (lack of goal-directed behavior such as daily self care and ADLs)

Once the problem behaviors have been identified, the social worker must identify the goals and the behaviorally based objectives that can be used to measure whether the identified problems have indeed been addressed and resolved. If the problem behavior is ambivalent feelings that impair general task completion, the main goal may be to help the client decrease feelings of ambivalence. It is important, therefore, to document a behavioral objective that clearly articulates a behavioral definition of ambivalence, ways that the ambivalence will be decreased, and the mechanisms used to determine if the behavior has been changed. The therapeutic intervention involves assisting the client in developing specific and concrete tasks that are geared towards decreasing this behavior and meeting the objective. The outcome measure simply becomes establishing whether the task could actually be completed. Table 7.4 provides a sample intervention plan for dealing with the client who has schizophrenia. It is important to note that this intervention is not designed to be all-inclusive, but rather

TABLE 7.4   Sample Intervention Plan

Objective	Intervention	Time frame	Responsibility
Verbally identify task that needs to be completed.	• Assist client in planning how and when task can be completed.	Upon admission assessment Insert date	Social worker, intervention team, client/support, system rep.
Verbalize trust in the support/ care role of staff.	• Assist client in developing list and writing down support/care issues the client will allow. • Probe possible causes for outbursts or noncompliant behaviors	Date	Social worker, team, client
Take antipsychotic medications consistently, with or without supervision.	• Assist in arranging for follow-up of medication regimens. • Monitor side-effect profiles that might decrease compliance. • Educate client about importance of taking medications, side effects, and benefits.	Ongoing	Team, client
Understand necessity of taking medication.	• Educate client about medicines that are being taken. • Help client understand the importance of taking medications. • Help client establish plan or routine for taking medications (identify rewards)	Date	Team, social worker
Report diminishing or absence of hallucinations.	• Monitor medication effects and need for readjustment. • Explore feelings or events that might trigger episodes. • Assist in restructuring irrational beliefs by using reality-based approach.	Date Client Social worker	Social worker
Increase family or system support for clients needs.	• Provide education about client's needs to family/support system. • Encourage family/support system and participation in care. • Refer for family therapy. • Conduct formal discharge problem-solving session prior to discharge	Date	Social worker

TABLE 7.4   *(continued)*

Objective	Intervention	Time frame	Responsibility
Verbalize that symptoms are related to an illness not a deliberate act.	• Provide one-on-one supportive therapy to address fears and reduce feelings of isolation. • Refer for group therapy to increase skills and socialization.	Date	Team, social worker

to provide the social worker with guidelines for effective documentation of the assessment and intervention process.

SUPPORTIVE INTERVENTIONS WITH SCHIZOPHRENIA

Many social workers are challenged by the task of how to best help the client with schizophrenia. Most agree, however, that medication treatment for the active symptomology of schizophrenia and the other psychotic disorders is an absolute necessity. Any type of verbal therapy by social workers or other mental health professionals is not productive until the client is stabilized, the psychosis is reduced, and some semblance of reality is restored. Once the client is stabilized, social work interventions that emphasize problem-solving methods may be used to address the significant problems that affect the daily lives of clients with schizophrenia. Strict behavioral intervention strategies may be employed that help clients become aware of their actions and the consequences on their levels of daily functioning (Sensky et al., 2000).

Interventions that involve the family or the client's support system are considered essential for many clients, because at times they alienate friends and family unknowingly. The aspects of the disease itself can be isolating as well. The splitting of mood or response that is characteristic of the disease may scare family and friends, and simply dealing with disturbances of affect and mood can be problematic. This may prevent the client's family or support system from assisting the client or demonstrating the affection and support that is so desperately needed. These strained relationships are based on a lack of understanding and an inability to control the symptoms of the disease and make education a critical component of any intervention strategy. Once made aware, families and support systems may become more tolerant of the eccentricities that are common in the condition. Social workers must understand the complexities of schizophrenia, the medications that are often used, the resistance that may be exhibited by the client, and the best ways to help the client adjust to his or her situation.

SUMMARY AND CONCLUSIONS

The field of social work has been forced to examine its treatment methods and modalities with a new vigor, as have many other disciplines. To compete successfully in the health care arena, social workers must provide effective and accountable practice. Assessment and diagnostic skills as well as information on medication usage and possible side-effect profiles must be taken into account. For the client with schizophrenia the unpredictable nature of the condition repeatedly alienates family and friends and often exhausts any type of support system that may have once been available. One glimmer of hope for increasing effective treatment strategy is the development of the new antipsychotic medications. It is important to remember, however, that despite the value of these medications, reliance on drug therapy alone may never be enough. Even with the advent of the new antipsychotic medicines, it is essential to remember the importance of emphasizing the uniqueness of the individual in his or her situation or environmental context. To rely on medication intervention alone denies the importance of the behavioral, biological, and social factors that are inherent to the individual. After the negative and positive symptoms of the illness have been controlled by drug therapy, individuals can benefit from the therapeutic help that counseling provides in order to achieve effective levels of functioning. Some essential ingredients provided by counseling modalities include education and problem-solving skills for both the client with schizophrenia and his or her family. Families need support during this difficult time, and all of the client's social, biological, psychological, and spiritual needs must be considered.

The social worker is often a catalyst in helping the client increase his or her functioning and in assisting the client to establishing or reestablishing a support system. Social workers can be important health care team members who provide advice and recommendations on those medications that will complement the current therapy being provided (Dziegielewski & Leon, 1999) and therefore need to be familiar with the current diagnostic guidelines and medications that are used in the treatment of schizophrenia.

It is crucial that social workers understand the inherent dynamics of blame and stigma experienced by both clients and their families. Family members, especially parents, often feel responsible for the client's illness and need to be reassured and educated to increase their understanding of the complex etiology of schizophrenia and other psychotic disorders. In these situations, it is important that social workers stress the essential role that families play in caregiving, emotional support, and problem solving (Walsh, 1996). Frustrating experiences with previous mental health agencies and other helping professionals often leave clients and family members skeptical and feeling powerless in any new attempts to address the illness. This anger and frustration can complicate the implementation of new and different types of intervention that might prove productive for the client.

Clients and their family members are faced daily with the stigma attached to mental illness. Many people view the mentally ill, especially people with schizophrenia, as dangerous. The use of words like maniac, schizo, and psycho by uninformed media enforces this viewpoint. The media often present the mentally ill as dangerous individuals just waiting for the opportunity to explode, when in reality people who do not have such illnesses commit 95% of all homicides. Those with schizophrenia are more likely to harm themselves than someone else (Ferriman, 2000). This tendency to harm oneself often rests with the guilt that many clients feel as they blame themselves for their illness.

A working knowledge of medications in today's practice environment is essential for social workers who must be prepared to consider the various types of medications and dosages a client may be taking. To effectively help clients with schizophrenia social workers must be familiar with side-effect profiles, dosage routines, and the potential for noncompliance and to assist clients in obtaining and maintaining the most therapeutically productive treatment possible. They must be able to recognize potential problem areas in order to refer the client for adequate or revised treatment. Social workers must stay updated on changing trends in the field and understand how these new medications can affect the client and the therapeutic relationship.

REFERENCES

American Psychiatric Association. (1994). *Diagnostic and statistical manual of mental disorders* (4th ed.). Washington, DC: American Psychiatric Press.

APA studies focus on side effects, efficacy of antipsychotics. (2000, January). *Outcomes and Accountability Alert, 5*(1), 5–6.

Apfledorf, W., & Alexopoulous, G. (1998). Psychopharmacology and psychotherapy. In W. R. Hazzard, J. P. Blass, W. H. Ettinger, J. B. Halter, & J. G. Ouslander (Eds.), *Principles of geriatric medicine and gerontology* (4th ed., pp. 1369–1378). New York: McGraw-Hill.

Armenteros, J. L. (1997). Risperidone in adolescents with schizophrenia: An open pilot study. *Journal of the American Academy of Child and Adolescent Psychiatry, 36*, 694, 697.

Barnes, T. R., & McEvedy, C. J. (1996). Pharmacological treatments strategies in non-responsive schizophrenic patient. *International Clinical Psychopharmacology, 11*, 117–121.

Berstein, J. G. (Ed.). (1995). *Handbook of drug therapy in psychiatry* (3rd ed.). St Louis, MO: C. V. Mosby.

Bently, K. (1998). Psychopharmacological treatment of schizophrenia: What social workers need to know. *Research on Social Work Practice, 8*, 384–405.

Breier, A. (1996). Introduction and overview. In A. Breier (Ed.), *The new pharmacotherapy of schizophrenia* (pp. xix–xx). Washington, DC: American Psychiatric Press.

Breier, A., & Buchanan, R. W. (1996). Clozapine: Current status and clinical applications. In A. Breier (Ed.), *The new pharmacotherapy of schizophrenia* (pp. 1–14). Washington, DC: American Psychiatric Press.

Buchanan, R. W., Brandes, M., & Breier, A. (1996). Treating negative symptoms: Pharmacological strategies. In A. Breier (Ed.), *The new pharmacotherapy of schizophrenia* (pp. 179–204). Washington, DC: American Psychiatric Press.

Brzustowicz, L., Hodgkinson, K., Chow, E., Honer, W., & Bassett, A. (2000, April 28). Location of major susceptibility locus for familial schizophrenia on chromosome 1q21–q22. *Science, 288*, 687–682.

Carpenter, W. T. (1996). Foreword. In A. Breier (Ed.), *The new pharmacotherapy of schizophrenia* (pp. xvii-xviii). Washington, DC: American Psychiatric Press.

Carpenter, W. T., Conley, R. R., & Buchanan, R. W. (1998). Schizophrenia. In S. J. Enna & J. T. Coyle (Eds.), *Pharmacological management of neurological and psychiatric disorders*. New York: McGraw-Hill.

Davis, J. M., & Casper, R. (1997). Antipsychotic drugs: Clinical pharmacology and therapeutic use. *Drugs, 12*, 260–282.

Dziegielewski, S. F. (1998). *The changing face of health care social work: Professional practice in the era of managed care*. New York: Springer.

Dziegielewski, S. F., & Leon, A. M. (1998, Winter). Psychopharmacology knowledge and use with social work professionals: A continuing education evaluation. *International Journal of Continuing Education, 1*(3), 31–40.

Empfield, M. (2000). Pregnancy and schizophrenia. *Psychiatric Annals, 30,* 13–17.

Farmer, R. L., Walsh, J., & Bently, K. J. (1998). Schizophrenia. In B. A. Thyer & J. S. Wodarski (Eds.), *Handbook of Empirical Social Work Practice: Vol. 1. Mental Disorders* (pp. 245–270). New York: Wiley.

Farmer, R. L., & Pandurangi, A. K. (1997). Diversity in schizophrenia: Toward a richer biopsychosocial understanding for social work practice. *Health and Social Work, 22,* 109–116.

Ferriman, A. (2000). The stigma of schizophrenia. *British Medical Journal, 7233,* 522.

Flaum, M. (1995). In C. L. Shriqui & H. A. Nasrallah (Eds.), *Contemporary issues in the treatment of schizophrenia* (pp. 83–108). Washington, DC: American Psychiatric Press.

Harvard Mental Health Letter. (1999, January). In brief: Olanzapine preferred. *Harvard Mental Health Letter, 15,* 7.

Hippius, H. The history of clozapine. *Psychopharmacology, 99,* S3–S5.

Hoffman, R. E. (2000, March 25). Transcranial magnetic stimulation and auditory hallucinations in schizophrenia. *Lancet, 355,* 1073–1076.

Jongsma, A. E., & Peterson, L. M. (1995). *The complete psychotherapy treatment planner.* New York: Wiley.

Kane, J. M. (1996). Conventional neuroleptic treatment: Current status, future role. In A. Breier (Ed.), *The new pharmacotherapy of schizophrenia* (pp. 89–104). Washington, DC: American Psychiatric Press.

Karper, L. P., & Krystal, J. H. (1996). Augmenting antipsychotic efficacy: New approaches. In A. Breier (Ed.), *The new pharmacotherapy of schizophrenia* (pp. 105–132). Washington, DC: American Psychiatric Press.

Kaplan, H. I., & Sadock, B. J. (1990). *Pocket handbook of clinical psychiatry.* Baltimore: Williams & Wilkins.

Kapur, S., Mieczkowski, T., & Mann, J. J. (1992, December). Antidepressant medications and the relative risk of suicide attempt and suicide. *Journal of the American Medical Association, 268,* 3441–3445.

Lam, Y. W. F. (2000, February). Ciprofloxacin may inhibit metabolism of olanzapine. *Psychopharmacology, 11,* 2, 1.

Lambert, L. (1998). New medications aid cognition in schizophrenia. *Journal of the American Medical Association, 280,* 953.

Malhotra, A. K., Pinsky, D. A., & Breier, A. (1996). Future antipsychotic agents: Clinical implications. In A. Breier (Ed.), *The new pharmacotherapy of schizophrenia* (pp. 41–56). Washington, DC: American Psychiatric Press.

McGrath, J. (1999). Treatment of schizophrenia. *British Medical Journal, 319,* 1045.

Moore, D. P., & Jefferson, J. W. (1997). *Handbook of medical psychiatry.* St. Louis, MO: Mosby.

Physicians' Desk Reference. (2000). *Physician's desk reference* (54th ed.). Montvale, NJ: Medical Economics.

Schulz, S. C. (2000). New antipsychotic medications: More than old wine and new bottles. *Bulletin of the Menninger Clinic, 64*(1), 60–75.

Sensky, T., Turkington, D., Kingdon, D., Scott, J. L., Scott, J., Siddle, R., O'Carroll, M., & Barnes, T.R. (2000). A randomized controlled trial of cognitive behavioral therapy for persistent symptoms in schizophrenia resistant to medication. *Archives of General Psychiatry, 57*, 165–172.

Siris, S. G. (2000). Management of depression in schizophrenia. *Psychiatric Annals, 30*(1), 13–17.

Saklad, S. R. (2000). APA studies focus on side effects, efficacy of antipsychotics. *Psychopharmacology Update, 11*(1), 1.

Stomwall, L. K., & Robinson, E. A. (1998). When a family member has a schizophrenic disorder: Practice issues across the family life cycle. *American Journal of Orthopsychiatry, 68*, 580–589.

Torrey, E. F. (1988). *Surviving schizophrenia: A family manual.* New York: Harper & Row.

Walsh, F. (1996). Families and mental illness: What have we learned? In B. Abosh & L. Collins (Eds.), *Mental illness in the family.* Toronto, Canada: University of Toronto Press.

PART III

Special Topics in Psychopharmacology and Social Work Practice

CHAPTER 8

Medications and Special Populations

The chapters in Part II of this book presented medication considerations as they relate to specific mental disorders. Each chapter has illustrated the importance of understanding a mental disorder, its symptoms, and the medications that may be most effective in treating the illness or disorder. The authors now wish to draw attention to the unique characteristics presented by two special populations that frequently receive psychotropic medications, namely children and older people. These two groups represent opposite ends of the developmental continuum and as such present unique challenges for professionals who prescribe medications that are intended to improve an individual's mental health. The decision to feature these two groups to the exclusion of other special populations such as women and HIV clients reflects the authors' extensive clinical work with these client groups.

Although medication concerns and considerations identified throughout this book apply to all client populations, the distinctive biological and physiological processes of children and older people warrant a closer examination of the impact that medications can have on these two groups. This chapter is intended to sensitize social worker practitioners to the unique considerations that are frequently encountered when these populations are prescribed medication and to highlight the importance of combining medication therapy with counseling when addressing the mental health needs of children and older clients. Furthermore, the authors would be remiss if they did not include some direct discussion of cultural diversity and working with minority clients and the issues and unique considerations relevant to this special population group in clinical practice (Devore & Schlesinger, 1999).

CULTURAL INFLUENCES

Most social workers would agree that culture is the "sum total of life patterns passed from generation to generation within a group of people and includes institutions, language, religious ideals, habits of thinking, artistic expressions, and patterns of social and interpersonal relationships. Aspects of culture are often related to people's ethnic, racial and spiritual heritage" (Kirst-Ashman, 2000, p. 11). This chapter is not meant to be exhaustive and therefore provides only an overview of the cultural issues that social workers should be aware of when working with children and older individuals who are taking mental health medications. The authors encourage the reader to seek out additional information pertaining to clinical practice and medication therapy with a focus on special populations, including minority clients. Although there is extensive literature on medications, more information is needed about how certain medications will respond in other special populations such as women, certain minority groups, children, and older people.

SPECIAL CONSIDERATIONS AND SERVICES FOR CHILDREN

During the late 1980s and early 1990s, mental health professionals acknowledged that there was a need for increased research with regard to the mental health needs of children and adolescents as well as accessibility to mental health services. The National Plan for Research on Child and Adolescent Mental Disorders (National Institute of Mental Health [NIMH], 1990) actively encouraged the development of research grants to study mental health service delivery among this population. In 1992, the Comprehensive Community Mental Health Services Program for Children and Adolescents with Severe Emotional Disturbances provided a mechanism for NIMH to develop a research initiative that reinforced the need for developing a base of knowledge that would yield essential information on effective mental health strategies for this population. Researchers and clinicians in the area of clinical services for children and adolescents have provided more information on effective mental health strategies for social work practitioners and other mental health professionals to use with this population (Ruffolo, 1998). Despite this progress there is still much to be learned about these mental health problems, effective counseling strategies, and patterns of medication use with this population: More than half of the prescription drugs that are likely to be prescribed to children have not been adequately tested or labeled for this type of use (Nordenberg, 1999a).

Social work professionals must consider many factors when providing clinical services to children and adolescents. Children present a rich, complex, and evolving biopsychosocial picture that compels social workers to remember that because of the developmental fluctuations these clients can be an ongoing "work-in-progress" (McAdoo, 1997). Throughout childhood, children are continuously developing and learning to understand their minds, bodies, emotions, and social patterns. Aggression, shyness, and a combination of low self-esteem and poor concentration are just some of the behaviors that are frequently seen (Harper-Dorton & Herbert, 1999). Children should have a variety of exposure and experience many opportunities that will allow development of the coping skills that are required for adjustment and adaptation to the world around them. Many normal behaviors that reflect conflict, lack of control, and opposition patterns may be mistaken for psychopathology by parents, school systems and mental health professionals (Maxmen & Ward, 1995). Roemmelt (1998) warns that addressing these behaviors by depending primarily on the use of medications can disguise what the child is really experiencing and also give parents and professionals a false sense of control that limits normal childhood development. It is therefore imperative that social work practitioners tread cautiously when assessing and treating the problems and disorders presented by children.

Historically, social workers in clinical practice have been accustomed to using various assessment and diagnostic tools on children that were originally intended for use with adult clients. Recently, however, this trend has changed, and with the introduction of child-focused assessment and diagnostic instruments, social workers are able to capture and interpret the signs and symptoms presented by children more accurately in clinical practice. While most of these child-sensitive instruments have been developed as tools for psychologists, social workers must not only be aware of them but also must aid in the interpretation process throughout the helping relationship. The increase in managed care and the emphasis on rapid assessment and treatment has forced social workers to shorten the length of the biopsychosocial assessments to include salient information on the child's past and current mental health functioning. Woolston (1999) warns of the dangers that can result from using only psychopharmacology to address the problems that a child is experiencing. He also highlights the danger that can result from fragmented care as a child moves from one health care setting to another. This makes the assessment critical and forces practitioners to focus on identifying the significant aspects of the child's presenting problems and highlighting the specific behaviors and circumstances that surround the impaired functioning.

It has become increasingly important for social workers and other helping professionals who work with children to become aware of the behavioral, cognitive, and physiological effects that medications can have on children. Social workers are frequently expected to assist children who are taking medications, and many times their symptoms and problems can occur in the school setting as well as in the home environment. Any adverse effects of medications that might be witnessed in school can be referred to the school psychologist or social worker. Social workers who provide clinical services to children will also have more occasion to work with children who are taking medications. The social worker will be expected to consult with other professionals and to help make decisions such as whether to use medications at all or modify current treatment schemes.

To facilitate an accurate and complete assessment of the child's behaviors, social workers need to record specific and behavior-focused information about the following: (a) the problem presented by the child; (b) behaviors that demonstrate the problem; (c) the intensity, frequency, duration, and specific environmental circumstances that accompany or appear to be linked to the problem; (d) areas that are affected by the problem; (e) previous coping skills and problem-solving methods used to address the problem and behaviors; and (f) any previous and current medication and counseling interventions prescribed.

USING THE *DSM-IV*

The *Diagnostic and Statistical Manual for Mental Disorders* is another tool used by social work practitioners in the assessment process to identify clearly those categories that are applicable to children and to caution the professional on developmental differences that prevent the use of some diagnostic codes with children (American Psychiatric Association, 1994). Goldman (1998) proposes a quick and practical schema that allows the practitioner to apply the *DSM-IV* diagnoses to children. He proposes that the clinician first confirm the full criteria in the *DSM-IV* and then consider using the following questions as a way to assess children.

1. *Where is the problem located?* Distinguish between problems generated within the child such as ADHD as an internal difficulty and environmental (V codes) or school-related difficulties.
2. *Is the child's problem a reaction to a specific and identifiable stressor?* This helps the clinician to rule out adjustment disorders and posttraumatic stress disorders.
3. *What are the basic areas affected and impaired by the problems?* In answering this question, Goldman suggests that the clinician is able to distinguish between behavioral, mood, and dissociative disorders.
4. *Are the symptoms reflective of long-standing difficulties?* In these cases the practitioner is probably observing disorders reflective of axis 2 diagnoses, which are usually found in older adolescents.

Johnson (1998) identifies various steps that clinicians can take in order to use the *DSM-IV* more effectively with minority children. He emphasizes that clinicians should recognize that cultural and ethnic factors can influence the manifestation of symptoms in children very similar to the way they affect adults; identify and understand how the child has acculturated to his or her environment and to mainstream society; assess how acculturation and racial issues are reflected in symptom formation; and utilize the appendix of culture-bound syndromes provided by the *DSM-IV*.

Culture-bound syndromes are extreme forms of cultural expression that may be perceived as dysfunctional by individuals who are outside the cultural context (Leon & Dziegielewski, 1999). Two examples of culture-bound syndromes that have been identified in children are brain fag (APA, 1994, p. 846) and *mal de ojo* or evil eye (APA, 1994, p. 847). According to the *DSM-IV* brain fag is a syndrome found among West African adolescents who are reacting to school pressures. The symptoms are primarily somatic in nature and include blurred vision, neck and head pain, difficulty in concentration, and an overall sense of "brain tiredness." *Mal de ojo* or the evil eye is a syndrome that affects many children in Caribbean and Mediterranean cultures. The belief is that due to their physical and psychological vulnerabilities, children and infants are at high risk or serve as receptacles for attracting evil thoughts or wishes intended for other adult members of the family. Symptoms in this syndrome include disruptive sleep, crying without cause, vomiting, diarrhea, or fevers.

Children do not operate in a vacuum and frequently reflect the belief systems and perceptions of their parents and their social environments

(Canino & Spurlock, 1994). Clinicians working with this population must be aware of and incorporate the cultural issues and perceptions of medication use that influence the course of counseling among ethnic and minority children (Dziegielewski, Leon, & Green, 1998). Dziegielewski et al. (1998) illustrate an example of this when they assert that African American children may learn that it is not culturally acceptable to seek help for mental health problems from formal institutions and professionals outside the family or culture.

Another way that clinical practice with a child differs from that with an adult is the nature of the psychopathology experienced. The symptoms experienced by children can be different from adults, and information that reflects exactly how children should respond is limited. In addition, the child's parents or guardians generally determine treatment issues such as the duration of treatment and medication intervention decisions. Therefore, parents or primary caretakers of the child strongly influence the mental health process, and this influence begins during the assessment phase and continues through the termination phase. Parents who cannot fully understand or accept the value of counseling and medication therapy can change or terminate these strategies, so it is essential that social work practitioners learn to include the parents or caregivers in the child's treatment process from the beginning. This becomes especially important when practitioners identify resistance to treatment by the child or the parents. For example, if a child's family of origin is not supportive of mental health treatment, the child learns not to ask for help (Dziegielewski et al., 1998). Oftentimes compliance issues emerge in relation to the parents' own perceptions of the medication or fears and concerns related to the potential for addictive patterns in the child.

Another significant difference when working directly with children as opposed to adults is that the clinician relies heavily on the information gathered. Assessment, treatment and termination information is needed from collateral contacts, which include parents, the school system, the community, and other informants who can potentially provide vital information pertaining to the child's difficulties and the impact of treatment and medication. This necessitates eliciting and incorporating feedback from these individuals within the child's environmental system in order to complete a comprehensive assessment of the child in his or her current environment.

One paramount issue that may complicate this assessment process is the parents' or caregivers' knowledge and expectations of what constitutes normal developmental behavior for a child of that age. Parents can expect more—or less—from a child than he or she is capable. When gathering information to supplement the assessment it is essential to note the parents' levels of expectations in terms of what is considered normal human growth and development for a child of similar age.

Mental health professionals should not make general assumptions that are based on adult guidelines when it comes to symptoms and presenting problems demonstrated by children, because there are clear differences between children and adults in the manifestation of psychological and emotional difficulties. A comprehensive assessment needs to include significant information on the specific behavioral, emotional, and psychological problems presented by children. The accuracy of this information will help the social worker and the medication prescriber to determine the nature of the child's mental disorder and whether medication therapy is indeed warranted.

CHILDREN AND MEDICATION

Social workers and other mental health professionals work regularly with children and adolescents who present with mental disorders that require both counseling and medication interventions. Unique to this population is the interaction between the child, the family system, and additional components in the child's environment (e.g., the school system). Medication should not be prescribed without the ongoing support and combination of various interventions, which include family therapy, parent-child work, and marital counseling (Boyd-Webb, 1991). Even when medication is effective and alleviates the presenting symptoms, children must be helped to understand the different facets of their difficulties and should be equipped with new coping skills to address the same or similar difficulties that may arise in the future. Medication prescribers also must be certain that the medication given is indicated by an accurate diagnosis and not simply to appease parents and school system. This requires a thorough assessment that takes into account an interview with the child and an examination of the child's behaviors in the home, school, and community environments. It is not uncommon for social workers to encounter parents and teachers who complain about a child's behavior and request medication as the sole intervention for behavior modification. In these cases the social worker's role as an educator comes into play. It is essential that the social worker provide information regarding the nature of the child's problems and stress the importance of integrating multiple interventions that could affect the child's behavior.

Because a child's emotional and physiological response to medication can vary, many mental health providers who prescribe medications do so in a cautious and conservative manner. In the debate over granting limited prescription privileges to psychologists, Kubiszyn (1994) reveals that despite the caution in prescribing to children there is little empirical research that illustrates the efficacy of pediatric psychopharmacology. Others report that one of the biggest concerns in prescribing patterns for children is that the majority of medication prescribers for child and adolescent clients tend to be nonpsychiatric physicians (Baldessarini, 1990; Barkley et al., 1990). Primarily general practitioners they are not specifically trained to deal with children and often have limited knowledge of child development and child psychopharmacology.

Rushton, Clark, and Reed (2000) found that the type of nonspecialist physician a child sees predicts the treatment types offered. These authors report that physicians are more likely to refer the child to a specialist. Similarly Ruston et al. (2000) found that 42% of family physicians had prescribed an antidepressant to at least one child in the last six months compared to 25% of pediatricians. Clearly these prescribing patterns provide grounds for further investigation. In fact, 80% to 90% of children in hospital or residential settings are on at least one medication, with almost 50% on two or more (Lyons, 2000).

Because a child's response to a medication can vary, it is important that the prescriber not ascertain information on the basis of adult symptoms and doses. Children are different developmentally from adults. Social work professionals dealing with children and adolescents who take medications as the sole modality or as a supplemental treatment should be aware and be trained on issues related to child development, child psychopathology, and child psychopharmacology. This is especially true in the case of pediatric pharmacology where it is clearly not appropriate to prescribe medications to this population using adult guidelines and patterns.

Social workers should take active measures to educate themselves about those medications that are appropriate for childhood disorders. They should also assist children and their families in understanding the nature of the illness, the side effects of medications, and the efficacy of combining medication and psychosocial interventions, which require a working understanding of the mental disorders commonly presented by children. The following section will provide a sampling of some of the *DSM-IV* diagnoses frequently identified in children and will highlight the medications commonly used to treat these disorders. In reading this section it is important to keep in mind that each child may respond differently to medications and is different in terms of the presenting problem and the combination of medical and psychological problems that can result (Dulcan, 1999). This means that dealing with children and the medications they take is an ongoing process of constant reassessment and evaluation.

ATTENTION DEFICIT HYPERACTIVITY DISORDER AND MEDICATIONS

Although many children are referred to health and mental health facilities for ADHD-like symptoms, only 5% to 9% of school-age children are actually affected by the disorder (Barkley, 1990). Children with ADHD present with many different types of symptoms, most of which are behavioral and cognitive in nature. According to Anastopoulos (1999), the clinical picture of what constitutes ADHD is blurred by (a) the wide range of assessment instruments with varying levels of reliability and validity; (b) the fluctuation of ADHD symptoms dependent on specific situations; (c) the amount of structure provided in each situation; (d) the existence of co-morbid conditions such as conduct disorders and learning disabilities; and (e) changes in parenting methods and styles.

There are several types of medications that can be used in the treatment of this disorder. The two types of medications that are most commonly used include the stimulants and antidepressants, which address the neurochemical imbalances thought to precipitate the symptoms of ADHD (Anastopoulos, 1999). The stimulants, which include methylphenidate (Ritalin), d-amphetamine (Dexedrine) and pemoline (Cylert), are the most commonly used. Basically, taking this type of medication helps the child to pay attention, stay calm, and follow instructions. Of these stimulants Ritalin is more commonly known among parents and is the faster-acting medication, taking effect within 30 to 45 minutes after being ingested. The effects of Ritalin generally will last from three to seven hours (Anastopoulos, 1999). This medication is available in tablet and capsule form and can be purchased in doses of 5, 10, or 15 mg. When used to treat ADHD, Ritalin and other types of stimulant medications need to be taken on a regular basis and the prescriber should be contacted before the medication is adjusted (Kent, Blader, Koplewicz, Abikoff, & Foley, 1995). When a child is taking these medications most physicians want to see the child on a fairly regular basis. In order to ensure adequate monitoring and follow-up, it is important for the social worker to ask the child and his or her family when the last visit was with the prescribing physician and when the next one is planned.

Recognizing that stimulants may not be effective for all children who present with ADHD symptoms and that there may be unwanted side effects, some medication prescribers have chosen to utilize the longer acting group of medications known as tricyclic antidepressants. A commonly prescribed tricyclic antidepressant is imipramine (Anastopoulos, 1999).

Other types of tricyclic antidepressants used are:

Brand name	Generic name
Tofranil	imipramine
Pamelor or Aventyl	nortriptyline
Norpramin or Pertofrane	desipramine
Elavil or Endep	amitriptyline
Anafranil	clomipramine

Listed in order of how they are prescribed (Dulcan, 1999).

Antidepressants may take longer to be effective and are usually taken twice a day, once in the morning and once in the evening. Although antidepressant medications are not generally the first choice for the long-term treatment of ADHD, these medications have produced positive results in decreasing impulsivity as well as aggressive moods and behaviors.

Regardless of how ADHD is treated, social work practitioners should use an approach that when combined with medication therapy can produce effective management of the ADHD symptoms. Some of these interventions include (a) using interviews and behavior scales to conduct a thorough assessment; (b) directly observing the child's behaviors; (c) parent training aimed at helping parents provide the necessary structure needed by ADHD children; (d) coordination with teachers and schools for classroom management plans; and (e) individual, family, and marital counseling for parents.

DISRUPTIVE BEHAVIORS AND MEDICATION

Social workers and other mental health professionals frequently get referrals of children with disruptive behavior disorders diagnosed with either oppositional defiant disorder or conduct disorder. As the milder of the two disorders, oppositional defiant disorder (ODD) consists of negative, defiant, and hostile behavior directed at authority figures (Kronenberger & Meyer, 1996). In order to diagnose a child with ODD, evidence of significant impairment must be demonstrated, because the behaviors presented in ODD are so common and can be confused with some of the normal oppositional behaviors characteristic of developmental growth. It is important that social work practitioners learn to identify the behaviors that distinguish ODD from normal developmental changes in children at different stages of growth. The *DSM-IV* identifies that for a period of six months or longer children with ODD present with significant impairment in academic, social, or occupational functioning and demonstrate behaviors that include loss of temper, arguing with adults, anger, deliberately annoying other individuals, and evidence of vindictive behaviors (American Psychiatric Association, 1994). Although there is a separate diagnostic category, diagnosing ODD in accordance with the *DSM-IV* standards can be complicated because ODD shares many of the characteristics in the conduct disorder (CD) category. Furthermore, it is not uncommon for some children with ODD to develop symptoms characteristic of conduct disorder. Similarities in the characteristics between these two diagnoses become important during the assessment process when the social work practitioner must distinguish between them and identify the symptomology of each. Despite this, conduct disorder is the more severe diagnosis and warrants more intensive psychosocial and medication interventions. Children with conduct disorders frequently display symptoms that indicate a disregard and violation of the rights of others. Its symptoms include physical aggression, cruelty to people and animals, breaking of laws, destruction of property, substance abuse, theft, and lying (Kronenberger & Meyer, 1996). Generally disruptive in school or community settings, these children usually have academic problems, anger management problems, and are prime candidates for developing antisocial personality disorder during adulthood (Myers, Burket, & Otto, 1993).

The literature on psychopharmacotherapy has identified a co-morbid relationship between the disruptive disorders and ADHD, and the psychostimulants are the most common class of medications used to treat ODD and CD. The most well-known and successful stimulants to reduce the impulsive and aggressive behaviors in these disorders include Ritalin, Dexedrine, and Cylert. Kronenberg and Meyer (1996) report that Ritalin is more commonly used and can be prescribed in doses to be administered three times a day, while Cylert is prescribed once a day usually in the morning. Social workers need to be aware and educate clients and their families about the side effects of stimulants, which include changes in appetite, sleep, and mood. Because Cylert is prescribed only once a day, it may increase the client's compliance in following the medication regimen while also decreasing the potential for medication abuse. Other medications used to treat symptoms in ODD and CD include the use of lithium for aggressive behavior, Tegretol for ADHD symptoms, Catapres for low frustration tolerance and aggressive behaviors, and Tenex to reduce overactivity and aggression (Kronenberger & Meyer, 1996).

Another medication that can be used to assist with behavior problems is Wellbutrin. Traditionally this medicine has been used for several purposes including treating depression in adults. This medication is now being used to treat emotional and behavioral problems in children, including depression and attention-deficit/hyperactivity disorder as well as conduct disorder in children and adolescents (Dulcan, 1999). The antidepressants Desyrel (trazodone) and Serzone (nefazodone) are also now being used in children to address emotional and behavioral problems including depression, insomnia (difficulty falling asleep), and disruptive behavior disorders by helping to decrease depression, irritability, and aggression (Dulcan, 1999). For additional information on each of these medications in the treatment of ODD and CD, see Table 8.1.

Like ADHD, the disruptive behaviors also require a multidimensional approach to treatment. Social workers must include medication therapy, cognitive behavioral techniques, parent management training, and family therapy in order to successfully treat oppositional defiant and conduct disorders.

Medications that are used as an intervention modality with children need constant monitoring and reevaluation, and the social worker must be keenly aware that not all medications used for children have printed information available that directly relates to their use with children. The information often is not available because the medications are not approved by the Food and Drug Administration for use in children. There may be many reasons for this, with the primary consideration being the time and expense involved in obtaining this type of approval. Absence of this pertinent information, however, does not mean that the medication is dangerous or does not work (Dulcan, 1999). It does mean that particular attention must be given to assessment and reassessment and to the side

TABLE 8.1   Common Pediatric Mental Health Medications

Brand name	Generic name	Type of medication	Conditions treated	Common side effects
BuSpar	buspirone	antianxiety	anxiety disorder, social phobia	nausea, headache
Catapres	clonidine	antihypertensive	ADHD, Tourette's syndrome	sedation, headache, nausea, dry mouth, constipation
Cylert	pemoline	psychostimulant	ADHD, autism, conduct disorder	appetite reduction (very infrequent)
Depakene	valproic acid	anticonvulsant	bipolar disorder, conduct disorder	upset stomach, nausea, vomiting, weight gain, sedation, tremor
Dexedrine	dextro-amphetamine	psychostimulant	ADHD, enuresis, autism	appetite reduction, delay in falling asleep, irritability, dry mouth, headaches, weepiness, increased heart rate
Elavil	amitripyline	tricyclic antidepressant	depression	same as Tofranil but less frequent
Eskalith	lithium	salt	bipolar disorder, conduct disorder	nausea, vomiting, diarrhea, mild tremor, fatigue, acne, weight gain
Norpramin	desipramine	tricyclic antidepressant	ADHD	similar to Tofranil but less frequent
Pamelor	nortriptyline	tricyclic antidepressant	ADHD, depression	similar to Tofranil and Norpramin but less frequent
Paxil	paroxetine	SSRI	depression, obsessive-compulsive disorder	nausea, diarrhea, weight loss, insomnia, upset stomach, excess sweating, jitteriness
Ritalin	methylphenidate	psychostimulant	ADHD, conduct disorder, autism	appetite reduction, delay in falling asleep, headaches, weepiness, increased heart rate

(continued)

TABLE 8.1 *(continued)*

Brand name	Generic name	Type of medication	Conditions treated	Common side effects
Tegretol	carbamazepine	anticonvulsant	bipolar disorder	double vision, drowsiness, poor concentration, mild nausea
Tenex	guanfacine	antihypertensive	ADHD, Tourette's syndrome	similar to Catapres but less frequent
Tofranil	imipramine	tricyclic antidepressant	ADHD, eating disorders, enuresis, depression	sedation, dry mouth, changes in blood pressure, constipation
Welbutrin	bupropion	atypical antidepressant	ADHD	similar to Ritalin and Dexedrine but less frequent

effects that are reported by the child, parents, school teachers, and others that come in regular contact with the child who is taking the medicine.

SPECIAL CONSIDERATIONS AND SERVICES FOR OLDER PEOPLE

Many physical, cognitive, psychological, social, and emotional changes accompany the process of aging (Beaver & Miller, 1992; Kane, Ouslander, & Abrass, 1999). Similar to the child client, the older client is in a state of constant flux characterized by the deterioration of biological, physical, and cognitive processes. While all individuals do not age in the same manner, many of the clients that social workers and other mental health professionals work with are experiencing major changes in their development. This is especially true for those who are in nursing homes and long-term care facilities that provide medical services to meet the basic daily living needs of their clients. Given these natural changes and the additional mental health problems experienced by older clients, it is important for social work practitioners to acquire an understanding of human development and how changes that occur during the life cycle can affect these clients.

Older individuals frequently attach primary importance to their health concerns and this helps explain why they use hospital services, physician services, and long-term care services more than any other age group (Rhodes, 1988). From a physician's perspective, dealing with clients who are 65 and older has become a practice reality because this age group now makes up more than one third of all primary care visits (Kane, Ouslander, & Abrass, 1999).

In an archival study conducted on 298 clients who were treated by a mental health center, three issues predominated among older clients: family conflicts, poor physical health, and feeling as if they were not in control of their lives (Mosher-Ashley, 1994).

Developing a chronic condition is generally an older person's worst fear, because this type of condition frequently results in a gradual loss of activity or unaided mobility (Rhodes, 1988). Chronic conditions found in the elderly are either of a physical (biological) or mental (psychological) nature. Although this is a simplistic distinction, it is important to note that physical and mental health conditions are often related and interdependent (Dziegielewski & Harrison, 1996).

In the natural process of aging, the individual becomes more vulnerable to changes in areas of functioning that include physical abilities, cognitive, and social skills. Issues like increasing reliance on others and medical problems become troublesome and often lead to feelings of loss. Normal feelings of loss related to diminishing health, diminishing independence, retirement, changes in socioeconomic status, and the loss of spouse and friends can sometimes turn into serious depressive episodes that require treatment (Dziegielewski & Harrison, 1996). Working with older clients who present with depression can potentially sensitize social workers to their own fears of losing their mental abilities, contracting illnesses, experiencing helplessness, and depending on others. Social workers may fear that they too will become depressed during their later years (Leon, Altholz, & Dziegielewski, 1999).

DEPRESSION AND DEMENTIA IN OLDER PEOPLE

According to Butler, Lewis, and Sunderland (1998) as many as 20% of those 65 years or older suffer from various mental health disorders. Depression in older people is sometimes difficult to diagnose and has traditionally been linked to physiological and medical changes resulting from the aging process. Difficulties in accurately assessing depressive symptoms can also stem from complications presented by other illnesses, which can mask or precipitate depression. Illnesses commonly associated with depression in the older population are hypertension, coronary problems, Alzheimer's disease, Parkinson's disease, diabetes, certain types of cancers, rheumatoid arthritis, chronic constipation, and sexual dysfunction (Butler et al., 1998).

Although depression is considered a common problem among older people, it is frequently associated with physical symptoms and illness (Rhodes, 1988). However, there is little consensus among researchers regarding the prevalence of this condition and how best to recognize this condition in this age group (Ban, 1987; Reynolds et al., 1994). According to Belsky (1988), who interpreted the results of various community surveys, anywhere from 5% to 50% of the older population suffer from some level of depression. Although some researchers believe that the incidence of depression does not appear to increase directly with age (Blazer, 1999), it is important to remember that there is a disproportionately high suicide rate among older people (Ban, 1987), with the highest rate found among males 75 and older (Apfeldorf & Alexopoulous, 1999; Blazer, 1999). Because depression is treatable, it is unfortunate that older individuals may avoid seeking treatment or minimize the symptoms they are experiencing for this or other mental health conditions (Maldonado, 1987; Belsky, 1988).

Common signs and symptoms of depression include feelings of sadness, loneliness, guilt, boredom, marked decrease or increase in appetite, lack or increase in sleep behavior, and a sense of worthlessness (American Psychiatric Association, 1994; Kane, Ouslander, & Abrass, 1999). When the etiology of depression is related to life circumstances, it is generally considered situational in nature. Situational depression presents a particular problem for older people because they have endured many tragic experiences including the loss of loved ones, jobs, status, independence, and other personal disappointments. When dealing with situational depression, it is essential to note that using medication alone is probably a disservice to the client. Perodeau and du Font (2000) warn that prescribing psychotropic drugs alone is not an adequate response to the distress expressed by seniors. The addition of social work intervention and counseling can provide the ability to achieve greater life satisfaction for many of these individuals. Social workers can assist those suffering from situational depression by teaching them to control the frequency of their depressive thoughts. Relaxation techniques such as imagery and deep muscle relaxation (as discussed in the chapter on anxiety) can be used to help clients calm down during times of anxiety. Concrete problem-solving and behavioral contracting can be implemented to help the older client change problem behaviors. Whenever possible, family members should be included in treatment contracting to provide support and to assist in recording and observing behaviors that the client seeks to change.

Depression is not always situational or reactive, however; it also can be related to internal causes, which is referred to as endogenous depression. The etiology of depression is not always clear and may result from a combination of situational and internal factors. For example, many chronic medical conditions often found in the elderly are accompanied by depression. Some of these conditions include hypothyroidism and congestive heart failure. Furthermore, if they are taking multiple medications it is possible that the symptoms of depression are the by-products or side effects of other medications (Belsky, 1988). The American Psychiatric Association (1994) has warned that the diagnosis of depression in the elderly can be particularly problematic because the symptoms of dementia in the early stages are very similar to depression. Loss of interest and pleasure in one's usual activities, disorientation, and memory loss are common in both conditions. Although many of the same signs and symptoms can exist in both cases, the individual suffering from early stages of dementia usually will not improve with treatment.

Psychopharmacotherapy for older people with depression usually involves some type of antidepressant medication. (See chapter 4 on depression for a list and clinical explanation of the antidepressant medications that are most frequently used.) When specifically addressing this type of medication use among older people, it is believed that at least 60% will respond with improvement of depressive symptomatology; however, even among responders many continue to have significant residual symptomology (Rabins, 1999). Side-effect profiles may be magnified, and these clients may be more likely to develop delirium, constipation, urinary retention, dry mouth, and orthostatic hypotension. For this reason the initial dose is generally lower than that used for younger adults, the medication should continue at a slower pace, and it should last longer (7 to 9 weeks) than that used for younger adults (Rabins, 1999).

All of the major depressant medications discussed in chapter 4 can be used with the elderly. Again, caution should always be exercised, and according to Apfeldorf and Alexopoulos (1999), the antidepressant medications that are generally used with older individuals include tricyclics (e.g., nortriptyline, desipramine as these have lower anticholinergic and sedative effects); and the selective serotonin reuptake inhibitors fluoxetine, steraline, and paroxetine, which are recommended for a broad spectrum of depressive disorders.

When working with older clients who are believed to be suffering from depression, social workers should gather as detailed a medical and medication history as possible. It is also critical to remember that medications often used with older clients do not have established safe, effective prescription doses. It was not until August of 1997 that the FDA made it mandatory for drug manufacturers to include a separate section in the drug literature that addresses "geriatric use" directly (Nordenberg, 1999b). Depressed older clients should always be referred for a medical exam to rule out any physical causes of depressive symptoms. Although depression is a problem that often goes unrecognized by professionals, treatment for depression in older people can be as effective when implemented as that with other age groups (Reynolds et al., 1994).

The type of mental disability known as dementia is acknowledged to be the most devastating and debilitating condition affecting the aged (Steuer & Clark, 1982; Corvea, 1987) with at least a hundred different possible causes (Kawas, 1999). Approximately 1 million older people have this chronic condition (Steuer & Clark, 1982). Dementia can lead to death, and it remains the fourth leading cause of death for those aged 65 and older (American Association of Retired Persons, 1993). It is estimated that the growing older population and increased life expectancy will serve to double the number of older individuals in our society; a similar increase will occur in the number of cases of dementia (Kawas, 1999). In the case of mental impairment related directly to dementia, confusion, which is characteristic of this disease, generally precipitates admission to long-term care facilities (Dziegielewski, 1991). This disease is particularly problematic because it can affect an individual's functional independence, requiring that every need be met by others. The American Psychiatric Association (1994) described the essential feature of this condition as a loss of intellectual abilities of a sufficient nature to interfere with social or occupational functioning, thus limiting an individual's judgment, abstract thought, intelligence, and orientation.

Unfortunately, the term dementia has been used as a catchall phrase when discussing older people. The professional community has not always attempted to diagnose or differentiate which type of dementia an individual is experiencing. The possible reasons for this may be that the person is

sometimes viewed as hopeless, helpless, and unworthy of careful evaluation and treatment; or that the general approach in dementia is to treat
symptoms as they appear because remedial treatments and cure are not
available (Corvea, 1987). Conditions such as dementia of the Alzheimer's
type (DAT) and vascular dementia, previously referred to as multi-infarct
dementia (MID), are frequently linked, although their etiology is different
(American Psychiatric Association, 1994). DAT is the most common form
of dementia (American Retired Persons, 1993) with a gradual deterioration
for which there is no known cure.

Differential diagnosis of dementia is important, although frequently
neglected and avoided. Professionals who seek early and improved diagnosis of older individuals can contribute to an increased understanding and
perhaps an eventual cure.

Social workers should be aware of the different forms of dementia and
the signs and symptoms this progressive disease presents. As members
of the health care team, social workers have the unique opportunity to
educate and provide counseling and support for individuals suffering from
dementia and to provide support and education to their families and care
givers, thereby increasing support networks for all involved (Dziegielewski, 1990, 1991). Furthermore, the medications now being used to assist
individuals who are experiencing cognitive difficulties have improved.
Although there is no known medication that can cure or completely reverse
the devastating effects of the illness, there is some promising research
that might indeed make it possible one day (Allian, Bentue-Ferrer, Gandon,
LeDoze, & Belliard, 1997; Nordberg, 1996). The two most commonly
used medications to assist with cognitive decline are Aricept (donepezil),
which is given in 5–10 mg dosages once a day; and Cognex (tacrine),
which is administered in divided doses of 20–160 mg. Both are for mild
to moderate cases of cognitive decline.

Unfortunately, most of the clients who respond to these medications
only receive modest clinical benefits that include mild memory enhancement, increased social interaction, and heightened attention (Kawas, 1999).

ASSESSMENT AND MEDICATIONS FOR OLDER PEOPLE

The use and misuse of prescription medication can present particular
problems for older individuals, and social work professionals must stay
informed on the subject. An older person for whom medication is prescribed may have a different reaction than a younger person taking the

same medication and dosage. They generally have slower metabolic rates, possibly related to decreased activity or physiological losses (Belsky, 1988). Medications taken to treat chronic conditions such as arthritis, ulcers, heart conditions, and hypertension can cause depression when taken alone or with other medications. Common prescribed medications also can present side effects such as irritability, sexual dysfunction, memory lapses, and a general feeling of tiredness (Harrison, 1988; Kane, Ouslander, & Abrass, 1999).

Older clients frequently take more than one medication and are often told to take them on complex dosing schedules (Kane, Ouslander, & Abrass, 1999). The number of side effects and contraindications increases dramatically when taking more than one medication. These individuals may be seeing more than one physician, and one doctor may not be aware of what another has prescribed. When taking multiple prescriptions, it is not uncommon for older individuals to simply forget that prohibited foods and drinks can lead to a toxic drug reaction. The number of medications complicates the problem of remembering what is being taken and for what purpose, and those who take many medications daily are more likely to forget whether they took them (Rost & Roter, 1987).

It is of utmost importance for social workers to be aware of any medications the older client is taking. The side effects should be explored and examined in relation to the social or interpersonal problems being presented by the individual, and before beginning any type of intervention, the social worker needs to explore whether the symptoms are medication-related. Recently, for example, researchers have begun to document cases of older individuals who have been given antipsychotic medications to control their symptoms of dementia (Magnuson, Roccaforte, Wengel, & Burke, 2000), and although it was originally believed to be rare, it now appears that the symptoms of dystonia (slow, sustained muscular contraction or spasm) do occur.

When assessing the problems of an older client, it is essential to do the following: (a) help older individuals stay as active, independent, and psychologically stable as possible (Beck, Freedman, & Warshaw, 1994); (b) keep assessment time and evaluations as brief as possible and determine the changes in behavior that have occurred over time (Beck et al., 1994); and (c) include the perceptions of family members or those in the immediate support system and recognize the effect that these individuals can have on the intervention regimen (Beck et al., 1994; Dziegielewski, 1990, 1991).

There are several important factors that social work practitioners and other mental health professionals must consider when providing psychosocial and medication interventions to this group of clients. First, the developmental tasks inherent in the aging process can often produce emotional and psychological problems unique to this population. For example, as one becomes older it is appropriate to begin evaluating one's life, goals, and accomplishments (Newman & Newman, 1995). This requires the older client to recognize that they are at the final developmental stages of their lives and that feelings and issues may emerge related to unaccomplished goals and dreams, regrets about decisions, and anxiety about the changes in physical and cognitive abilities. Though not all changes during this stage have a negative impact on the individual, social workers must help the client during this adjustment period to minimize the suffering experienced by the client. Social workers can help these clients by aiding them in reevaluating their lives, by offering counseling and medication strategies, by helping their clients set new goals for the remaining years, and by encouraging them to pass their knowledge and wisdom on to the younger generation.

Brody and Brody (1987) say, "Probably no factor is of more immediate concern to older persons than physical health" (p. 99), and many fear the loss of individual, unaided activity or perceived independence (Bruce, 1998). The numerous chronic medical problems experienced by these clients complicates the course of mental health assessment and treatment, because many of these clients are already taking other prescribed medications for medical problems, which may adversely interact with psychotropic drugs. Social workers need to conduct a thorough assessment of past and present medical and mental health problems presented by these clients. Because of cognitive and psychological difficulties, many older clients are poor informants of vital information that would provide the helping professional with an accurate picture of the client's biopsychosocial functioning. In these cases, it is extremely important that social workers seek out other family members and support systems who can fill in the gaps. Whenever possible a home visit is recommended, which allows the client to show the social worker all the medications that have been or are being taken. Older clients often amass and hold on to large quantities of medications that have been prescribed, believing they are important or too expensive to throw away.

Prescribers must be sensitive to the developmental changes that affect the clients' understanding of and compliance with medication. For example, changes in vision may prevent the client's being able to read the directions or to identify correctly the different medications prescribed. In these cases it is helpful if the social worker advocates medications that are color coded, have large, easy-to-read directions, and that are placed in easily distinguished containers of different sizes. In addition, it is critical that all older individuals be able to open the bottles, especially ones that are designed to be child resistant.

In explaining psychotropic medications, social workers should take the time to illustrate how the medication works to alleviate the symptoms (sometimes graphic pictures are helpful) and have the client practice explaining the dosage and frequency (Kane, Ouslander, & Abrass, 1999).

Although they warn that there is no simple rule for prescribing medications to older people, Kane, Ouslander, and Abrass (1999) make the following observations:

1. There can be multiple factors that are age-related that can influence pharmacology.
2. The way individuals age and the changes they experience can be varied, thus making precise predictions with an elderly individual difficult.
3. The clinical (physical health) status of each client must be considered on an individual basis such as nutrition, hydration, cardiac output, intrinsic renal, and liver disease in addition to the effects of aging.
4. As research with the newer drugs continues, specific attention needs to be given to the results with older individuals and when this is done more specific recommendations can be made.

The mental disorders and psychotropic medications discussed in other chapters were not specific to older clients, yet many of the principles still apply. Social workers need to acknowledge the developmental changes manifested in the physical, cognitive, emotional, psychological, and social spheres of the client's functioning. A sound knowledge of adult development will enable the social worker to conduct an accurate assessment and provide valuable input regarding the types of mental health medications that may benefit the client best.

Knowing the hallmarks of development and assessing the client's situation can help the practitioner determine if psychopathology is actually present and if medications are needed. Keep in mind that many medical problems may mimic psychological or emotional difficulties. For example, when older clients have vision or hearing problems they might misinterpret information around them. If the professional does not carefully examine this misinterpretation of information, it can lead to a misunderstanding. In one such case an older woman reported to her daughter and physician that she was being watched daily by a stranger in her backyard, whom she feared was waiting for her to fall asleep so he could rob her. During the next visit to her primary care physician, she told him of her fears and asked if anything could be done to help her. The physician interpreted her statements as paranoia, especially after her daughter stated that she lived in a very safe neighborhood and doubted seriously that anyone was actually hanging around. The physician was prepared to prescribe a low dose of the psychotropic medication Haldol to help alleviate the feelings of paranoia. Fortunately, as part of an interdisciplinary approach, he notified the social worker who was assigned a home visit to assist with possible placement in supervised living. At the time of the visit, it appeared as if the woman had taken care to clean her house before the social worker's arrival, but there were crumbs and numerous small items on the floor and counters. During the interview it became obvious that the client's vision was impaired. She did not notice the crumbs that had fallen on the table while she was eating her lunch, and as she wiped the table with a cloth she simply sprinkled all of the crumbs to the floor. When asked about her last eye exam, she stated that it had been about ten years ago, and when asked if she wore glasses she said that she did when she was younger but had stopped wearing them when they broke years ago. The client spent a great deal of time sitting in a chair near the window, and the social worker asked her to sit in the chair and talk about the man who was watching her. Shortly after sitting down the client became quite flustered and said, "There he is, can you see him, he is watching us now. And look, I think there is someone with him." There was no one outside, but the reflection in the window did show two people standing there: the client and the social worker. It was easy to see how this client with limited vision could mistake the reflection for someone watching her. The social worker helped her to get an eye exam, and the client's ability to care for herself improved dramatically with the new glasses. She no longer reported that anyone was watching her, although she did hire someone to clean her windows. It was decided that she did not need supervised placement at this time and no medication was prescribed.

It is also essential to take the necessary steps to educate the older client on the medication regimen. Providing simple, clear, easy-to-read and easily followed directions will facilitate medication compliance among this population (Kane, Ouslander, & Abrass, 1999), because two thirds of adults over the age of 65 use one or more drugs daily and older adults use an average of three prescription and nonprescription drugs at a given time (Cohen, 2000). Although there is debate about whether this level of medication use is excessive, these prescribing trends appear strong. The use of multiple prescription and over-the-counter medications remains a significant problem (Larsen, 1999). Generally speaking, older individuals use more medications than younger ones because of the multiplicity of the acute and chronic conditions that seem to manifest as people get older (Willams, 1997). Whenever medication is given to older clients the well-known precaution "start low and go slow" should be applied (Cohen, 2000). When asked, many clients reveal long histories of adverse drug reactions. In patients age 60 and older, about half of all deaths are caused by some type of adverse drug reaction (Cohen, 2000; Larsen, 1999). This is generally related to the fact that older individuals often metabolize medications slower and it takes longer for medication to be metabolized by the liver and excreted by the kidneys. Knowing that lower than recommended doses can be effective, social workers can help clients encourage their physicians to provide more individualized care and attention. Older clients can also be educated to identify whether a medication is working, and when adverse reactions occur they can inform their physician. This type of education can facilitate medication compliance, assisting both the client and the intervention team.

Finally, the social work practitioner should educate clients and their families about the importance of combining psychosocial treatments such as counseling strategies with medication therapy. Families can also be instructed on the client's drug regimen and can assist with compliance and structure. Practitioners should not assume that the advanced age and developmental stage of the older client prohibits the use of counseling, in conjunction with medication therapy, to enhance the client's biopsychosocial functioning (Leon et al., 1999).

SPECIAL CONSIDERATIONS IN A CULTURALLY DIVERSE POPULATION

Social work practitioners encounter a wide range of ethnic and minority clients who present varied mental health problems and concerns. Although the authors cannot do justice to the unique characteristics, issues, and challenges that each of these groups present, it is important to ensure that practitioners are aware of the major considerations related to mental health practice with these populations. This section will sensitize the reader to some of these considerations and how they can affect the course of medication regimens in mental health practice. The authors strongly encourage the reader to seek out other information about additional considerations in the mental health treatment of minority clients. The *DSM-IV* cautions clinicians not to diagnose individuals without taking cultural considerations into account, and it provides information on culture-bound syndromes (American Psychiatric Association, 1994).

To further exemplify the importance of cultural diversity and minority concerns, Leon and Dziegielewski (1999) identify two culture-bound syndromes that are of particular importance when working with Hispanics. These two conditions are *ataque de nervios* (nerve attacks) (p. 847) and *susto* (fright or soul loss) (p. 848) and are listed as culture-bound syndromes in the *DSM-IV*. These conditions often exist within the culture and can resemble certain mental disorders but they may be interpreted as dysfunctional in mainstream society by the professional who is unaware (American Psychiatric Association, 1994). Yet these syndromes are not considered mental disorders (although they may resemble the signs and symptoms of certain mental disorders) and are commonly accepted among many Hispanic cultures.

Social workers and other mental health professionals are encouraged to become familiar with the culture-bound syndromes during the assessment and treatment process. Knowledge of these syndromes can prevent clients from being misdiagnosed and can help practitioners understand the role that culture plays in the client's manifestation of symptoms and behaviors.

The beliefs of individuals about the role of drug therapy in curing or controlling their disease or in promoting their health are intimately linked to their beliefs about disease causation (Eisenhauer, 1998).

While differences exist among minority clients, it is essential that social work practitioners integrate the following major points when working with all minority clients. First, an understanding, appreciation and assessment of cultural differences is required to enable mental health providers to develop culturally compatible services for a variety of clients (Gonzalez-Ramos, 1990; Rogler, 1989; Smart & Smart, 1995). Practitioners must learn about the client's cultural background and develop an understanding of how the client's unique value and belief systems shape who the client is, how emotional and psychological problems are manifested, and how the individual perceives mental health services. The minority client's perceptions, fears, and concerns about psychosocial and medication interventions will influence treatment compliance and ultimately determine treatment success. Professional helpers must be aware of a probable tendency to base their assessments on their own values, beliefs, societal biases, and stereotypes rather than on the client's (Boyd-Franklin, 1989; Dupper, 1992). Providing culturally sensitive practice utilizing a narrow cultural lens can result possibly in interpreting a minority client's traditions and problem-solving processes as abnormal or dysfunctional.

Second, social workers must recognize that many minority clients rely on informal systems that provide nontraditional therapeutic services. An example of this is the role of a spiritualist for Hispanic clients. The spiritualist listens, encourages ventilation, supports, and provides empathy while also providing specific rituals and herbal remedies to cure the emotional and psychological ills. For other minority groups such as African Americans, the church and clergy serve the same role as the spiritualist. Informal systems such as the spiritualist or the church serve important functions in providing emotional and psychological help to minority clients. It is imperative therefore that social work practitioners ask clients directly about other helping systems used to cope with mental health problems and find ways to integrate these systems into the client's treatment plan. For example, including a spiritualist or clergy person in the client's treatment plan may increase compliance with both psychosocial and drug interventions.

A third consideration when working with minority clients who seek mental health services requires that social workers become aware of the oppression that minority clients have encountered. Efforts should be made to understand how institutionalized oppression has affected the minority client's perception of helping professionals outside their culture or race, as well as the perception and the utilization patterns of mental health services (Lee, 1996). According to Lee (1996), this includes active discussions with the client on how oppressive factors have contributed to the client's current problems.

Finally, social workers should not take a cookie-cutter approach with all minority clients. The diverse range of minority clients and the regional differences that exist within larger ethnic minority groups requires that practitioners pay attention to the unique differences reflected by diversity in age, gender, region, education, and personal experiences. These variables account for distinctive differences between clients of the same minority group who on the surface appear to be similar but on closer examination have clear differences in their language, values, and belief systems. At no time has the statement "start where the client is" been more relevant than when addressing culturally sensitive practice in the field of social work.

For example, two Hispanics, one a Puerto Rican and another Mexican, will have different political and socioeconomic history, dialect, and belief systems. Acknowledging these differences allows the social work practitioner to examine carefully the applicability of current treatment models and determine if a relevant therapeutic framework is being used with minority clients. Rogler, Malgady, Costantino, and Blumenthal (1987) advocated culturally or ethnically sensitive services that include focused, therapeutic models and emphasize short-term problem-solving approaches when working with Hispanic clients. Many of these approaches are useful in helping Hispanic and other minority clients cope with the socio-environmental problems they encounter.

ASSESSMENT AND MEDICATIONS WITH MINORITY POPULATIONS

Yamamoto and Lin (1995) stress the importance of understanding the relationship between psychopharmacology and ethnic and cultural factors in the United States as it becomes increasingly diverse. Although there is a scarcity of literature on the influence of culture on psychopharmacological interventions, existing literature suggests that ethnicity may influence the metabolization of medications in some minority groups (Keltner & Folks, 1992). For example, Lin and colleagues (1986) identified that metabolizing rates are higher (32%) in Asians than in Whites and Blacks (9%). Studies have identified that Hispanic and African American clients on tricyclic antidepressants experience side effects before reaching full dosages of the medications, which implies that these groups may require lower dosages of the antidepressants (Marcos & Cancro, 1982; Rudorfer & Robins, 1982). Another medication that requires a change in dosage based on ethnicity is haloperidol (Haldol). Based on slower rates of metabolism, this neuroleptic used to treat anxiety should be given at one half to two thirds of the normal dosage when prescribed to Asian clients (Yamamoto & Lin, 1995). Similarly, higher levels of toxicity have been found in African

Americans prescribed lithium carbonate for treatment of bipolar disorders (Yamamoto & Lin, 1995).

Beyond the biological relationship between psychotropic medications, culture and rates of metabolism, social work practitioners need to be aware of how cultural differences may affect compliance with the medication regimen. Social work practitioners must acknowledge that for many minority clients such as Hispanics, Asians, and African Americans, the family unit is a strong influence and can reinforce or weaken compliance with psychosocial and medication interventions. It is important therefore that family members of minority clients be included in the treatment process and educated about the value of medication therapy. Another consideration when working with minority clients is understanding that for many of these clients, medication therapy and counseling may be perceived as signs of weakness and vulnerability. If viewed in this negative light, it may dissuade clients from taking medication or result in their discontinuing a medication regimen. Taking this potential resistance into account, it is essential that social workers explain the purpose of the medication and help the client to see how medication therapy can be integrated into the client's cultural context.

Compliance can become a more complicated issue when minority clients cannot see immediate results and when they are skeptical about the traditional form of intervention being used. The client may not think the medication is going to work in the first place, and the lack of quick reinforcement can become a reason for noncompliance or discontinuance. It is important at the beginning of treatment for practitioners to educate clients about the dosage patterns and the estimated length of time required for achieving effective therapeutic results. Some Hispanic and Asian clients defer to the medical authority figure and do not question the purpose, directions, or side effects of the medications. In these cases, the role of the social worker is to provide clients with the necessary medication information without devaluing the client's cultural beliefs. If a client is not comfortable asking questions of the provider, then clearly it can be the role of the social worker to empower clients to seek answers related to the medication regimen.

To best provide culturally sensitive practice to clients who are taking medications as part of the intervention process, social workers need to take the following steps.

The social worker needs to become familiar with the minority client's ethnic and cultural background. It is important to remember that even though a client may belong to a certain cultural group, there is variation within that group as well. Social workers should start all intervention efforts by taking into account "where the client is," always noting what the client wants, and recognizing that any intervention efforts are a reciprocal process where the client and social worker contribute to developing the goals and objectives for continued and lasting change.

Although the information is very limited, it is essential that social workers be aware of any studies that specifically target the minority group they are working with. While it is not known if there are differences in metabolism rates between men and women and among different people of color, little has been done to test medications of effectiveness and efficiency on these groups. Social workers clearly should advocate for more research in this area and report any side effects when working with these specific populations. Recording these events will bring more attention to these specific needs and encourage more systematized research to address potential problems.

The importance of the values and belief systems of the client should always be considered and addressed in all counseling and medication interventions. Clients who understand what they are taking and how it relates to their own health will be more likely to take the medication. Demonstrating respect for the client's beliefs and expectations is essential for creating an atmosphere of trust and encouraging continued compliance.

Include the client's family system as a way of increasing compliance with the medication regimen. The client's support system is very concerned about the client's welfare, and they also have a great deal of influence on what the client does and will continue to do. The best example of this is a client with diabetes whom one of the authors worked with. This Hispanic male had been given directions many times on how to take his insulin and what foods to avoid but repeatedly violated the dietary restrictions. In frustration his physician sent him to the social worker for counseling. During the first interview it became obvious that the client was indeed noncompliant with regard to his diet. When this was discussed with him he stated that he did not do the cooking, his wife did. When asked if she had ever seen the dietitian, he said no but that he had on five occasions. The importance of involving his wife in the dietary educational sessions was explained, and he agreed to invite her with him to meet the dietician. After this meeting the physician reported that the client had made remarkable progress in terms of his dietary restrictions. The client's wife also went to several of the sessions and reported to the physician that although she was "not perfect yet," she was working very hard at performing her duties in preparing her husband's diet.

Finally, the social worker must be aware of mental health diagnoses and how individuals from different races and cultures may not fit into a specific therapeutic mold, and that traditions and beliefs can be misinterpreted. As social workers, it is important to become more aware of cultural mores and expectations as well as the cultural influences that affect the diverse clientele that practitioners encounter. Social workers should be keenly aware that their own cultural beliefs can result in a client's being diagnosed incorrectly.

SUMMARY AND CONCLUSIONS

This chapter has provided an overview of several considerations for providing mental health services and especially medication therapy to children, older people, and culturally diverse clients. A brief discussion on the unique characteristics, challenges, and considerations when prescribing mental health medications has been provided. This chapter only begins to identify some of the salient considerations to motivate the reader to seek additional information on these special populations. Social work practitioners will discover that the developmental and cultural differences identified for each of the groups provide significant information for social workers who provide mental health counseling. Of equal importance is recognizing that social workers must be familiar with the special attributes of these three special populations in order to assess clients accurately, develop treatment plans, participate in medication recommendations, and help clients monitor the effects of prescribed drugs. This requires a sound knowledge of specific developmental characteristics and milestones when working with children and older clients and an understanding of ethnicity and culture when working with minority clients.

REFERENCES

Allian, H., Bentue-Ferrer, D., Gandon, J. M., LeDoze, F., & Belliard, S. (1997). Drugs used in Alzheimer's disease and neuroplasticity. *Clinical Therapeutics, 19*, 4–15.
American Association of Retired Persons. (1993). *Coping and caring: Living with Alzheimer's disease* [Brochure]. Washington, DC: Author.

American Psychiatric Association. (1994). *Diagnostic and statistical manual of mental disorders* (4th ed.). Washington, DC: American Psychiatric Press.

Anastopoulos, A. D. (1999). Attention-deficit/hyperactivity disorder. In S. D. Netherton, D. Holmes, & E. C. Walker (Eds.), *Child adolescent psychological disorders: A comprehensive textbook* (pp. 98–117). New York: Oxford University Press.

Apfeldorf, W., & Alexopoulos, G. (1999). Psychopharmacology and psychotherapy. In W. R. Hazzard, J. P. Blass, W. H. Etinger, J. B. Halter, & J. G. Ouslander (Eds.), *Principles of geriatric medicine and gerontology* (4th ed., pp. 1369–1378). New York: McGraw-Hill.

Baldessarini, R. J. (1990). Drugs and the treatment of psychiatric disorders. In A. Goodman Gilman, T. W. Rall, A. S. Nies, & P. Taylor (Eds.), *The pharmacological basis of therapeutics* (8th ed., pp. 383–435). New York: Pergamon Press.

Ban, T. A. (1987). Pharmacological perspectives in therapy of depression in the elderly. In G. L. Maddox & E. W. Busse (Eds.), *Aging: The universal experience* (pp. 127–131). New York: Springer Hill.

Barkley, R. A. (1990). *Attention deficit hyperactivity disorder: A handbook for diagnosis and treatment.* New York: Guilford Press.

Barkley, R. A., Conners, C. K., Barclay, A., Gadow, K., Gittelman, R., Sprague, R. L., & Swanson, J. (1990). Task Force report: The appropriate role of clinical child psychologists in the prescribing of psychoactive medication for children. *Journal of Clinical Child Psychology, 19(Suppl.),* 1–38.

Beaver, M. L., & Miller, D. A. (1992). *Clinical social work practice with the elderly.* Belmont, CA: Wadsworth.

Beck, J. C., Freedman, M. L., & Warshaw, G. A. (1994, February). Geriatric assessment: Focus on function. *Patient Care,* 10–32.

Belsky, J. (1988). *Here tomorrow: Making the most of life after fifty.* Baltimore: Johns Hopkins Press.

Blazer, D. G. (1999). Depression. In W. R. Hazzard, J. P. Blass, W. H. Etinger, J. B. Halter, & J. G. Ouslander (Eds.), *Principles of geriatric medicine and gerontology* (4th ed., pp. 1331–1400). New York: McGraw-Hill.

Boyd-Franklin, N. (1989). *Black families in therapy.* New York: Guilford Press.

Boyd-Webb, N. (1991). *Play therapy with children in crisis.* New York: Guilford Press.

Brody, E., & Brody, S. (1987). Aged. In A. Minaham (Ed.), *Encyclopedia of Social Work: 18th ed.* (pp. 106–126). Silver Spring, MD: NASW.

Bruce, D. G. (1998). Increasing frailty in the elderly patient: An approach to management. *Journal of Clinical Medicine, 41*(5), 41.

Butler, R. N., Lewis, M. I., & Sunderland, T. (1998). *Aging and mental health: Positive psychosocial and biomedical approaches.* Needham Heights, MA: Allyn & Bacon.

Canino, I., & Spurlock, J. (1994). *Culturally diverse children and adolescents: Assessment, diagnosis and treatment.* New York: Guilford Press.

Cohen, S. J. (2000). Avoiding adverse reactions—effective low dose drug therapies for older patients. *Geriatrics, 55*(2), 54.

Corvea, M. (1987, Fall). Senile dementia of the Alzheimer's type and multi-infarct dementia: A clinical comparison. Florida State University.

Crichton, J. (1987). *The age care source book: A resource guide for the aging and their families.* New York: Simon & Schuster.

Devore, W., & Schlesinger, E. G. (1999). *Ethnic-sensitive social work practice.* Needham Heights, MA: Allyn & Bacon.

Duke, W. M., Barton, L., & Wolf-Kleing, G. P. (1994). The chief complaint: Patient caregiver and physician's perspectives. *Clinical Gerontologist, 14*(4), 3–11.

Dulcan, M. K. (Ed.). (1999). *Helping parents, youth and teachers understand medications for behavioral and emotional problems: A resource book of medication information handouts.* Washington, DC: American Psychiatric Press.

Dupper, D. (1992). Separate schools for black males. *Social Work in Education, 14*(12), 75–76.

Dziegielewski, S. F. (1990). *The institutionalized dementia relative and the family member relationship.* Unpublished doctoral dissertation, Florida State University, Tallahassee.

Dziegielewski, S. F. (1991). Social groupwork with family members of elderly nursing home residents with dementia: A controlled evaluation. *Research on Social Work Practice, 1*, 358–370.

Dziegielewski, S. F., & Harrison, D. F. (1996). Counseling the aged. In D. F. Harrison, B. A. Thyer, & J. Wodarski (Eds.), *Cultural diversity in social work practice* (2nd ed.). Springfield, IL: Charles C Thomas.

Dziegielewski, S. F., Leon, A. M., & Green, C. E. (1998). African American children: A culturally sensitive model for group practice. *Early Child Development and Care, 147*, 83–97.

Eisenhauer, L. A. (1998). Psychosociocultural aspects of drug therapy. In L. A. Eisenhauer & M. A. Murphy (Eds.), *Psychosocial aspects of drug therapy* (pp. 37–52). New York: McGraw-Hill.

Goldman, S. M. (1998). Preface. In G. P. Koocher, J. C. Norcross, & S. Sam (Eds.), *Psychologists' desk reference.* New York: Oxford University Press.

Gonzalez-Ramos, G. (1990). Examining the myth of Hispanic families' resistance to treatment: Using the school as a site for services. *Social Work in Education, 12*, 261–274.

Harrison, D. F. (1988). The institutionalized mentally ill. In H. G. Gochros, J. S. Gochros, & J. Fischer (Eds.), *Helping the sexually oppressed* (pp. 191–209). Englewood Cliffs, NJ: Prentice-Hall.

Harper-Dorton, K. V., & Herbert, M. (1999). *Working with children and their families* (Rev. ed.). Chicago: Lyceum.

Johnson, R. (1998). Clinical assessment of ethnic minority children using the *DSM-IV*. In G. P. Koocher, J. C. Norcross, & S. Sam (Eds.), *Psychologists' desk reference* (pp. 103–108). New York: Oxford University Press.

Kane, R. L., Ouslander, J. G., & Abrass, I. B. (1999). *Essentials of clinical geriatrics* (4th ed.). New York: McGraw-Hill.

Kawas, C. H. (1999). Alzheimer's disease. In W. R. Hazzard, J. P. Blass, W. H. Etinger, J. B. Halter, & J. G. Ouslander (Eds.), *Principles of geriatric medicine and gerontology* (4th ed., pp. 1257–1269). New York: McGraw-Hill.

Keltner, N. L., & Folks, D. G. (1992). *Psychotropic drugs.* St. Louis: Mosby-Year Book, Inc.

Kent, J. D., Blader, J. C., Koplewicz, H. S., Abikoff, H., & Foley, C. A. (1995). Effects of late-afternoon methylphenidate administration on behavior and sleep in attention-deficit hyperactivity disorder. *Pediatrics, 96,* 320–325.

Kirst-Ashman, K. K. (2000). *Human behavior, communities, organizations and groups in the macro social environment.* Pacific Grove, CA: Brooks/Cole.

Kronenberger, W. G., & Meyer, R. G. (1996). *The child clinician's handbook.* Needham Heights, MA: Allyn & Bacon.

Kubiszyn, T. (1994). Pediatric psychopharmacology and prescription privileges: Implications and opportunities for school psychology. *School Psychology Quarterly, 9*(1), 26–40.

Larsen, P. D. (1999). Polypharmacy and elderly patients. *AORN Journal, 69*(3), 619.

Lee, J. A. B. (1996). The empowerment approach to social work practice. In F. J. Turner (Ed.), *Social work treatment: Interlocking theoretical approaches* (pp. 218–249). New York: The Free Press.

Leon, A. M., & Dziegielewski, S. F. (1999). The psychological impact of migration: Practice considerations in working with Hispanic women. *Journal of Social Work Practice, 13*(1), 69–82.

Leon, A. M., Altholz, J. A., & Dziegielewski, S. F. (1999). Compassion fatigue: considerations for working with the elderly, *Journal of Gerontological Social Work, 32*(1), 43–62.

Lyons, J. (2000, February). A call for outcomes data: Psychopharmacology with children. *Outcomes and Accountability Alert, 5*(2), 12.

Magnuson, T. M., Roccaforte, W. H., Wnegel, S. P., & Burke, W. J. (2000). Medication-induced dystonias in nine patients with dementia. *Journal of Neuropsychiatry, 12,* 219–225.

Maldanado, L. A. (1987). Mexican immigrants and Mexicans: An evolving relation. *Contemporary Sociology, 16,* 682–683.

Marcos, L., & Cancro, R. (1982). Pharmacotherapy of Hispanic depressed patients: Clinical observations. *American Journal of Psychotherapy, 36,* 505–512.

Marsiske, M., Franks, M. M., & Mast, B. T. (1998). Psychological perspectives on aging. In L. Morgan & S. Kunkel (Eds.), *Aging: The social context* (pp. 145–182). Thousand Oaks, CA: Pine Forge Press.

Maxmen, J. S., & Ward, N. G. (1995). *Essential psychopathology and its treatment* (2nd ed.). New York: W. W. Norton.

McAdoo, H. (1997). *Black families*. Thousand Oaks, CA: Sage.

McCullough, P. K., & Cody, S. (1993). Geriatric development. In F. S. Sierles (Ed.), *Behavioral science for medical students* (pp. 163–167). Baltimore: Williams & Wilkins.

Mosher-Ashley, P. M. (1994). Diagnoses assigned and issue brought up in therapy by older adults receiving outpatient treatment. *Clinical Gerontologist, 15*(2), 37–64.

Myers, W. C., Burket, R. C., & Otto, T. A. (1993). Conduct disorder and personality disorders in hospitalized adolescents. *Journal of Clinical Psychiatry, 54*, 21–26.

National Institute of Mental Health. (1990). *National plan for research on child and adolescent mental disorders* (DHHS Publication No. ADM 90-1683). Rockville, MD: Author.

Nordberg, A. (1996). Pharmacological of cognitive dysfunction in dementia disorders. *Acta Neurologica Scandanavia Supplementum, 168*, 87–92.

Nordenberg, T. (1999a). Pediatric drug studies: Protecting pint sized patients. *FDA, 33*(3), 23–28.

Nordenberg, T. (1999b). Protecting older patients. *FDA, 33*(3), 25.

Newman, B., & Newman, P. (1995). *Development through life: A psychosocial perspective*. Pacific Grove, CA: Brooks/Cole.

Perodeau, G. M., & du Font, G. G. (2000). Psychotropic drug use and the relation between social support, life events, and mental health in the elderly. *Journal of Applied Gerontology, 19*(1), 23–41.

Rabins, P. V. (1999). Miscellaneous psychiatric disorders. In W. R. Hazzard, J. P. Blass, W. H. Etinger, J. B. Halter, & J. G. Ouslander (Eds.), *Principles of geriatric medicine and gerontology* (4th ed., pp. 1365–1368). New York: McGraw-Hill.

Reynolds, C. F., Frank, E., Perel, J. M., & Miller, M. D. (1994). Treatment of consecutive episodes of major depression in the elderly. *American Journal of Psychiatry, 151*(12), 1740–1743.

Rhodes, C. (1988). *An introduction to gerontology: Aging in American society*. Springfield, IL: Charles C Thomas.

Roemmelt, A. F. (1998). *Haunted children: Rethinking medication of common psychological disorders*. Albany, NY: State University of New York Press.

Rogler, L. H., Malgady, R. G., Costantino, G., & Blumenthal, R. (1987). What do culturally sensitive mental health services mean? *American Psychologist, 42*, 565–570.

Rogler, L. H. (1989). The meaning of culturally sensitive research in mental health. *American Journal of Psychiatry, 146,* 296–570.

Rost, K., & Roter, D. (1987). Predictors of recall of medication regimen and recommendations for lifestyle change in elderly patients. *Gerontology, 27,* 510–515.

Rudorfer, M. V., & Robins, E. (1982). Amitriptyline overdose: Clinical effects on tricyclic antidepressant plasma levels. *Journal of Clinical Psychiatry, 43,* 457–460

Ruffolo, M. C. (1998). Mental health services for children and adolescents In Janet B. W. Williams & Kathleen Ell (Eds.), *Advances in mental health research: Implications for practice* (pp. 333–419). Washington, DC: NASW Press.

Rushton, J., Clark, S., & Reed, G. (2000, April). Primary care role in the management of childhood depression: A comparison of pediatricians and family physicians. *Pediatrics, 105,* 957–962.

Smart, J. F., & Smart, D. W., (1995). Acculturative stress of Hispanics: Loss and challenge. *Journal of Counseling and Development, 73,* 390–396.

Steuer, J., & Clark, E. (1982). Family support groups within a research project on dementia. *The Clinical Gerontologist, 1,* 87–95.

U.S. Senate Special Committee on Aging. (1981). *Development in aging: 1981 (vol. I).* Washington, DC: U.S. Government Printing Office.

Williams, R. D. (1997, September–October). Medications and older adults. *FDA Consumer,* 15–18.

Woolston, J. L. (1999). Combined psychopharmacotherapy: Pitfalls of treatment. *Journal of the American Academy of Child and Adolescent Psychiatry, 38*(11), 1455.

Yamamoto, J., & Lin, K. (1995). Psychopharmacology, ethnicity, and culture. *American Psychiatric Press Review of Psychiatry, 14,* 529–541.

CHAPTER 9

Complementary Medications, Herbal Healing: An Introduction for Social Work Professionals

There has been a pronounced movement toward taking charge of one's own physical and mental health. The underlying premise in accepting this responsibility is that good health now involves not only promoting but also maintaining wellness.

Use of plants and herbs in particular constitutes an ancient form of medicine that has been practiced for thousands of years. Many individuals use herbs, vitamins, minerals, and the new so-called functional foods to enhance and support their well-being. It is difficult not to be influenced by these products, which have become a multibillion-dollar industry that continues to grow at an unprecedented rate (Tyler, 2000). This blossoming market has attracted national attention, and Americans have joined the people of many other countries to make alternative or herbal strategies the medicine of choice for at least 70% of the world's population (Goeddeke-Merickel, 1998a, 1998b, 1998c).

One of the biggest concerns facing social workers who accept and support these types of medicines is the client's assumption that herbals are natural and therefore must be safe. Yet considering their long history and tradition as medicinal remedies, it is surprising that so little research has been done to quantify their effectiveness.

Most people do not realize that many prescription medications are created from similar ingredients and that approximately 25% of all drugs used today are derived from herbs (Greenwald, 1998). Furthermore, many prescription and OTC medications adapt and freely utilize a herbal base in their composition. Aspirin is derived from the bark of the white willow tree, and there is a cancer treatment medication known as Taxol that comes directly from the Pacific yew tree. Yet, while aspirin is a powerful medication derived from herbal products to relieve pain and inflammation, it can also have numerous interaction effects. The belief that a remedy is harmless because it comes from a plant or tree may lull consumers into thinking that these ingredients are completely safe, regardless of other medications they may be taking.

The worst-case scenario of combining herbal remedies and prescription medicines deserves some attention, because of serious toxic results that might present severe health risks for clients. Most people are not aware that although herbal medicines and traditional medicines can be beneficial at one dose, the same medications can be toxic at another (Henkel, 2000). Fugh-Berman (2000) reports that the consumer must be aware of interaction effects between herbs and drugs that can result in increased toxic or pharmacological effects in either component. It is possible that complementary medicines of all types not only supplement the effects of medication, but can also augment the negative effects of medications, which could result in toxic reactions. For example, drinking grapefruit juice seems safe enough but when someone is receiving dialysis treatments, it appears that drinking grapefruit juice can prohibit the absorption of medications (Goeddeke-Merickel, 1998a, 1998b).

The implications of the "natural is safe" assumption requires further exploration and study because clients may be unaware that they are taking preparations that can create problems when combined with prescription drugs. Furthermore, mixing herbal remedies and prescription medicine does not always have a negative outcome: At times these mixtures can result in positive combinations that complement the other medications being taken. But because it is possible for these complementary medications to supplement, interact, or augment the negative or positive effects of medications, caution should be taken when using herbal and natural products.

CASE EXAMPLE: USING A NATURAL REMEDY

JoLee was a 52-year-old graduate-level accountant who reported that she had suffered from depression for approximately the past 10 years. Upon arriving for her third session with the social worker, JoLee stated that she was very excited because she had found the answer to all her depression problems. JoLee proceeded to thank the social worker for her time, saying that she was ready to try a new and different approach to life. In an excited voice she told the social worker how thrilled she was about her recent discovery. She was convinced after sharing the news of her discovery that the social worker would also want to immediately purchase the product.

In the assessment phase, it became obvious that JoLee had a history of depressive episodes. These episodes began approximately 10 years earlier, after she divorced her husband. Although the episodes were recurring, each episode was associated directly to situations or events that directly disturbed her usual levels of interaction. For example, JoLee reported that she felt as if the "rug had been pulled from under" her after the divorce, and these negative feelings returned each time she was forced to interact with her ex-husband and his new wife. JoLee was devastated by the ending of her 15-year marriage and humiliated by the fact that her husband married a woman more than half JoLee's age. In the initial interview JoLee was in tears, stating that the woman her ex-husband married was only 2 years older than her oldest child. She was often frustrated and embarrassed when she was forced to act cordial toward her husband's new wife at family functions. During the first two sessions JoLee was able to express her anger, and progress was noted. JoLee stated that with the help of counseling she was now aware that she had never allowed herself to get over the divorce and disruption it had caused.

Immediately after the divorce JoLee's physician prescribed an antide-pressant and later an antianxiety medication to help her cope. She stated that she liked the medications because they always made her feel "a little numb" and that when she felt that way nothing really mattered or affected her. Initially JoLee stated that she was content with her life, and it was her daughter's insistence that persuaded her to seek counseling. Her daugh-ter was concerned that JoLee had few friends, very few outside interests, and she was concerned because her mother had been taking prescription medication for depression and anxiety for the past 10 years. JoLee agreed with her daughter and after stopping both her antidepressant and anxiety medication decided that she had better give counseling a try. During the first few sessions, an intervention plan and contract were established, which involved JoLee's contracting to do some outside activities and to see her physician for a physical and reevaluation of her need for medication.

Now on the third visit with the intervention progressing well, the social worker was shocked by JoLee's announcement. JoLee was convinced that her recent discovery of a natural product provided a better, effortless plan in which her body would be able to self-heal naturally. JoLee stated that she had come across the literature about SAM-e, a new natural remedy her friend was taking. According to JoLee, her friend had been depressed for a very long time and was feeling "better than ever." Based on how well it worked for her friend, JoLee was eager and willing to give it a try. She said she had been taking it for more than a week and could already feel the natural results of a subsequent lift in energy.

When the social worker asked her about information on the effectiveness of the product she was taking, JoLee was quick to report that SAM-e had clearly helped millions of individuals to fight off feelings of depression. She shared the advertisement and research information she had received with the social worker. Upon reviewing the literature, the social worker agreed that there were indeed numerous research studies that had been conducted on the effectiveness of the product. Unfortunately, however, all of the reported studies had been conducted in Europe and other foreign countries. The social worker had received research training in her graduate program and knew that foreign medical trials did not have nearly the same scientific rigor as those in the United States. The social worker pointed this out to JoLee whose reply was "Research is research, isn't it?" The social worker clarified that research conducted in other countries is not subject to the tight limitations enforced by the U.S. Food and Drug Administration (FDA). The lack of regulation elsewhere allows clinical trials to be less rigorous with limited monitoring and is probably one of the biggest criticisms of complementary medicine.

The article JoLee was reading also warned about the lack of governmental regulation of SAM-e and said it was essential to ensure that active ingredients were present in the product. Consequently, without a clear reason and depending on the manufacturer, cost varied significantly from approximately $2.50 a dose to $18.00. Due to the expense and the fact that it was not covered by insurance, JoLee chose one of the least expensive brands. The social worker was concerned because the literature clearly stated that the natural medicine was broken down primarily in the intestines, so coated medications were needed to protect against partial digestion in the stomach. The brand of SAM-e JoLee selected had no protective coating, which is a cost-cutting method used by many manufacturers. There was also no expiration date stamped on the container, making it impossible to determine the shelf life of the product, whereas federally regulated products require an expiration date. Given the current lack of standardization, the most helpful advice the social worker could give JoLee was to avoid using imported products because some of these products have been shown to contain lead and other toxic materials. The literature pointed out that this natural remedy would probably not help you if you were not depressed. Since the social worker herself had no history of depression, she found it interesting that the client initially had suggested that she also take it.

In the last line of the article it stated that "many of us could arm ourselves against low moods, bad joints and weak hearts simply by upping our intake of B vitamins . . . that may sound less exciting than taking a miracle supplement . . . but with luck . . . it could keep you from ever needing one" ("St. John's Wort and SAME-e," 2000, p. 50). This statement implied that the supplement being promoted was no more effective then simply increasing the intake of the B vitamins. The social worker recommended that the client speak to a physician about her choice of a natural remedy because it really was not well tested or proven for effectiveness. In addition, the social worker suggested that JoLee reconsider returning to the behavioral contract whether she continued to take the herbal medicine or not. Despite her current upbeat mood, there were still many issues that needed to be addressed therapeutically.

CHOOSING MEDICAL TREATMENTS

Medical treatments in this country are varied and can range from home remedies shared among family and friends to medications that are prescribed by a physician. Basically, there are four primary approaches to the delivery of medical care: traditional mainstream medicine, complementary medicine, alternative medicine, and integrative medicine.

Broad Categories of Medical Care Approaches and Intervention

1. **Traditional medicine:** Standard drug therapies and surgical interventions
2. **Complementary medicine:** Mind and body interactions such as traditional medicine, meditation, and yoga
3. **Alternative medicine:** mind and body therapeutic touch (e.g., acupressure), chiropractic approaches, and herbal and natural remedies
4. **Integrative medicine:** using complementary and alternate therapies

TRADITIONAL MAINSTREAM MEDICINE

Historically, in this country, traditional interventions generally involve standard drug therapies and surgical interventions. This type of traditional mainstream medicine, and the practices that reflect it clearly require the skill of a trained professional. Traditional medicine is frequently referred to as mainstream American medical practice. Today the majority of medical physicians in this country share this philosophical approach to medicine and their primary training is in this area. It is believed that this type of training can create bias in the health care provider, discouraging him or her from approving of and using nonmainstream practices. Clients may sense this reluctance and may not want to tell the provider about the herbal or nontraditional treatments they are utilizing. These individuals may fear that the health care provider will not support the treatment, so they avoid discussing it. Clients may also believe that the health care provider doesn't know enough about these alternative treatments and therefore could not assist properly in identifying the client's individual needs.

Although there may be multiple reasons for using supplemental treat-ments to traditional medicine, the trend to supplement medical care with herbal treatments, products, and services is a significant one. All practicing social workers (these authors included) are well aware of how many clients are now actively using complementary approaches to medicine and steering away from solely traditional methods. The most common reason cited for this increased attention is that conventional medicine and practice ignores the human side of medicine. Managed care has empha-sized rapid assessment, rapid treatment, and less input from the client about his or her care. Consequently, clients are identifying other ways to prevent diseases, which has influenced the use of traditional medical regimens. Conventional methods have often come under attack for being too invasive. For example, heart disease has been conventionally treated through surgery, yet this intervention entails the risk of stroke or heart attack. Because the complications can be so serious, many are electing not to have this invasive procedure. Rather, they are choosing alternative treatments that are clearly less invasive such as low-fat and vegetarian diets, stress management, moderate exercise, and group counseling (Good-man, 2000; McCall, 1998). In some cases, it appears that these methods work as effectively and provide reasonable alternatives to the more inva-sive state-of-the-art surgical procedure.

Many people with chronic conditions realize there will not be a quick cure and are eagerly seeking ways to better address their needs while maintaining continued comfort. Since chronic conditions are painful, re-curring, and long lasting, the desire to avoid pain puts clients who suffer from chronic and complicated conditions in a vulnerable position. They tend to become the prime targets of fraudulent claims and products that promise a quick and easy cure.

Professionals who practice medicine—whether they specialize in tradi-tional approaches or newer, holistic methods—would agree that when traditional medical interventions have been proven to work, it is best to use them (Zahourek, 1999). For example, conventional therapies can yield an 80% cure rate in childhood leukemia; therefore, it seems unreasonable to switch to something that is not considered to have as a good chance of success. Generally, this is not the type of client who will leave traditional medicine, but rather the person who suffers from a complicated or chronic condition. These individuals are tired of receiving minimal relief and want new and different "get-and-stay-well" approaches. For so many people, the thought of being pain free or symptom free is so seductive that they will drop the more conventional therapies and give it a try as a means to address what ails them.

COMPLEMENTARY MEDICINE

A second type of medicine practiced in this country is referred to as complementary medicine. In this approach to medical care, clients generally receive traditional adjuncts to therapy such as prescription medications, which are often complemented by noninvasive approaches that use the mind-body interaction (Cheng, 1995). Strategies like those described in chapter 6 for anxiety that involve deep breathing, meditation exercises, yoga, and other means of relaxing are frequently used.

ALTERNATIVE MEDICINE

A third approach to medical care that has recently gained significantly in popularity is alternative medicine and the alternative approaches. These are varied but frequently involve such techniques as touch therapy and massage (acupressure), chiropractic, magnets, herbals, and naturopathic remedies. Herbal preparations and spiritual healing are also used that allow for mind and body control.

Despite the controversy and the reluctance of those from the traditionalist perspective, the use of these alternative herbal medicinal preparations continues to grow. In the past, modern medicine has referred to herbal preparations and natural remedies with disdain, believing that these methods were quackery, and these alternative practice were not considered threatening to mainstream medical practice because they had little if any scientific basis to support their use. With the subsequent shifts to avoid the traditional medical model, many other avenues are now being viewed as reasonable alternatives. People want control of their lives and in many cases want to take an active role in securing what is good for their individual sense of well being. Clients are saying, "I want more than management of my symptoms. I want someone to care about me and to look at me as an individual and to realize that I have unique needs." The traditional more aggressive therapies are being avoided and gentler, more user-friendly alternatives are being sought. Of concern to many individuals is the fact that although tighter controls on prescription medications have been implemented for more than 50 years, there are still serious side effects and unusual interaction effects that many clients would prefer to avoid. These consumers want to try a more natural substitute. Today well over 60 million Americans actively use alternative practices as part of their medical regimens and many people consider alternative medicine as the intervention of choice.

Touch Therapy and Massage

When describing touch therapy and massage, it can be broken down into several distinct types. Acupressure is generally considered the most common form of touch therapy. Shiatsu is a very old form of massage that applies pressure to various key points on the body. Many clients become confused about the difference between acupuncture and acupressure. In acupressure the fingers rather than needles are used to apply pressure. Obviously it is beyond the scope of this chapter to introduce all the techniques of acupressure and massage. For more detailed information on how to secure resources for clients who wish to apply these techniques see *The Prevention How-To Dictionary of Healing Remedies and Techniques* (1996) edited by John Feltman. Although it has been shown that touch therapy can help to fight disease and it is frequently accepted as an adjunct to traditional medical approaches, the provider should be licensed or certified to perform it. Licensing or certification can be verified by placing a call to the National Certification Board for Therapeutic Massage and Body Work at (800) 296-0664. All social workers should recommend that clients consult a physician or have a physical exam prior to beginning any type of alternative practice or exercise routine. These treatments can be helpful in making clients feel that they are participating in maintaining efforts toward continued health and wellness.

Several different types of acupressure include:

- Do-In: A system of stretches, breathing, and acupressure techniques that is easy to learn. It involves exercises that can be done every day by clients for a type of acupressure workout.

- Acu-yoga: This approach uses yoga postures to increase an individual's ability to apply pressure with the fingertips as in traditional acupressure. The yoga position allows the individual to use concentrated pressure to designated areas.
- Jun Shin Jyutsu: This form of self-help allows for gentle cradling of the body rather than massage-like movements.
- Shiatsu: In Japanese the word Shiatsu means finger pressure. In this most common form of acupressure, there is rhythmic pressure on acupressure points for periods up to 10 seconds. The thumb is used because it provides the greatest pressure.
- Zen Shiatsu: Zen is a form of Buddhism that originated in Japan and often involves repeated daily exercises that could result in hours of meditation per day. Zen Shiatsu is also strenuous and adds yogalike stretches while striving to achieve an overall balancing of the body. *Information taken from Chen (September 1999) "An Alternative Way to Ease Pain" in *Health.*

Chiropractic Medicine

Chiropractic medicine is an alternative practice geared toward musculoskeletal problems that are generally related to the neck and upper and lower back. Generally, chiropractors use a wide variety of techniques that align the spine and are designed to alleviate pain and disease. Although the literature is lacking on research to support the technique as a cure for disease, it does seem to be very beneficial in treating lower back pain (Goeddeke-Merickel, 1998a; McCall, 1998). It is important to remember that a chiropractor is not considered qualified to diagnose many medical conditions, and a misdiagnosis or delay in achieving a proper diagnosis could be particularly problematic. Clients seeking this type of intervention should call the American Chiropractic Association at (703) 276-8800.

Magnets

Many individuals claim that magnet therapy can cure or alleviate their aches and pains. The process can be linked to Chinese healers as far back as 2000 B.C. and entails physically attaching a magnet to the problem area or directly on it. It is believed that the magnets correct unhealthy flow in the body and balance *chi* or energy. Studies appear fruitful and magnets offer promise particularly for those who suffer from chronic pain.

In a recent study, Collacott (2000) examined 20 patients, breaking the sample into two groups of individuals with long and extensive histories of chronic lower back pain. One group was treated with bipolar permanent magnets, and the control group was treated with a placebo device. The double-blind study was conducted in 1998 and 1999 and ran for 15 months with individuals from both groups alternating one week with the device and one week without it. At the end of 15 months, the data analysis showed no cumulative treatment differences in either group, and those who used the device reported treatment gains similar to those who did not. Although this is considered a pilot study because the sample size is so small, more studies are needed in this area. Future studies need to take into account the various magnetic strengths being used as well as the placement of the magnets and duration. The market is being targeted by a media storm that promotes the sale of permanent magnets for treatment, and once again it is a case of "buyer beware" as the research remains limited to support the effectiveness of this method. Even though research to validate the use of magnet therapy is limited, $5 billion in sales worldwide have made this a large and profitable industry (Collacott, 2000).

When working with clients who have chosen to use magnets as a mode of treatment, it is important that they be aware of the tendency of manufacturers to make unrealistic claims about the benefits of magnet use while convincing consumers to buy an overpriced product. Beware of advertisements for magnets that claim they can cure arthritis or restore sexual vigor because there is little, if any, formal research to support such claims. According to the physicist James Livingston, "If magnets truly can lessen pain, a strong refrigerator version ought to work . . . try one that can move a paper clip from half an inch away" (cited in Cheng, 1999, p. 64).

HERBAL AND NATURAL REMEDIES

It has become apparent to many social workers that clients are starting to rely on herbal medications and preparations in order to obtain an increased sense of control over their physical and mental health and wellness. At a recent workshop, it was obvious to these authors just how much interest there was in learning more in this area. The workshop was scheduled for 7:30 A.M. and was titled "Herbal Medications and Social Work Practice." It was held at a state conference sponsored by the National

Association of Social Workers in spring of 1999. Because the workshop was scheduled early in the morning and attendance was optional, few participants were expected, and only 30 handouts were prepared for distribution. Can you imagine the presenters surprise when the room filled to standing room only with more than 200 hundred individuals? Although many questions centered on client issues, other questions during the workshop focused on the herbal remedies that the social work professionals were taking. The consensus was that although many things were unknown about these preparations, many of their clients relied heavily on their use. After the presentation, many of the participants commented on their lack of knowledge regarding the interpretation and identification of possible prescription, OTC, and drug–herb interactions. Extensive concern was apparent over the lack of controlled information and testing with regard to herbal preparations, especially with the increase in the number of clients that were actively using these preparations.

LACK OF STANDARDIZED TESTING

For the most part herbal medicines are derived from plants, leaves, roots and flowers. There are well over 600 medicinal herbs available to the consumer (*Physicians' Desk Reference for Herbal Medications,* 2000) without much regulated and standardized testing to clearly establish their effectiveness. Table 9.1 lists many popular herbal medicines. In the United States, the Dietary Supplement Health and Education Act of 1994 (DSHEA) allows herbs to be sold legally as long as they make no claims for disease treatment on the label (Kroll, 1997). For example, Saint-John's-wort, a very popular product used primarily for the treatment of depression, states in ambiguous terms that it is used "for mental well being" or "to improve mental health." Because of an upsurge in interest in the 1990s, herbal medications have drawn the attention of the FDA. It probably won't be long before herbal preparations are regulated like their prescription counterparts to ensure efficiency and effectiveness for the conditions they purport to address. The need for more controlled studies has been recognized in the United States and will continue to increase (Bender, 1996).

Today the herbal industry is a booming one with few if any government requirements. Due to the competition in the herbal market, manufacturers are coming out with herbal combinations to prevent rival manufacturers from duplicating their product. According to Professor Varro E. Tyler

TABLE 9.1   Popular Herbal Medicines

**Black pepper: (Piper nigrum extract) reportedly enhances absorption and increases blood levels of nutrients and medications

Capsicum: (dried ripe fruit [cayenne]) muscle spasms, arthritis, topical shingles (decreases itching)

Cascara: (dried bark) constipation

Chaste tree berry: (fruit of the Vitex angus-castus) premenstrual syndrome

Dong quai: (dried root) menopausal symptoms, premenstrual syndrome

Echinacea: (purple coneflower) immune system booster, topical, preventative

Feverfew: (dried leaves) migraines

*Garlic: (fresh dried bulb) cholesterol

Ginger: (fresh dried root [rhizome]) nausea and vomiting, digestive aid, used in chemotherapy

Ginkgo: (dried extract from dried leaves) short-term memory, concentration

Ginseng: (fresh, dried root) fatigue, stress

Goldenseal: (dried root [rhizome]) upper respiratory, cold and flu

Gotu kola: (dried above ground plant parts) memory, concentration

Green tea: (steamed, dried fresh leaves) cancer, hypertension, dental caries

Guarana: (dried crushed seed paste, plant parts) high caffeine content, considered a "cerebral stimulant"

**Jiaogulan: (Gynostemma pentaphyllum, China's "immortality" herb) used as a tonic and antioxidant

Kava: (dried root [rhizome]), anxiety, stress, sleep enhancement

**Maca: (Lepidium pervianum tonic) impotence, menopausal symptoms

**Puncture vine: (Tribulus terrestris, common American weed) reportedly increases testosterone levels

Saint-John's-wort: (dried above-ground plant parts) mild depression

Valerian: (fresh underground plant parts) sleep disorders

---

*The reader is referred to an article in the Mayo Clinic Health Letter (1998) that evaluates garlic and its numerous and complicated effects on the body.

**These are new herbs that were introduced at the Herbal Conference of Botanicals in Amsterdam in 1999 (as cited in Tyler, 2000).

from the Purdue School of Pharmacy, competition has caused two problems (cited in Tyler, 2000). First, the market is being inundated with combination herbal products. The combination of these products is not always necessary and can lead to the second problem: confusion about what combination is best and why. It is important for clients and social workers and other professionals to understand that many of these multiple herbal preparations have not been tested as such. Because of this lack of formalized testing, it is not clear what each product contributes and whether the combination of ingredients is as beneficial as advertised. Without quality standards to monitor the production of herbal medicinal products, it is impossible to tell why an herb does or does not do what is expected. The product's failure to provide relief may not be directly related to the use of the herb, but rather to a poor manufacturing process (Tyler, 2000).

Most of the herbal products are exempt from federal regulation because they are not considered medications. Advertising a product as a medication allows the FDA to monitor and evaluate its production, and in order to avoid this regulation many of the manufacturers are careful to refer to their herbal products as dietary supplements. Unfortunately, avoiding government regulation can lead to confusion and misinformation (Reaves, 2000). And because there are no requirements for product standardization, there are no assurances that the product's ingredients are active. No professional regulating body is examining these preparations in terms of bioavailability and efficacy; nor is any testing required in terms of combining herbal preparations with OTC and prescription drugs. Based on limited monitoring and regulation it is clear the consumer *must* beware.

Furthermore, pharmaceutical companies are making big profits producing and selling these preparations. To prevent increased competition from the herbal manufacturers, prescription and OTC manufacturers can encourage roadblocks to prevent competition from the herbal manufacturers. For example, if a dietary supplement such as the red yeast that is grown in China could actually reduce cholesterol, it would capture interest and market shares from the current available prescription medications (Barrett, 1998). Traditional manufacturers have begun to feel this pressure. Herbal remedies have begun to compete for the market consumer who previously only took the prescription drugs. This competition with prescription drug manufacturers could discourage the introduction of new herbal products. Thereby prohibiting the initiation of the expensive and time-consuming testing that would be required in order for an herbal preparation to be recognized for its medicinal purposes in the United States.

Probably the single largest concern for social workers whose clients are taking these preparations is the lack of formal regulation. Although many people don't like the ideal of regulation of any kind, it is critical when dealing with herbal products to ensure that adequate controls are implemented to decrease the possibility of toxic reactions that can happen in a nonregulated environment. Because these products are referred to regularly as dietary supplements they are shielded from government oversight, and very little premarket testing is conducted. Most of the testing that is used to support a medication's efficacy is conducted at the time of the introduction of the brand name product; a generic medication requires little if any additional testing. Once created, a generic medicine does not have the same stringent rules for testing, because it is believed to have undergone adequate controlled testing when the brand-name medication was tested and marketed.

Keep in mind the reservations that many professionals express over the lack of standardized and uniformed testing on generic medications and apply this context to the herbal preparation. Imagine the creation of an herbal preparation that has many of the same essential ingredients as a brand name prescription medication yet little standardized testing will ever be conducted. Confound this process further with nonstandardized regulation and limited batch testing with almost no assurances that the product contains fresh, active ingredients. If there are negative effects from using the preparation, they will not be discovered until well after the product is on the market and numerous individuals have used it. The lack of clear rules to ensure standardization allows for variation in each product, and the reactions clients experience can be quite diverse. Furthermore, without controlled studies there is no way to know who is taking the medicine, what the relative potency is, and without a professional evaluation, whether the client has the problem that the herbal remedy is designed to help.

Because many of the herbal products undergo limited testing, there are no direct links to safety and efficacy. To avoid legal penalties it is common for herbal and natural product manufacturers to use vague terminology such as "supports body function" or "safely balances emotions." What do these descriptions actually mean?

Lack of regulation can also lead to limited standardization in terms of harvesting, processing, and packaging. The increase in the popularity of supplements has put pressure on manufacturers to increase the supply of their herbal extracts, which according to the *Manufacturing Chemist* means that "the producer has verified that the active ingredient in the herb is present in the preparation and that the potency and the amount of the active ingredient is assured" ("Herbal Drugs: Medicines or Food Supplements," p. 1). Ensuring that the ingredients are active is essential for effective quality and ensuring that they stay active is just as important. For example, when baking bread from scratch, if the yeast is not active the bread will not rise. Applying the same principle to herbal preparations, if the ingredients are not active you will not get the same results. Without regulation there is no obligation to ensure that a product is fresh or that the packaging is sufficient to maintain the active ingredients at a therapeutic level (Kroll, 1997). This can be a particular problem when substances are brought in bulk or remain in stores for an extended period of time.

The lack of regulation also can lead to products of poor quality. It has been documented in several case studies (LaPuma, 1999) and reported by the FDA that in the past some imported herbal products have been known to contain by-products or trace metals that can prove harmful when ingested. Ingesting lead, for example, could clearly lead to lead poisoning or toxic reactions that might not be traced easily to the herbal product that introduced it. In monitoring minimal levels, the FDA has already established harmful links to products such as ephedra, comfrey, chaparral, licorice, pennyroyal, sassafras, and senna, just to name a few. To investigate further the efficacy of herbal products, American Chemical Society researchers found that variations existed in Gingko biloba herbal products. On the United States market, the products that these researchers tested "contained only trace amounts of active ingredients—ginkolides and bilobalide—and the rest was made up of other compounds (*Manufacturing Chemist*, 2000, p. 2). Clearly, the consumers of these products need to be aware of the efficacy and potential adverse effects associated with the use of herbals, as well as the fact that the labels may not accurately reflect the true contents.

As interest of herbal products continues to grow, so do reports of fraudulent health-care claims. Consumers want so much to find a cure for what ails them or improve their well being that they may be taken in by magazine ads and TV infomercials. The FDA describes health fraud as "articles of unproven effectiveness that are promoted to improve health, well being, or appearance, and these articles can be drugs, devices, foods, or cosmetics for human or animal use" (Kurtzweil, 1999, p. 22). Social workers need to help clients be objective consumers. According to Kurtzweil (1999) special attention should be paid to any advertising that makes the following claims or uses certain strategies:

1. *This product can do it all.* Encourage clients to be suspicious of products that claim to cure a wide range of unrelated health conditions, particularly serious conditions such as cancer and diabetes. Unfortunately, there are no cures for most diseases and medical conditions, only treatments and interventions that can help manage symptoms. Individuals with cancer, AIDS, diabetes, or other serious diseases are easy targets, because of the devastating nature of their condition.

This product is . . . extremely beneficial in the treatment of cancer . . . heart trouble, diabetes, and more . . .

2. *This product is a quick fix.* Social workers should discourage clients from believing product promotions that suggest a quick or immediate cure for potentially serious disease or illness (Cerrato, 2000). Even with traditional and other proven treatments, few diseases or conditions can be addressed that quickly. If the product promoter uses ambiguous language to describe their treatment, they are less likely to be held accountable by legal action.

. . . eliminates skin cancer in days.

3. *"My husband tried the product and now in just 22 days he is mowing the grass . . . he is more like himself again."* A product that uses personal testimonials to proclaim the effectiveness of the product is probably the weakest type of advertising, with little evidence of scientific validity. Whether the testimonies are real or fraudulent, desperate individuals may magnify their impression of the product's benefit, or the disease may go into remission on its own, leading them to believe a cure has been effected.

4. *This product is simple and natural.* The term natural is often used fraudulently to catch the reader's attention. There are many natural substances that can be grown quite simply and ingested yet are deadly. As mentioned repeatedly in this chapter, if something is potent enough to have an effect and work like a drug, it is certainly strong enough to cause side effects.

This product provides a simple, natural way to . . .

5. *Satisfaction guaranteed.* Product manufacturers promise your money back, no questions asked, and if it sounds too good to be true because it probably is. If a product is fraudulent the manufacturers will not stay in business or in the same location for very long, and many people cannot get their money back when they try.

Guarantee: If after thirty days . . . your money will be returned to you in full with no questions asked.

6. *Time tested newfound treatment.* Beware of product claims for a new, unprecedented discovery or miracle cure. If it were so, it would be well reported in the media and would be the topic of scientific discussion.

This revolutionary innovation can make a difference because it is based on 200 years of medical science.

7. *Meaningless medical jargon is designed to fool the consumer.* Many claims and scientific terms may sound impressive but usually mean nothing. The FDA warns that many times scientific terms are removed from articles in scientific journals but if consumers were to check the term they would find it has nothing to do with the claim the product is making.

Hunger stimulation point (HSP) . . .
Thermogenesis, which converts stored fats into soluble lipids . . .

8. *Paranoid accusations* convince people to buy a product by suggesting that "health care providers and legitimate manufacturers are in cahoots with each other promoting only the drug companies' and medical-device manufacturers' products for financial gain" (Kurtweil, 1999, p. 23).

It seems these million dollar companies all have one relentless competitor in common as they all fear natural remedies.

A NATURAL SUPPLEMENT

Earlier in this chapter we presented a case where a client was excited about her use of a naturally occurring substance called SAM-e. The way this natural product is processed in the body is worth discussing because it presents an unusual perspective of how natural remedies can be created and utilized to support functions that already exist in the body. SAM-e (known formally as S-adenosylmethionine) is not an herb or a naturally occurring hormone. It is a molecule that is present in all living cells. Our bodies produce it on a regular basis when they are functioning in a healthy state. This molecule is important in a process known as methylating where molecules are combined and both the donor and the recipient change in the process (St. Johns Wort and SAM-e: The mood menders, 2000). It is believed that this necessary function affects everything from fetal development to brain function. Among other things, it helps to regulate the actions of various hormones and neurotransmitters, including those related to mental health and alertness such as serotonin, dopamine, and adrenaline. It also has been noted to assist in arthritis and liver disease (Gower, 2000). Although there are many different methyl donors that create the catalysts, SAM-e is considered the most potent, but as we get older SAM-e levels decrease. (Children have about seven times the level of SAM-e that adults do.) As we continue to age, our bodies make this molecule naturally from methionine, an amino acid found in protein-rich foods. Once SAM-e loses its methyl grouping, it will break down to form homocysteine, which can be very toxic if it accumulates in the cells. With the help of the B vitamins (B_6, B_{12}, and folic acid) this eventually converts back into methionine. Keeping the body well nourished in terms of the elements it needs to create SAM-e is a healthy practice (Cowley & Underwood, 1999). By eating well and including these factors in the diet, an individual could actually produce its own levels of SAM-e without taking it as a supplement at all.

It appears that when SAM-e is abundant in the system it tends to enhance the mood-elevating neurotransmitters such as serotonin and dopamine by speeding up production or helping to foster linkages towards initiating thoughts, feelings, and actions. Even though we are not sure exactly how the entire process works, most researchers will agree that SAM-e can indeed help prevent depression (Heusel, 2000). Its action is similar to Saint-John's-wort, though some studies found it to be effective on more severe cases of depression.

What most people don't realize, however, is that because SAM-e acts in the same way as the newer antidepressants discussed in chapter 4, users of SAM-e should always take the same precautions. For example, by decreasing depressive mood like the other newer antidepressants, SAM-e might actually trigger a manic episode (Heusel, 2000). Aside from that, the most serious side effect documented so far is stomach upset. The most serious drawback to using SAM-e is that almost no research about its effectiveness has been conducted in the United States, which means that the scientific validity of the product is questionable.

In addition, SAM-e varies dramatically in price depending on the brand name one buys. The minimal regulation that exists in terms of active-ingredient standardization leaves the consumer little to go on (Reaves, 2000). Paying $25 a dose rather than $2 does not guarantee a better product.

Most professionals agree that most clients should start with approximately 400 mg and increase the dosage to 1,600 mg to treat depression most effectively. It is probably also a good idea to take this medication on an empty stomach and to look for a brand that is coated. SAM-e is usually absorbed in the intestine, and coated pills will help prevent the active ingredient's being absorbed in the stomach. As social workers, probably the most important thing is to advise clients who are interested in taking this natural substance to decide first if it is relevant to their health needs because it will not help anyone who is functioning normally. Taking it simply to encourage or promote wellness does not appear to be indicated.

SUMMARY AND CONCLUSIONS

Most alternative approaches are frequently defined as any medical practice or intervention that lacks sufficient documentation with regard to its safety and effectiveness against certain diseases and conditions. Today, complementary approaches need to be mixed with complementary approaches. Many practitioners today prefer to use the word complementary as opposed to alternative approaches so traditional and alternative can be used in conjunction (Zahourek, 1999).

The number of individuals using alternative therapies appears to be rising (Cary, 1998). One factor that remains particularly frightening, however, is that 80% of those using these types of treatments and herbal preparations are using conventional medicine concurrently without a physician's knowledge. Poor communication can make it difficult for social workers to assess the needs of the individual and what needs to be done. The lack of unsupervised care can complicate current treatment regimens, putting the client at significant risk for interactions and synergistic effects that cannot be anticipated.

For many traditionally trained physicians, informal learning about alternative medicines is a sign of the times. This lack of formal professional training in the area of herbal remedies was highlighted in a recent University of Mississippi study, which revealed that 60% of the retail pharmacists interviewed learned about herbal medicines from their patients, and only 25% had learned about them during their professional schooling (Kroll, 1997). This means that many times clients are expected to educate professionals about the herbal medications they are taking and why they are taking them, despite the lack of controls and the conflicting, ambiguous information that abounds in this area of health care. If professionals are having trouble sorting it all out, how can clients be expected to?

Many clients desire more effective, less troublesome treatments for chronic or terminal conditions especially when conventional therapies have fallen short. They want a chance to try something different and promising in addition to their traditional treatment by using herbal remedies and other forms of alternate treatment. When looking closely at alternative or complementary medicine, it is easy to see why they have captured interest. Though conventional treatments can be limited in terms of cost and effectiveness, this does not mean that all alternative treatments provide an answer for everyone. The alternative treatments can also have potentially negative side effects or outcomes depending on the seriousness of the illness.

There is a growing movement to integrate alternative and conventional care, which can help bridge the gap between two very different approaches to health care. In the meantime, it is extremely important that people share information about what they are taking with their physicians. Combining herbs and other supplements with prescription drugs can have unpleasant and even hazardous consequences. If physicians and other health care providers are not informed about what their clients are taking, the professional will be unable to use his or her expertise to help the clients determine if this is the best remedy for them. It is important for social workers to encourage their clients to inform health care providers of all natural remedies they are taking so that the health care professional can also become familiar with the effects these natural remedies are having on the clients. The social worker should also encourage the client to make informed decisions in terms of what is best for them. Clients do not have to accept and automatically commit to a traditional approach to medical care (Seligson, 1998). Social workers should assist and encourage clients to seek information that allows them to make informed choices. If health care providers seem resistant to a method of intervention, encourage the client to ask the providers to explain their reasoning. By understanding that there may be reluctance within the mainstream medical community to discuss the use of natural remedies, social workers can help clients prepare for such discussions by role-playing to decide what to say and how best to say it.

Effective, efficient, and comprehensive helping relationships require that social workers recognize other forms of treatments that could potentially be more effective for their clients. Alternative forms of intervention can also serve as a preventive measure to ensure a client's well being. As providers of stress management strategies, relaxation techniques, and psychosocial interventions that can be incorporated into alternative therapies, social workers need to be aware of these techniques and remedies. Keeping abreast of all forms of treatment is important to provide the best possible care for our clients, while discouraging the use of medications and herbal preparations as the only form of intervention when other alternatives can be just as effective.

APPENDIX: RESOURCES FOR COMPLEMENTARY/ ALTERNATIVE MEDICINES

Benson, H., & Stark, M. (1996). *Timeless healing. The power and biology of belief.* New York: Scribner.

Bloomfield, H. H. (1996). *Hypericum and depression.* Los Angeles: Prelude Press.

Blumenthal, M. (1998). *The Complete German Commission E Monographs. Therapeutic Guide to Herbal Medicines.* Austin, TX: American Botanical Council.

Bradley, P. (1992). *British herbal compendium.* Vol. 1. British Herbal Medicine Association.

Bratman, S. (1997). *The alternative medicine sourcebook.* Los Angeles: Lowell House.

Brinker, F. (1996). *The toxicology of botanical medicines* (2nd ed.). Sandy, OR: Eclectic Institute.

Brinker, F. (1997). *Herb contraindications and drug interactions.* Sandy, OR: Eclectic Institute.

Brown, D. J. (1996). *Herbal prescriptions for better health.* Rocklin, CA: Prima.

Cassileth, B. R. (1998). *The alternative medicine handbook.* New York: W. W. Norton.

Clark, C. C. (2000). *Integrating complementary health procedures into practice.* New York: Springer Publishing Co.

Collinge, W. (1996). *The American holistic health association complete guide to alternative medicine.* New York: Time Warner.

Copeland, M. E. (1992). *The depression workbook.* Oakland, CA: New Harbinger.

Davis, M., Eshelman, E. R., & McKay, M. (1988). *The relaxation & stress reduction workbook.* Oakland, CA: New Harbinger.

Duke, J. A. (1997). *The green pharmacy.* Emmaus, PA: Rodale Press.

Fugh-Berman, A. (1997). *Alternative medicine: What works.* Baltimore: Williams & Wilkins.

Goldberg, I. (1994). *Functional foods.* New York: Chapman & Hall.

Goleman, D. (Ed.). (1993). *Mind/body medicine.* Yonkers, NY: Consumer Reports Book.

Khalsa, D. S. (1997). *Brain longevity.* New York: Time Warner.

Moyers, W. (1993). *Healing and the mind.* New York: Doubleday.

Murray, M. (1995). *The healing power of herbs.* Rocklin, CA: Prima Publishing.

Pert, C. B. (1997). *Molecules of emotion.* New York: Scribner.

The physician's desk reference family guide to nutrition and health. (1995). Montvale, NJ: Medical Economics.

The physician's desk reference for herbal preparations. (1988). Montvale, NJ: Medical Economics.

Reiter, R. J., & Robinson, J. (1995). *Melatonin.* New York: Bantam Books.

Sahelian, R. (1995). *Melatonin, nature's sleeping pill.* Marina del Rey, CA: Be Happier Press.

Sapolsky, R. M. (1993). *Why zebras don't get ulcers.* Stanford, CA: Stanford Alumni Association.

Schulz, V., Hansel, R., & Tyler, V. E. (1998). *Rational phytotherapy.* New York: Springer Publishing Co.

Stay, F. P. (1996). *The complete book of dental remedies.* New York: Avery.

Tyler, V. (1993). *The honest herbal.* New York: Hayworth Press.

Tyler, V. (1994). *Herbs of choice.* New York: Hayworth Press.

Weil, A. (1997). *Eight weeks to optimum health.* New York: Random House.

Werbach, M. R., & Murray, M. T. (1994). *Botanical influences on illness.* Tarzana, CA: Third Line Press.

Wichel, M. (Ed.). (1994). *Herbal drugs and phytopharmaceuticals.* Stuttgart, Germany: Medpharm.

REFERENCES

Barrett, A. (1998). Hot war over herbal remedies. *Business Week, 33581*, p. 42.

Bender, K. J. (1996, October). St. John's Wort evaluated as a herbal antidepressant. *Psychiatric Times.* [On-line], July 6, 1999. Available: http://www.mhsource.com/edu/psytimes/p964058.html

Cary, C. (1998). St. John's Wort—The happy flower. Times-News [On-line]. Available: http://www.timesnewsfreedom.com/news/stjohnwort.html

Cerrato, P. (2000). Diet and herbs for BPH (benign prostatic hyperplasia). *RN, 63*(2), 63.

Cheng, J. (1995, August). Old medicine, new cures. *Free China Review*, pp. 45–51.

Collacott, E. A. (2000). Bipolar permanent magnets for the treatment of chronic low back pain: A pilot study. *Journal of the American Medical Association, 283*, 1322–1327.

Cowley, G., & Underwood, A. (1999, July 5). What is SAM-e? *Newsweek*, pp. 46–50.

Feltman, J. (1996). *The prevention how-to dictionary of healing remedies and techniques.* New York: Berkly Books.

Fugh-Berman, A. (2000). Herb-drug interactions. *Lancet, 355*, 134.

Goeddeke-Merickel, C. M. (1998a, March/April). Herbal medicine: Some Do's and Don'ts for dialysis patients. *For Patients Only*, pp. 22–23.

Goeddeke-Merickel, C. M. (1998b, May/June). Alternative medicine and dialysis patients; Part II. *For Patients Only*, pp. 19–20.

Goeddeke-Merickel, C. M. (1998c, July/August). Alternative medicine and dialysis patients: Part III. *For Patients Only*, pp. 22, 30.

Goodman, S. (2000). The new face of medicine—why Andrew Weil is driving so many doctors nuts? *Modern Maturity, 1*, 46–51.

Gottelieb, B. (1995). *New choices in natural healing.* Emmaus, PA: Rodale Press.

Gower, T. (2000, February). The new happy pill. *Better Homes and Gardens*, pp. 99–104.

Greenwald, J. (1998). Herbal healing. *Time, 152*(21), 59–68.

Henkel, J. (2000, May/June). Health claims for soy protein, questions about other components. *FDA Consumer*, 13–20.

Heusel, C. (2000). Hot natural remedies. *Good Housekeeping, 230*, 164.

Kroll, D.J. (1997, September). St John's Wort: An example of the problems with herbal medicine regulation in the United States. *Medical Sciences Bulletin, 240*, 1–5.

Kurtzweil, P. (1999). How to spot health fraud. *FDA Consumer, 33*, 6, 22–26.

LaPuma, J. (1999). Danger of Asian patent medicines. *Alternative Medicine Alert: A Clinician's Guide to Alternative Therapies, 2*(6), 71.

Manufacturing Chemist. (2000, January). Herbal drugs: Medicines of food supplements? *Manufacturing Chemist, 16,* 1–3.

Mayo Clinic Health Letter. (1998, October). Garlic, the latest on this legendary herb. Author, p. 7.

McCall, M. D. (1998). *Alternative medicine: Is it for you?* Orlando Sentinel, May 12, 1998, Orlando, FL.

Physicians' Desk Reference. (2000). *Physicians desk reference for herbal medications* (2nd ed.). Montvale NJ: Medical Economics.

Reaves, J. (2000). If you choose the herbal life, it's buyer beware. (2000, January 6). *Time Daily* (n.d.).

Seligson, S.V. (1998, May/June). Melding medicines. *Health,* pp. 64–70.

St. John's Wort and SAM-e: The mood menders. (2000). *Psychology Today, 33*(2), 50.

Tyler, V.E. (2000). Herbal medicine 2000. *Prevention, 52*(1), 93–95.

Zahourek, R. P. (1999). An experience of healing: A clinical perspective. *Alternative Health Practitioner, 5*(1), 5–17.

CHAPTER 10

Conclusion: Pulling It All Together

The overriding message for social work professionals is clear: a knowledge of medications is now essential for social workers in order to deliver and monitor effective and efficient services. The social workers' position is a unique one as they are frequently the first professionals to see the client. Therefore, they can be the first to complete an assessment that takes into account the general mental health status of the client, the medications that may be indicated, and the side-effect profiles that can trigger recommendations for change. The role of the social worker is multifaceted and complements diverse skills that become available to the client when a interdisciplinary team is used to provide care. This is particularly true in rural areas where a social worker with a wide range of skills can assist in providing improved communication, coordination, and referral between primary health, mental health, and community-based programs (Van Hook, 1996).

PRESCRIPTION MEDICATIONS

With the wide array of medications available today, a broad knowledge of the types of medications a client is taking and how they can affect the helping process is essential. These authors believe, however, that knowing prescription medications only can be shortsighted. As stated earlier in this book, statistics show that at least three out of every four visits to a physician will result in the client's taking a prescription home, with approximately 2.8 billion prescriptions dispensed in the year 1999 alone (Friebert & Greeley, 1999). The sheer number of prescriptions being written is also impacted by the extensive and complicated array of prescription drugs now available to the consumer. The *Physicians' Desk Reference*

(2000) lists more than 6,000 of these preparations, and with the FDA approving drugs at a faster rate than ever this number will surely increase (Nordenberg, 1999). In the year 1999 alone, 28 new therapeutic agents were marketed (Hussar, 2000). Unfortunately, 50% of all individuals will not take these medicines as prescribed (Friebert & Greeley, 1999).

Compared to other forms of mental health treatment, psychotropic medications are the newcomers. Social workers with clients who are experiencing mental health difficulties must have knowledge of these types of medications, which can help in the fight against mental illness and its subsequent emotional, psychological, and social problems. The upward trend over the last 30 years has been fueled by controlled-medication-based studies that support the assertion that medication alone can be viable as a solitary form of treatment.

It is obvious that professionals cannot be expected to be familiar with all the medications a client is taking. However, they should be well versed in the ones that are most commonly used to treat specific problems in client populations and have some basic knowledge of the effects of medications on the human body. Social workers must also know their own limits and are expected to look up a medication they are unsure about or refer to another interdisciplinary team member. It is also considered essential for the experienced social worker to be familiar with the PDR and to use it. In all cases, to help the client effectively, it is important and social workers are encouraged to admit to the client when they are not familiar with a drug. There is no stigma attached to looking up a medication and in fact there can be very negative consequences for not doing so. Most clients are unable to use the PDR as a resource because it is often too complicated and technical for them to (McGrath, 1999). Besides, the side-effect profiles in the PDR may frighten even the most experienced professional and cause the client unnecessary anxiety. When a client is seeking additional information, it is best to help the client gain access to more user-friendly information. When clients pick up prescriptions, most find that pharmacists can provide the most easily read and understandable literature that explains the medications, directions for usage, and potential side effects. It is important to remind the client to read and save these descriptions, which can be used to explain medications to their families and friends and to other professionals trying to assist them.

The National Institute of Mental Health provides a user-friendly publication for clients and professionals that gives basic information about numerous mental health medications and what they are used for. The full text for NIMH Publication No. 95-3929 is also available on line at *http:// www.nimh.nih.gov/publicat/medicate.cfm*. Social workers should help clients access this type of information and answer questions and help interpret it. Information for NIMH Publication No. 95-3929: You can order the booklet from NIMH Public Inquiries, Room 8184, MSC 9663, 6001 Executive Boulevard, Bethesda, MD 20892-9663 or fax a request to 301-443-4279.

AVOIDING PRESCRIPTION ERRORS

Social workers do not prescribe medications; however, their role in protecting clients who use prescription medications is crucial for promoting comprehensive and preventive practice. Approximately 125,000 deaths occur each year as a result of not taking medication as directed (Buppert, 2000). In a recent study, in-depth interviews were conducted with 20 prescribers about communicating information to clients, and several themes emerged (McGrath, 1999). The first was the debate about how much information should be given to clients, and time constraints were reported as the most important reason for not sharing information. The professionals who were interviewed said that sharing information also depended on the client, on whether the client wanted the information, and what kind of psychological impact knowing the side effects of a medication would have on their taking it.

Another had to do with the sources of information that were available to clients. Most prescribers felt that the more questions a client asked the better, and that much of the necessary information could be shared by other health care professionals (pharmacists, nurses, and other members of the health care team). These prescribers also expressed concerns about the type of information available and thought that clients should be careful about believing everything they read because much of the available information may not be well referenced and that television advertisements and pamphlets promoting specific products could be misleading.

Social workers need to take a more active role in this area in order to protect and educate their clients. McGrath's study (1999) highlights that prescribers are interested in increasing compliance and the availability of medication information to their clients. Yet a frequent debate in the medical industry asks, Who is actually responsible for counseling patients on the negative results of a drug interaction? Physicians and pharmacists say that they do not have the time (Barnes, 1999), which means that other members of the health care team may need to deal with this issue. To address some of the problems that can occur from medication interactions and the need for education in this area, other resources like the *Physicians' Desk Reference: Companion Guide* (1999) are used. This book gives the common medications and the interaction effects that can occur with their use. In addition, some pharmacies utilize computer support to further analyze individualized drug interactions (De Angelo, 2000).

Buppert (2000) from the *Gold Sheet* makes the following suggestions for health care providers to reduce prescription errors and catch mistakes that might be hazardous to a client's health.

- Be sure that the prescriber has the medical record or an accurate history and update of all medications a client is taking, including a listing of any known drug allergies.
- Be sure that the list of medications a client is taking is updated. If it cannot be easily tracked in the client's record, other ways of providing this information should be instituted. For example, the social worker can help the client to create an index card that lists current and past medications. The client should have the card available for review at every appointment with a health care provider. Be sure that all medications are listed including the name, dose, number, and date of last refill. By ensuring that all providers are aware of what a client is taking, problems with duplicate prescriptions, drug interactions and side effects, contraindicated medications, and errors in dosages can be avoided.
- Help the client to write down information about when refills and medication changes were ordered and why these changes were made. This information should be given to the prescriber to assist with making informed medication decisions.
- Each time the social worker visits with the client, it is important to ask what medications he or she is on and if any changes have been made. Don't forget to ask about over-the-counter and herbal preparations as well.
- When a client reports that they have been given a new medication, ask the following questions. What is the medication for? Did you get any written information about the side effects or interaction effects? Would you like to review the information you were given with me? Do you know what to do if you miss taking a dose or

decide not to take it anymore? For documentation purposes be sure to note that this information has been discussed.

- If a client is noncompliant with a medication, try to find out why. Are they forgetting, or can they not afford to purchase them? It is critical that social workers be aware of circumstances in the environment that can prohibit compliance. Once identified, efforts to improve compliance simply become part of competent, ethical, and comprehensive practice.

- Ask female clients of childbearing age if they are using birth control and about the probability of pregnancy. Some medications can delay menses and women may not know they are pregnant. Medications can cause the most damage to fetal development in the first trimester, so early detection is critical.

NONPRESCRIPTION MEDICATIONS

There are more than 600 over-the-counter preparations on the market, and well over $5 billion is spent in sales of over-the-counter drugs each year (Nordenberg, 1996). Although many social workers acknowledge the importance of being well versed on prescription medications, little emphasis is placed on the effects of nonprescription medications on the client's overall health and on the helping relationship. More nonprescription medications are becoming available to clients every day, and for many a trip to the pharmacy is fast becoming a substitute for a trip to the physician (Colino, 2000). Over-the-counter products taken by clients range from heartburn medications to nicotine patches, and the FDA has begun to review its policies on over-the-counter products in hearings that started in June of 2000 (Cauchon, 2000). During a similar review in 1972, more than 600 drugs were changed from prescription to nonprescription status, and similar results are expected from this review (Cauchon, 2000). The use of these OTC medications becomes more complicated because many clients believe that the nonprescription preparations cannot be harmful. It is critical for the social worker to remember that the interactions between OTC medications and prescribed drugs can produce powerful effects and that many of the OTC medications were once available only with a prescription.

The increasing numbers and continuing trends to use these medications compel social workers to fully appreciate these medications, their potential toxic interactions with other drugs, their effects on the mental disorder, and their impact on the treatment process. This requires the social worker and the treatment and intervention teams to be fully aware of the prescribed, OTC, and herbal medications that clients are taking. In addition, as clients make more self-help OTC purchases, storage can become problematic and clients should be warned that contrary to usual practice, OTCs and prescription medication should not be kept in the bathroom medicine cabinet. The cabinets are frequently in hot and humid bathrooms and are subject to temperature variations. A dark, dry place such as a linen closet is a better place for storing medications of any kind.

ALTERNATIVE MEDICINES

The authors of this text believe that any discussion of medications in today's practice environment should include herbal treatments and remedies. Herbal medications and remedies are not new; in fact, interest in these interventions for various health and mental health problems dates back extensively. The resurgence of interest in these strategies is clearly documented. The numerous alternative medicines and treatment strategies available to clients today reflect the attitude that educated consumers are increasingly concerned with the long-term effects of standard medications and that they want to rely less on traditional drugs and more on alternative or holistic means for their health and mental health wellness.

A significant number of Americans are self-medicating today with nonprescription medications and herbal medicines, and because herbal preparations are so easy to get, self-medication with herbal and natural remedies is rapidly becoming a practice reality. What remains questionable is the extent to which consumers are aware that while these products appear to be safe, they can indeed interact with prescription and nonprescription medications. Furthermore, the United States continues to lack a regulatory system for herbal products, particularly those that are marketed as food and dietary supplements (*PDR: For Herbal Remedies*, 2000; Zink & Chaffin, 1998). The fact that few legal standards are applied to their harvesting, processing, or packaging creates the potential for poor quality, adulteration, and contamination (Zink & Chaffin, 1998). Social workers must be prepared to educate clients about the potential adverse reactions when herbal remedies are combined with other pharmaceutical agents.

This multibillion-dollar health industry has attracted many consumers. Two groups that are at particularly high risk are teenagers and older

Americans. During adolescence, there is a great deal of emphasis on developing positive physical attributes and maintaining high self-esteem. Oftentimes, adolescents evaluate one another on the presence or lack of specific physical features that determine popularity and group acceptance. Consequently, many teenagers use diet pills, breast developers, or muscle-building aids that they believe will make them look or feel better (Stehlin, 1995). Rarely do adolescents reflect on the combination of medications or on the side effects that herbal remedies and other medications can produce. On the other hand, the older client who is typically plagued by chronic health problems may seek remedies and easy treatments that may provide immediate and cost-effective results (Stehlin, 1995).

The increased use of these preparations clearly reflects the attitude that clients are taking charge of their own health and mental health needs. Social work professionals have long since encouraged the process of client self-determination. However, when dealing with the use of all medications, including herbal remedy, social workers should empower clients by encouraging them to seek out additional information in order to determine if herbal remedies are appropriate for them. This requires that social workers not forget to ask clients about the specific medications they are on and that clients identify the issues inherent in the usage of these or any other medication.

Whether or not social workers acquire additional education to have limited prescription privileges (Dziegielewski, 1997), it is clear social workers must have a general knowledge of all medications and be familiar with side-effect profiles and dosage routines.

This book was never meant to be inclusive of all assessment and medication concerns that social workers will encounter. It is written in the hope that it will provide basic information for the health and mental health social worker and sensitize these professionals to some of the salient issues related to the process of assessment and medication prescribing. It is essential that social workers recognize that as biological determinants of mental illness continue to be uncovered, medication use as a therapeutic modality will constitute a rapidly growing and changing field of science that requires professionals to stay abreast of the changing trends and discoveries.

BUYING DRUGS ON THE WEB: A SIGN OF THE TIMES

Recent advances in modern technology, and especially the rise in computer literacy, have facilitated the purchasing of medications via the Internet

(Costello, 2000). Different from mail-order-pharmacy, purchasing with the aid of computers appeals to many individuals, especially those who cannot leave their homes or who live in rural areas (Henkel, 2000). With a simple faxed prescription or an on-line request, a client can have his or her medicines delivered the next day to his or her own home.

Although this is a convenient way for clients to receive medications and treatments, it can be problematic for those professionals who treat the individual. For example, a consumer can obtain a medication prescription without ever seeing a health care professional at some of the Internet sites by simply filling out a questionnaire. This type of purchase can result in problems for the client from misdiagnosis to purchasing or receiving incorrect medication (Carey, 2000). To demonstrate the negative effects that can result from this practice Chen (1999) described an official crackdown on one such site and found that the person authorizing the prescriptions was a veterinarian in Mexico. The Clinton administration allocated $10 million annually to crack down on illegal drug sales on-line. This fund is designed to identify and punish some of the site owners; however, this cannot stop foreign-based sites from engaging in the same practices (Carey, 2000). The rules and regulations for sites located in other countries are not the same as in the U.S., but they are available to anyone with Internet access (Henkel, 2000). Unfortunately, cases such as these give a bad name to reputable electronic pharmacies that provide a valuable service.

If clients decide to purchase their medications in this fashion, then social workers can help them consider ways to establish the credibility and reputation of an electronic pharmacy. For example, remind clients that reputable pharmacies will always verify the prescription with the physician who wrote it and provide the client with clear information about the risks and side effects. Advise clients to get the name, phone number, and professional license number of the on-line pharmacist and to keep this information in a safe place in the event of any problems. In addition, it is helpful to determine whether a site is approved by the National Association of Pharmacy Boards (NABP), which has developed a seal of approval for sites that meet the appropriate standards (Carey, 2000). Regardless of where clients get medication, before using it they should be sure that it has been dated and should check that outdated medications are not being used. Contact information for National Association of Boards of Pharmacy: Web site: www.nabp.net; Telephone: 847-698-6227.

INTERVENTION CONCERNS WITH SPECIAL POPULATIONS

There are special considerations related to inequities in the patterns of medication prescribing among certain client populations. These are important considerations as social workers need to ensure that factors such as ethnicity, gender, or age not determine the accessibility to medications or the overprescribing of drugs.

Second, do some physicians prescribe specific medications to certain people? For example, elderly people regularly get more medications than younger ones. This can be particularly problematic as these individuals often have slower metabolisms, numerous developmental changes, and more chronic illnesses, which require a combination of medications. Another concern that emerges is whether medications for the elderly replace the use of psychosocial interventions that may also be effective, especially when combined with drug therapy (Perodeau & du Fort, 2000). Regardless of the client's age, it is equally important that medication not be prescribed to the exclusion of other psychosocial counseling strategies. The notion that because of age and advanced development, older clients may not have access to aggressive or innovative medications is not foreign in a youth-oriented society such as ours.

Third, if a physician specializes in the treatment of a specific mental disorder is it more likely that individuals will be diagnosed and treated for that specific illness? Every now and then, the media reminds us of stories in which diagnosing based on a hospital or doctor's specialty and not the client's needs occurred.

Fourth, when working with special populations we cannot forget the changes that have resulted in primary care in which physicians act as gatekeepers of both care and medication. Many primary care physicians have not been extensively trained in the mental health medications now available, nor have they had ample experience with clients who present mental health problems. This lack of training may leave these primary care doctors at the mercy of high-pressured sales campaigns sponsored by drug companies seeking to market their product. Drugs introduced by pharmaceutical company agents who entice physicians with free samples can lead physicians to prescribing something that may not be individually suited for the special mental health needs of the client.

In the case of children diagnosed with attention deficit hyperactivity disorder, parents find that a referral to a neurologist is quickly followed by confirmation of the diagnosis and a recommendation to begin medication immediately, often without trying other psychosocial interventions that may prove effective and which eliminate the need for medication. Although some cases require medication, these authors wish to emphasize that there are also instances in which psychosocial interventions with the family and school environments should be attempted. It also highlights the need to ensure that a thorough assessment confirming the ADHD condition be performed. In these situations, the role of the social worker is to maintain sensitivity to cultural and diagnostic issues, and provide education and support on medication-related issues, while helping clients decide on the best course of treatment.

REALIZATION OF THE INTER–INTRA ETHNIC DYAD

Ethical and culturally sensitive practice requires the recognition of the factors that emerge when providing psychosocial services to a client from a different cultural background. Interethnic issues inherent in the client–social worker dyad must be addressed. First, clients who are unfamiliar with a certain helping system or facility may react with a sense of overcompliance and friendliness. They may feel that the social worker or members of the interdisciplinary team have power because they have privileged knowledge and authority, and are out to meet the client's own best interests; thus believing that health care professionals are somewhat omnipotent. For some clients, this can be problematic as they rely heavily and sometimes exclusively on the information provided by the health care professional and do not develop their right to self-determination and may shy away from asking questions or proposing alternative approaches. In these cases, the role of the social worker is critical as the social worker can validate the client's questions, fears, and concerns concerning medications. This role also enables the social worker to help the client develop enough assertiveness to seek direct information from the medication prescriber.

It is essential to preserve the ethical values of respect and dignity for all clients and to incorporate the client's cultural context into the helping process. This may sometimes be complicated when clients are struggling with acculturation issues or they may not be in tune with how their cultural backgrounds influence their behaviors, symptoms, or approach to treatment. The importance of integrating the client's cultural beliefs and practices can be illustrated by an incident experienced by one of the authors on a recent trip to Poland. The author's aunt, who was suffering from pneumonia and was given a prescription for antibiotics, also practiced a treatment that was culturally accepted and encouraged. This practice required using a very thick-rimmed glass, which is heated until it's red hot, and then placed on the person's back proximal to the lung that had the infiltrate. The glass cup burns the skin and once it cools, the glass releases the suction and falls off. The physician that had prescribed the antibiotic also prescribed this procedure. This physician understood that in order to encourage the client's compliance in his treatment regiment he had to demonstrate that he was accepting of her own faith and beliefs. By using this type of "cupping" treatment he showed the client that he had faith in her cultural practices. He used her beliefs to ensure that she would comply with what he considered essential in the intervention process. By integrating her cultural practice, the physician ensured her compliance with the antibiotic prescribed.

It is also important to realize that many times clients may distrust a practitioner who looks or acts differently from them. Therefore, it is important to discuss cultural differences and be sure the social worker is aware of her/his own cultural beliefs and mores and how this may conflict with that of the client's. Unfortunately, in a hurried health care environment and in a society that does not always appreciate differences, this may be overlooked. The social worker can be a vital link in ensuring that culturally based ethnic practices are used and that clients maintain their right to integrate cultural practices as they seek to establish self-determination in regard to health and mental health treatments.

A second major consideration for incorporating culturally sensitive practice goes beyond the client and the social worker. It has to do with the relationship between the client and his or her cultural system. For clients who seek health interventions such as medication, some resistance and lack of support may develop within the family system. What if a client's family does not believe in the treatment or intervention prescribed? What if they do not understand or support it? When the client's network is not supportive, will the client be as likely to follow the regime realizing that it might alienate him or her from family or friends? In the case of the author's aunt, although some of her relatives did agree that the "cupping" treatments might not have been effective for treating pneumonia, the procedure was still endorsed. These family members endorsed the intervention by providing emotional support and performing the treatments.

Whether or not practices such as the one described actually help to treat the medical or mental health conditions for which they are prescribed becomes less important than the client and the family believing they can help. An extremely helpful perspective to follow allows social workers working with culturally diverse clients to start where the client is. For example, in systems theory the helping activities of the social worker are generally divided into four concrete functions: educate, advocate, facilitate, and intervene. Education is critical in helping the client learn more about his/her own needs and the treatments that are available to alleviate symptoms and problems. Both medications and psychosocial interventions should be clearly integrated into the client's frame of reference, always encouraging the client to express how these two fit or don't fit together. Social work practitioners cannot assume that the medication and psychosocial intervention strategies that make sense to the worker or to clients of other cultures will be acceptable for a particular client. Advocacy provided to the culturally diverse client must involve maximizing the clients' support systems and using those individuals and organizations that are in the client's ethnic and cultural environment. From a strength-and-resiliency perspective, social workers must remember that culturally diverse clients have developed coping skills and systems in order to survive whatever difficulties they encountered prior to seeking formal help. These existing coping strategies should not be discarded but instead integrated into whatever new approaches the practitioner and client identify.

Lastly, effective intervention skills include those that help clients understand the systems responsible for medication prescribing and for delivery of psychosocial services. Beyond understanding mental health systems, clients must be helped to understand, how, when, and why medications need to be taken. Forcing clients to accept prescriptions without recognizing how individual and cultural differences will impact the client's willingness to accept the recommended treatment is a recipe for medication noncompliance and violates the basic self-determination rights of clients.

When working with ethnic or culturally diverse clients in terms of assessment and psychopharmacology it is critical to identify and evaluate (a) diet and nutritional factors, as they can directly influence metabolic activity; (b) patterns of consumption of cigarettes, caffeine, alcohol, herbs, and other psychoactive substances as they can influence drug metabolism and response patterns and rates; (c) an individual's sleep or activity/rest patterns as these patterns can influence when a medication should be taken; (d) a history of exposure to environmental toxins or pollutants; and (e) note previous reactions and exposure to psychological stress. For example, what does health and wellness mean to that individual? What is he or she willing to do to obtain it? Studies have shown that gathering this information is so important because certain groups tend to act similarly.

In summary, all individuals can be influenced by the concept of culture, which can be defined on the basis of ethnicity, race, gender, or age. The scarcity of studies on how culture influences psychopharmacology indicates that more research is needed.

THE IMPORTANCE OF WORKING WITHIN THE ENVIRONMENT

There are certain responses and reactions that will occur within the environment that should always be considered, and it is the social worker's ability to assess and identify environmental concerns that makes social work intervention an essential component of any interdisciplinary team.

It is important to understand how our societal attitudes towards the general use of medications have evolved. First, the notion of a quick fix or "pill" to alleviate stress and emotional problems has resulted in an abundance of medications that can be obtained by prescription, over-the-counter, or in the form of herbal remedies. Our society has become used to identifying and using medications to treat numerous chronic medical problems that include headaches, heartburn, coughs, allergies, and colds, as well as more complicated routine health problems (Nordenberg, 1999). Furthermore, herbal medications have attracted so much interest that more than 7.3 million Americans who were worried about the flu started swallowing a purple-petaled daisy native to the Midwest (echinacea). This trend is illustrated repeatedly by the fact that consumers spent more than $12 billion on natural supplements in 1997 alone. This is double the amount spent the year before, and that figure is expected to grow at the amazing rate of 10% per year (Greenwald, 1998).

Throughout this book we have stressed the important role of the social worker as educator. It may not be an easy task because many clients are searching for immediate solutions to their health and mental health problems. It is important to recognize that human beings are generally pleasure-seeking individuals who will consider medication as a way to avoid pain, discomfort, and distress. However, clients should also be educated on the disadvantages of taking medications in mental health treatment for the sole purpose of numbing painful emotions and thoughts, which may serve as crucial motivators for clients to examine their problems, make changes, and develop new coping skills to address these. Oftentimes emotional pain can generate energy for growth and learning that would otherwise be stunted by relying exclusively on mental health medication. The brain requires stimulation provided by learning through education and by experience that can be triggered by pain and pleasure (Kotulak, 1997).

For social workers the "medicalization" of simple body phenomenon such as stress must be anticipated. It is important always to help our clients and other members of the interdisciplinary team to understand the effects that this medicalization of symptoms can have on clients.

It is easy to question why counseling is needed when medications like Prozac can neurochemically "cure" mental illnesses such as depression. As previously mentioned in other sections of this book, psychotropic medications can help to alleviate and control the blatant symptoms of many mental disorders; however, attention must be paid to the underlying dynamics, causes, and feelings related to or caused by the illness. Let us imagine for a moment that we could indeed give a client a pill and cure the mental illness that he or she had been suffering from for many years. Everyone, including family and friends, would be thrilled when the client reports that he or she is feeling better and now has the energy to address his or her problems. On the surface the client's symptoms appear to be improving, but the impact and the adjustment process that the mental disorder has had on the client's environment and social spheres must also be taken into account. This is particularly true for the client's significant other who is now reporting difficulties dealing with the loved one. Since the client is now feeling better physically, the significant other who has been handling things throughout the client's mental illness does not understand why the partner has not started taking a more active role in the family system. Furthermore, family members see the marked improvement in the client's functioning and may be skeptical of the client's previous inability to function, believing that the client may have been able to perform at this high level all along. At work, the client initially had been assigned a lighter work load, but now that the client is feeling better supervisors and coworkers may expect an increase in work load and performance. We can use psychotropic medications to address a client's mental health problem from a biological basis, but all individuals are influenced by social, psychological, and environmental factors that must be addressed simultaneously.

The desire for a quick cure and the medicalization of normal emotions such as anxiety and stress are complicated by the fact that research methodology on the efficacy of medication intervention by itself is limited. Researchers and scientists with preconceived notions can make claims unintentionally and support findings that may not accurately demonstrate the efficacy of mental health medications. Although most scientists and researchers are honest they are under pressure to find results that support the funding they receive. At a presentation to physicians in 1994, David Kessler, the former Surgeon General, emphasized that the single greatest marketing technique and strategy for drugs is the testing. Therefore, it is important for social workers to look critically at these claims and not be afraid to ask questions that will support and protect the clients they serve.

Furthermore, drug companies tend to encourage gender-related or cultural stereotypes that perpetuate common beliefs, such as the one that menstrual cramping is not only normal but to be expected. For some women cramping is not a common symptom of the menstrual cycle. Another commonly held belief is that menopause will inevitably bring major and lasting changes in an individual's life that must be tempered with herbal or hormonal stimulation. Although these changes do occur in some cases, it is an inaccurate assumption that they will affect all women. The newer trend, popularized by television commercials for herbal remedies, characterizes the working woman as overloaded, stressed, and in need of herbal remedies that will provide a desired emotional balance. While economic, social, and family demands can result in increased stress for women, not all working women experience stress the same way, nor do they all require herbal interventions.

There is also a great deal of media hype about maintaining wellness. What exactly does preventing illness and maintaining wellness mean? Most professionals agree that the single greatest factor for promoting health and wellness probably is living a balanced life that includes a proper diet, exercise, and adequate sleep. Dietitians might agree that eating a balanced diet is all one really needs to maintain adequate nutritional intake. Yet many people take the additional vitamins, perhaps as a preventive strategy, realizing that they probably could get the same thing by eating right. Though in many cases (barring an overdose of vitamins) taking these supplements proves harmless, the bigger issue that emerges from this practice is that it supports our society's "take a pill and make it better" attitude.

DOCUMENTATION, RECORD KEEPING, AND TREATMENT PLANNING

Social workers find that there are many agency forms to document the overall progress made by clients who are receiving mental health medications and the accompanying psychosocial interventions. In most agencies, social workers will have to follow a uniformed recording or documentation format. The reader is referred to Dziegielewski and Leon (In Press) for a more comprehensive review of the formats that are available. In a recent survey done by a medical liability insurer, 40% of the medical records examined did not have clear documentation regarding patient education; 40% did not mention whether the client had any previous history of drug allergies; 49% were so poorly written that the handwriting could not be deciphered; 96% of the notes contained unidentified comments or documentation; and 66% had little information about when prescriptions were written and refilled (Buppert, 2000). Documentation problems like this are considered unacceptable and put the client, the family, and the providers at significant risk.

Dziegielewski and Leon (In Press) suggest that regardless of the type of format use, all record keeping should at a minimum contain the following information: (a) a description and assessment of the client's situation; (b) the reason for referral and purpose of service; (c) identification and description of measurable goals, objectives and tasks; (d) a clear intervention plan; (e) a plan for monitoring and evaluation of client progress; and (f) evaluation and presentation of treatment outcomes. When looking at the relationship of medications as part of the helping process, the importance of including this type of documentation cannot be overemphasized.

The social worker should be certain that client information (including information on medications) is accurate and complete. Good record keeping is essential to the ethical and legal aspects of practice (Buppert, 2000; Kagle, 1991). Every record must have basic information that includes the date and time of entry, interview notes that describe the client and the problem or situation that requires treatment, an assessment and initial treatment plan, and therapeutic objectives and treatment responses. A time frame for intervention must be clearly established and progress with regard to that time frame must be documented. When family interventions are included, the time, date, and who was involved should always be inserted. Also, when discharge services such as placement are addressed, they need to be formally documented in the record. Ongoing progress notes should always reflect the client's adjustment and compliance with the medication and indicate any side effects that may have emerged.

SUCCESSFUL COMPLIANCE

To increase compliance with medications the social worker should always explore, examine, and document the conditions or situations that might lead to noncompliance. First, ask the client what is keeping him or her from taking the medication, because the problem is usually a solvable one. For example, if a medication is causing decreased sexual interest or drive (as frequently occurs with the SSRIs), a client may decide simply stop taking the it. Once the side effect is identified, other medications can be suggested to eliminate the problem. Or the medication may be expensive, and the client is embarrassed to admit not being able to afford it (Trafford, 1999). In other cases the client may start to feel better and decide to stop taking the medication (McGrath, 1999). If the client is not taking it because he or she simply forgot, plans can be made to help remember. Using egg cartons to hold the weekly dose is just one way to assist.

Second, record how often the client is supposed to take the medication. Taking a medication once a day rather than twice a day may assist in increasing compliance, and liquid medication may be more tolerable for individuals who have trouble chewing or swallowing. Third, empower the client by helping him or her to fill out a medication card where the client becomes responsible for monitoring, recording, and updating the medications.

Finally, if cost is an issue consider advising the client to switch to a generic medication, or determine whether the client would benefit from a pharmacy assistance program, either through governmental agencies or pharmaceutical companies. These programs are particularly good for clients who are having difficulty paying for their medications. Some of these companies may provide medications directly to physicians for use with patients who cannot afford them. Buppert (2000) warns, however, that it is illegal for a health care provider to sell samples even at a reduced cost, or to give a client the full dosing supply of free samples. The primary criteria for participation in these programs are that clients must show they cannot afford to purchase the medications and that they have no health insurance coverage. Because other eligibility requirements vary depending on the program, it is best to call the specific program and find out the requirements.

Pharmaceutical companies that provide patient assistance:

DuPont 302-992-5000

Jansen, Inc. 1-800-652-6227

Pfizer, Inc. 1-800-646-4455

Roch Laboratories 1-800-443-6676

UpJohn Co. 616-323-6332

The social worker practicing in today's managed care environment must be aware of the direct link between service delivery, good record keeping, and treatment planning. Of special importance is that the documented record make reference to the original treatment plan and show evidence of outcome measurement. The process of assessing pretreatment, posttreatment, and follow-up measures of client progress or change must be clearly demonstrated through this written exchange. When symptom description is made, it must be stated clearly in observable, demonstrable terms that relate to the measurable treatment intervention presented. The treatment plan should always include a detailed description of client complaints with the specific interventions used to address them. The importance of the written record in health and mental health treatment cannot be overemphasized during this time of increased litigation, limited service delivery access, and controlled health care costs.

PROACTIVE PROFESSIONALS IN THE ERA OF MANAGED CARE

This book was written to review the basic concepts of clinical assessment and psychopharmacology from a social work perspective. Social work involves aspects of practice that include direct work with clients and their families in diverse settings such as clients' homes, communities, hospitals, clinics, private practice offices, and other health and mental health care institutions. However, changes in health care service and delivery that were created by managed care demands in the 1990s have presented social workers with numerous challenges and opportunities that must be embraced if social work practitioners are to survive and thrive in this fluctuating and complex environment (Dziegielewski, 1998).

This rapidly changing environment has challenged social workers to become significant players in this new era of competition for the provision of outcome-based service delivery. This requires that social workers demonstrate empirically the effectiveness of their interventions by validating and reporting that concrete and identifiable therapeutic gain was achieved in the most cost-effective way. This means that the treatment provided by social workers must be therapeutically effective and professionally competitive with other disciplines that use similar treatment strategies and techniques. Since the battle for delivering "more service with less resource" continues to rage, social workers must accept the changes in health care and become more PROACTIVE in acquiring as much knowledge as possible in all areas of mental health interventions, including medication therapy (Dziegielewski, 1998). The acronym "PROACTIVE" contains the following components essential for effective social work practice.

P: All social workers need to PRESENT and POSITION themselves as competent professionals with POSITIVE attitudes in all health care service settings, regardless of the type of practice being provided.

R: RECEIVE and acquire adequate training and continuing education in the current and future practice areas of health and mental health social work. This means being prepared to work with and assist clients who are taking prescription medication, over-the-counter preparations, and self-help remedies.
RESEARCH time-limited treatment approaches that can provide alternatives for social workers who are struggling to provide quality-of-care service while cutting costs. These strategies should be encouraged and supported to coincide with medication treatments. Therefore, medication as a sole modality of treatment seems to fall short of realizing the importance of the "person-in-environment" stance that has long been the cornerstone of social work practice.

O: ORGANIZE individuals and communities to help these client systems receive safe, accessible, and affordable health services. Help these individuals to feel comfortable questioning intervention strategy and encourage their active participation in intervention planning. ORGANIZE other social workers to prepare for the changes that are occurring, and develop strategies to continue to provide ethical, cost-effective service.

A: Help ADDRESS and identify the policies and issues that are relevant to providing ethical, effective, efficient, and cost-effective service.

Help clients to address their own needs and feel secure in questioning medication regimens that are prescribed. It is also essential to encourage clients to question claims that appear vague and unsubstantiated such as, "This product promotes wellness."

C: COLLABORATE with other health care professionals to provide services that utilize an interdisciplinary team approach for addressing client concerns and needs. Assist with medication monitoring and compliance issues for the team while helping to make the client fill a more active role in his or her own treatment regimens.

COMPLEMENT orthodox medical practices and techniques by utilizing holistic practices and alternative strategies that can help clients achieve increased health and wellness. Be aware of cultural mores and beliefs and how this can affect the client's adherence and continuance with treatment.

T: TEACH others about the value and importance of including social work services and techniques. Educate clients and team members about the importance of respecting the worth and dignity of clients while maximizing self-determination.

TAKE TIME to prevent professional burnout. Social workers need to remain productive and receptive professionals who can serve as good role models for the clients and other professionals. It is essential for social workers, like all health professionals, to remember that it is not possible to know all medications and the implications for usage and misuse. Rather, the key is to recognize what is not known and help the client to find the answers that are needed.

I: INVESTIGATE and apply innovative and empirically based approaches to current client-care problems and issues.

INVOLVE and make all social workers aware of the change process that needs to occur in order to affect changes in the traditional ways that health and mental health social work have been delivered in the past.

INTERVENE on behalf of clients to ensure that they not only get access to the services that they need but are also able to utilize such services in the future if the social worker is not available.

V: VISUALIZE and work toward positive outcomes for all those who are affected by behavioral managed-care health strategies.

VALUE the role of other health care professionals and support them as they face similar challenges and changes.

E: Responsibly EXPLORE supplemental therapies and strategies that clients can self-administer at little or no cost to treat chronic conditions and to preserve and enhance health and wellness.

Most important, EMPOWER our clients and ourselves by stressing the importance of EDUCATION to help client systems obtain the most effective and appropriate intervention strategies, while also encouraging clients to ask relevant questions related to medication and psychosocial interventions.

As health and mental health care continues to evolve, social workers will find that they can remain viable contributors in the field. The social work code of ethics ensures that services based on reasonable fees are provided to clients and allows social work practitioners to offer similar treatments at fees lower than those charged by other mental health professionals such as psychiatrists, psychologists, family therapists, psychiatric nurses, and mental health counselors. This fee structure can provide an incentive to managed care agencies to contract with social workers instead of other professionals. Having knowledge of medications provides an additional valuable skill to the repertoire of interventions used by social workers and may make social work practitioners more appealing to managed care companies who require continuous monitoring of client medications. Knowledge of medications is essential as it truly can affect psychosocial interventions and successful treatment outcomes.

SUMMARY AND CONCLUSIONS

In closing, the authors would once again like to stress the purpose of this book. It is not meant to be inclusive of all information related to the medications or preparations used by clients; rather it is written with the intention that social work practitioners develop an appreciation for the importance of acquiring and integrating such knowledge into the psychosocial intervention process. A working knowledge of the different types of medications, their side effects, and benefits can help social work practitioners monitor such issues as medication compliance and medication-related problems. Furthermore, having knowledge about current therapies can help prepare the social worker to educate clients and their families about responsible use of mental health medications (Matorin & DeChillo, 1984; Bently & Walsh, 1998).

Of all the professionals who work with clients, social workers often have regular and subsequent contacts with their clients. This continued contact is particularly important between physician follow-up visits because information gathered during these periods could and should be shared with the consulting physician/psychiatrist or the interdisciplinary team members. As a member of the team who has established rapport with the client and is also aware of pertinent social, emotional, family and environmental concerns, the social worker's input on the medication regimen, tolerance, and compliance should not be underestimated. The social worker serves a pivotal role obtaining the family's help and support throughout treatment, while also allaying the client's and family's fears (Bernheim, 1982). Moreover, with the increased availability and popularity of medication information, clients and their families have become increasingly assertive in questioning social workers about the use of prescription medications as well as over-the-counter and herbal preparations. Oftentimes clients and family members have limited information in these areas and are uncomfortable admitting to other health care professionals that they believe another mode of treatment might be better. The well-informed social worker can correct distortions and foster cooperation in the treatment plan and among treatment team professionals (May, 1976; Matorin & DeChillo, 1984). When social workers are knowledgeable or know where or how to get additional knowledge about a medication, they can help prepare as well as educate clients and family members about the responsible use and expectations of psychiatric medications.

Social work educators must consider incorporating medication knowledge into the social work curriculum as a way of preparing students to practice effectively (Beels & McFarlane, 1982). Social work students need updated information on the integration of medications in social work practice and should be encouraged to integrate this body of knowledge from both the curriculum and their field internship experiences. This type of learning can be offered through elective courses in specialized medications or by integrating medication knowledge and recent empirically based research on medication into core curriculum practice courses.

Schools of social work are strongly encouraged to include this type of course work in their curriculum and to encourage students to use social work clinical, educational, case management, research, and advocacy skills actively in response to the medication dilemmas of their clients. Regardless of how this information is conveyed, it requires that social work educators and professionals stay abreast of newer drugs (Dziegielewski, 1997, 1998) and remain conversant on some of the more controversial issues in the field of psychopharmacology (Matorin & De Chillo, 1984). Information regarding medications and the way these drugs can affect the client should not be obtained by chance; program administrators, educators, and practitioners must periodically arrange for dialoguing and sharing of current medication knowledge and expertise (Miller, Wiederman, & Linn, 1980; Levine & Dang, 1977).

More education is needed about medication use in order for the fast growing field of social work to compete in the professional arena (Dziegielewski, 1998). The knowledge of the practice of medications in the psychosocial counseling environment can only help social work professionals as they strive to achieve the highest standards of the profession.

REFERENCES

Barnes, P. (1999, June). Prescription for liability. *ABA Banking Journal, 85,* 40.

Beels, C., & McFarlane, W. R. (1982). Family treatment of schizophrenia: Background and state of the art. *Hospital and Community Psychiatry 33,* 541–550.

Bently, K. J. (1997). Should clinical social workers seek psychotropic medication prescription privileges?: No. In B. A. Thyer (Ed.), *Controversial issues in social work practice* (pp. 152–165). Boston: Allyn & Bacon.

Bently, K. J., & Walsh, J. (1998). Advances in psychopharmacology and medication management. In J. B. Williams & K. Ell (Eds.), *Advances in mental health research: Implications for practice* (pp. 309–342). Washington, DC: NASW Press.

Bernheim, K. (1982). Supportive Family Counseling. *Schizophrenia Bulletin, 8.*

Buppert, C. (2000). Avoiding prescription errors. *Gold Sheet, 2*(5), 1–4.

Carey, J. (2000, February). A crackdown on e-druggists. *Business Week, 3667,* 104.

Cauchon, D. (2000, April). FDA moves to make more drugs Rx-free. *USA Today* [On-line]. June 3, 2000. Available: http://www.usatoday.com

Chen, I. (1999, September). Worry box: Is it dangerous to buy drugs off the web? *Health, 30.*

Colino, S. (2000, April). The pharmacist is in. *Good Housekeeping, 230*(4), 185.

Costello, P. (2000, April). Easy drugs online. *Glamour, 102,* pp. 104 and 303.

De Angelo, M. (2000). Internet solution reduces medical errors. *Health Management Technology, 21*(2), 20.

Dziegielewski, S. F. (1997). Should clinical social workers seek psychotropic medication prescription privileges?: Yes. In B. A. Thyer (Ed.), *Controversial issues in social work practice* (pp. 152–165). Boston: Allyn & Bacon.

Dziegielewski, S. F. (1998). *The changing face of health care social work; Professional practice in the era of managed care.* New York: Springer.

Dziegielewski, S. F., & Leon, A. M. (in press). *Journal of Brief Therapy.*

Freibert, E., & Greeley, A. (1999). Taking time to use medications wisely. *FDA Consumer, 33*(5), 30–33.

Greenwald, J. (1998, November 23). Herbal healing. *Time*, pp. 59–68.

Henkel, J. (2000). Buying drugs on line: Its convenient and private but beware of "rouge sites." *FDA Consumer, 34*(1), 29.

Hussar, D. A. (2000). New drugs of 1999. *Journal of the American Pharmalogical Association, 40*(2), 181–221.

Kagle, J. D. (1991). *Social work records.* Belmont, CA: Wadsworth.

Kotulak, R. (1997). *Inside the brain: Revolutionary discoveries of how the brain works.* Kansas City, MO: Andrews McMeel.

Levine, C., & Dang, J. C. (1977). Psychopharmacology and social work skills. *Social Casework* (pp. 153–156).

Matorin, S., & DeChillo, N. (1984, December). Psychopharmacology: Guidelines for social workers. *Social Casework: The Journal of Contemporary Social Work*, pp. 579–589.

May, P. R. (1976). When, what, and why? Psychopharmacotherapy and other treatments in schizophrenia. *Comprehensive Psychiatry, 17*, 72.

McGrath, J. M. (1999). Physician's perspectives on communicating prescription drug information. *Qualitative Health Research, 9*, 731–746.

Miller, R. S., Weideman, G. H., & Linn, L. (1980). Prescribing psychotropic drugs: Whose responsibility? *Social Work in Health Care, 6*, 51–61.

Nordenberg, T. (1999). New drug label spells it out simply. *FDA Consumer, 33*(4), 29–32.

Perodeau, G. M., & du Fort, G. G. (2000). Psychotropic drug use and the relation between social support, life events, and mental health in the elderly. *Journal of Applied Gerontology, 19*(1), 23–41.

Physicians' Desk Reference. (1997). *Physicians' desk reference: For nonprescription drugs* (18th ed.). Montvale, NJ: Medical Economics.

Physicians' Desk Reference: Companion Guide. (1999). *Physicians' desk reference: Companion guide* (53rd ed.). Montvale, NJ: Medical Economics.

Physicians' Desk Reference. (2000). *Physicians' desk reference* (54th ed.). Montvale, NJ: Medical Economics.

Physicians' Desk Reference. For Herbal Medicines. (2000). *Physicians' desk reference for herbal medicines* (2nd ed.). Montvale, NJ: Medical Economics.

Stehlin, I. B. (1995). An FDA choosing guide for medical treatments. *FDA Consumer, 29*(5), 11–14.

Trafford, A. (1999, November 9). Health Talk: Prescription drug coverage. *Washington Post*, pp. B1–B5.

Van Hook, M. P. (1996). Challenges to identifying and treating women with depression in rural primary care. *Social Work in Health Care, 23*(3), 73–92.

Zink, T., & Chaffin, J. (1998). Herbal health products: What physicians need to know. *American Family Physician, 58*, 1133–1140.

Appendix A

Resources and Web Sites

Academy for Guided Imagery
PO Box 2070
Mill Valley, CA 94942
(800) 726-2070
www.healthy.net/agi

Alzheimer's Association
919 N. Michigan St.
Chicago, IL 60611
(800) 272-3900
www.alz.org

Alzheimer's Disease Education & Referral Ctr
PO Box 8250
Silver Spring, MD 20907-8250
(800) 438-4380
www.alzheimers.org/adear

American Botanical Council
PO Box 144345
Austin, TX 78714-4345
(512) 926-4900
(512) 926-2345 (Fax)
www.herbalgram.org

American Dietetics Association
216 W. Jackson Blvd.
Chicago, IL 60606-1600
(800) 877-1600
www.eatright.org

American Geriatrics Society
770 Lexington Ave., Ste. 300
New York, NY 10021
(212) 308-1414
(800) 247-4779
www.americangeriatrics.org

American Heart Association
7320 Greenville Ave.
Dallas, TX 75231
(214) 373-6300
www.amhrt.org

American Herbalists Guild
PO Box 70
Roosevelt, UT 84066
(435) 722-8434
(435) 722-8452
www.healthy.net/herbalists
http://ahgoffice@earthlink.net (E-mail)

American Herbal Pharmacopoeia
PO Box 5159
Santa Cruz, CA 95063
(408) 461-6317
(408) 438-7410
www.herbal-ahp.org

**American Psychiatric
Association**
1400 K St. NW
Washington, DC 20005
(202) 682-6000
(202) 682-6850 (Fax)
www.psych.org
e-mail: apa@site.org

**American Psychological
Association**
750 1st St. NE
Washington, DC 20002-4242
(202) 336-5500
www.apa.com

**American Sleep Disorders
Association**
1610 14th St. NW, Ste. 300
Rochester, MN 55901
(507) 287-6006
www.asda.org

**Anxiety Disorders Assoc of
America**
11900 Parkline Dr. Ste. 100
Rockville, MD 20852
(301) 231-9350
(301) 231-7392
www.adaa.org

**Association for Applied Psycho-
physiology & Biofeedback**
10200 W. 44th Ave. Ste. 304
Wheat Ridge, CO 80033
(303) 422-8436
www.aaph.org

Biofeedback Institute
3428 Sacramento St.
San Francisco, CA 94118
(877) 246-9357
(415) 921-6500
(415) 921-5457 (Fax)
biofdbk@itsa.ucsf.edu (E-mail)

Functional Food Program
Dr. Clare Hassler
Bldg ABL, Rm 103
1302 W. Pennsylvania Ave.
Urbana, IL 61801
(217) 244-7788

Herb Research Foundation
1007 Pearl St. Ste. 200
Boulder, CO 80302
(303) 449-2265
www.herbs.org

**Institute for Safe Medication
Practices**
(800) 324-5723

**National Alliance for the Men-
tally Ill**
2101 Wilson Blvd. Ste. 302
Arlington, VA 22201
(800) 950-6264
www.nami.org

**National Cholesterol Education
Program**
NHLBI Information Center
PO Box 30105
Bethesda, MD 20824-0105
(301) 251-1222
(301) 251-1223
www.nhlbi.nih.gov

National Institute on Aging
PO Box 8057
Gaithersburg, MD 20857
(800) 222-2225
www.nih.gov/nia

**National Mental Health
  Association**
1021 Prince St.
Alexandria, VA 22314-2971
www.nmha.org

**Office of Alternative Medicine
  (NIH)**
Bldg. 31, Rm. 5B-38
9000 Rockville Pike, Mailstop
  2182
Bethesda, MD 20892
(800) 531-1794

**Office of Alternative Medicine
  (NIH)**
PO Box 8218
Silver Springs, MD 20907
(301) 495-4957
www.altmed.od.nih.gov

**Office of Disease Prevention &
  Health Promotion**
National Health Information
  Center
PO Box 1133
Washington, DC 20013-1133
www.odphp.oash.dhhs.gov

US Pharmacopoeia
12601 Twinbrook Pkwy.
Rockville, MD 20852
(301) 881-0666

Accepts reports of adverse events
  at: (800) 487-7776
www.usp.org

ADDITIONAL HELPFUL WEB SITES AND CONTACTS

**Center for Complementary and
Alternative Medicine**
www.camra.ucdavis.edu

FDA Office of Women's Health
www.fda.gov/womens/tttc.html

FDA on the Internet
www.fda.gov

**FDA monitoring of product ad-
verse reactions**
www.fda.gov/medwatch

Quackwatch
Monitoringwww.quackwatch.com

**Special Nutritionals Adverse
Event System (SN/AEMS)**
http://cfsan.fda.gov/~dms/
aems.html

**NIH Office of Alternative
Medicine**
altmed.od.nih.gov

**National Library of Medicine
(MEDLINE)**
www.nlm.nih.gov

Centers for Disease Control and Prevention
www.cdc.gov

Herb Research Foundation
www.herbs.org

Alternative Therapists in Health and Medicine (journal)
www.healthonline.com/altther.htm

Medical Herbalism Website
http://medherb.com

FOOD SAFETY RESOURCES

U.S. Department of Agriculture, Meat and Poultry Hotline
1-800-535-4555

Food and Drug Administration
1-800-332-4010

On the internet:
www.foodsafety.gov/~dms/fs-toc.html
www.cfsan.fda.gov/~mow/foodborn.html
www.cdc.gov/ncidod/diseases/foodborn/foodborn.htm
www.fsis.usda.gov/OA/pubs/consumerpubs.htm

Appendix B

Sample Assessment for Medication Use

Name: _____

Social Worker: _____

Date: _____

1. I am taking the following prescription medication[s] (list them). (Please list the medications you have taken over the last 6 weeks. Give the dose, times per day, and when generally taken. Also include why you are taking the medication or what it is for.)

2. I am taking the following over-the-counter medication[s] (list them). (Please list the OTC medications you have taken over the last 6 weeks. Give the dose, times per day, and when generally taken. Also include why you are taking the medication or what it is for.)

3.   I am taking the following herbal or natural preparation[s] (list them). (Please list the preparations you have taken over the last 6 weeks. Give the dose, times per day, and when generally taken. Also include why you are taking the preparation or what it is for. Don't forget to include teas, etc. if they are used for a specific health reason.)

4.   I am taking the following vitamins and mineral supplements (list them).
      (Please list the supplements you have taken over the last 6 weeks. Give the dose, times per day, and when generally taken. Also include why you are taking the supplement or what it is for.)

5.   Overall, my medications/herbal preparations or supplements help me:
      a.   Feel less sad.
      b.   Feel less nervous.
      c.   Feel less bothered by bad thoughts I cannot control.
      d.   Other (list any other benefits).

6.   Before drinking any alcohol, whether beer, wine, whiskey, wine coolers, or taking over-the-counter/herbal preparations, I should:
      a.   Stop taking my medication.
      b.   Talk to my doctor about whether it is safe or not to mix alcohol with this medicine.

c. Read the label on the bottle or package containing the alcohol to see what I should do.

7. Of the conditions below, which **should** I inform my health care provider about?
   ____ a. I have a history of an eating disorder.
   ____ b. I have a history of seizures.
   ____ c. I am pregnant or want to become pregnant.
   ____ d. I am breast-feeding.
   ____ e. I am taking other medications.
   ____ f. I have certain allergies.
   ____ g. I have a history of heart problems or high blood pressure or have had a recent heart attack.
   ____ h. I have a history of kidney disease.
   ____ i. I have diabetes

8. If a friend asks me for a dose of my medications or herbal preparations, I should:
   a. Refuse and explain that the medicine may make him/her sick.
   b. Give one dose away just so the friend can see if it helps or not.
   c. Freely share my medicine with other people who have the same symptoms as I.

9. There are some side effects that I should immediately tell my doctor about. Which of the following fall into that category? (check all that apply)
   ____ a. High fever, chills, sore throat
   ____ b. Change in skin color
   ____ c. Any unusual bleeding
   ____ d. Swelling of feet and lower legs
   ____ e. Headache
   ____ f. Diarrhea

10. If my medication can be habit-forming, I **should:**
    a. Take the medication exactly as my doctor tells me to.
    b. Only take the medication when I feel desperate.
    c. Stop taking the medication as soon as I feel better.

APPENDIX C

Glossary*

Absorption: The basic process by which the bloodstream metabolizes a drug.

Acetylcholine: A type of neurotransmitter released by all neurons that controls bodily function such as the skeletal muscles, heartbeat, some glandular functions, mood, sleep, and memory. This neurotransmitter is important in the transmission of brain and spinal-cord messages.

Acute: Often related to a disease process in which there is a marked intensity or sharpness in symptoms that subsides over a short period of time.

Affect: An outward manifestation of a person's feelings or emotions. The general expression of mood (e.g., flat, blunted, etc.).

Agonist: A drug or substance having a specific cellular affinity that produces a predictable response.

Agoraphobia: A panic disorder that occurs when an individual becomes anxious about being alone, generally when away from the home. The panic or fear experienced is incapacitating. In addition, the individual suffering from agoraphobia can also fear having an unexpected panic attack in a public setting where withdrawal is difficult or embarrassing.

Agranulocytosis: A dramatic decrease in the number of infection-fighting white blood cells that fight infections. Agranulocytosis is a rare side effect

---

*The definitions and information in this glossary were modified from several sources including the *Physicians' Desk Reference* (2000); the *PDR Medical Dictionary* (1995); the *PDR for Herbal Medicines* (1998; 2000); the *PDR for Nonprescription Medications* (1997); Dulcan's Information Handouts printed by the American Psychiatric Press (1999); the *Diagnostic and Statistical Manual of Mental Disorders* (APA, 1994); and *Modell's Drugs in Current Use and New Drugs* (44th ed., 1998), by Beth Duthie, Springer Publishing Co.

that has been directly linked to the antipsychotic drug clozapine (Clozaril), although agranulocytosis affects only 1% to 2% of its users.

Akathisia: A side effect of the typical or traditional antipsychotic medications that results in an extreme internal sense of restlessness.

Akinesia: A feeling of fatigue or weakness in the arms or legs.

Alprazolam (brand name Xanax): A benzodiazepine with a rapid onset making it effective in dealing with episodic bursts of anxiety. Often used in the treatment of panic disorder.

Alternative medicine: A form of treatment offered referred to as Eastern medicine. Its practice is based on ancient beliefs and traditions such as faith healing and herbal remedies. The effectiveness of these treatments is unproven and not scientifically tested.

Alternate or alternative practices: The use of techniques such as acupuncture, accupressure, herbals, chiropractic techniques, magnets, and others.

Amitriptyline (brand name Elavil): A commonly prescribed tricyclic antidepressant drug. Also used in the treatment of bulimia.

Antagonist: Any agent such as a drug that exerts an opposite action to that of another or competes for the same receptor sites.

Antianxiety drugs: Includes several groups of medicines that are used to treat anxiety (nervousness). Generally, these drugs are used to treat the symptoms of anxiety and some can assist with sleep disorders as well. These medications can help address and decrease fears and excessive worry, allowing individuals minimal improvement in current occupational and social functioning.

Anticholinergic effects: Adverse effects that result from the suppressive action of certain mental health medications (antipsychotic and antidepressant medications) as well as other general medications (antihistamines). This affects the action of acetylcholine in the brain and peripheral nervous system. The actual side effects include dry mouth, blurred vision, constipation, and urinary hesitancy. This could present a particular problem when working with older people.

Anticonvulsants: Medications generally used to treat seizures (fits or convulsions) but can also be used to address behavior problems regardless of whether the client has seizures or not. If a client has a history of brain damage, these may be considered the medications of choice for addressing mood changes related to the behavioral problems. It is believed that the anticonvulsants can help to reduce anger, aggression, and severe mood swings. Examples of commonly used medications in this area include Tegretol (carbamazepine), Depakene or Depakote (valproate or valproic acid) and Clonopin (clonazepam).

Antidepressant drugs: A major class of psychotropic drugs with diverse chemical configurations including the monoamine oxidase inhibitors (MAOIs), the heterocyclic drugs (composed of mono-, di-, tri-, and hetero-cyclics), the serotonin reuptake inhibitors (fluoxetine, paroxetine, sertra-line, trazodone, and venlafaxine), and bupropion are more recent innovations. Antidepressants usually must be taken for several weeks to have the desired effect and they often have a low therapeutic index, so they must be closely monitored.

Antihistamine: A class of drugs that can impede the effects of naturally occurring chemical compounds in the body called histamines, which can dilate the capillaries, produce headaches, and decrease blood pressure. Antihistamines may be employed for their sedative and hypnotic properties and can be utilized to help address extrapyramidal symptoms.

Antipsychotic drugs: A major classification of drugs, most of which are dopamine receptor antagonists (with the exception of the newer antipsy-chotic medications), and are used to address disturbances in affect and mood such as psychosis, delusions, and psychotic depression.

Anxiety: This is generally related to a response that occurs without the presence of real threat; it is differentiated from fear, which is generated when the threat is considered serious and negative enough to impair psychological, occupational, or social functioning.

Anxiety disorders: A classification of disorders often characterized by persistent worry.

Anxiolytics: Medications used to treat anxiety, agitation, or tension. Also known as antianxiety drugs.

Arteriosclerosis: An age-related condition in which the walls of the arteries become thickened and more rigid; also called hardening of the arteries.

Ataxia: The loss of power or muscle coordination.

Autoimmunity: The tendency of the body to mistake its own tissues as foreign invaders and to attack and destroy them.

Behavior disturbances: Marked changes in a person's behavior patterns that are typical of psychotic disorders. The disturbances generally include withdrawal, apathy, and bizarre actions.

Benzodiazepines: A class of drugs that is most commonly used both for anxiety (nervousness) and as a sedative (generally used to treat sleep problems). When used in the treatment of anxiety, many counselors warn that the medication may create a type of euphoria or false sense of progress that can impede improvement. It is always a good idea to ask the client to contract for services prior to starting this class of medications. Benzodiazepine medications are used to decrease anxiety, panic and night terrors; for example: Ativan (lorazepam), Clonopin (clonazepam), Librium (chlordiazepoxide), Valium (diazepam), and Xanax (alprazolam). The benzodiazepine that is generally used to treat sleep problems is Dalmane (flurazepam).

Bereavement: Loss, due to death, of someone to whom one feels close and the process of adjustment to the loss. Often mimics depression.

Beta-blockers: A class of drugs that reduces the physiological analogs of anxiety by blocking the beta-receptors in the autonomic nervous system. The receptors blocked include those that stimulate heartbeat, dilate blood vessels, and dilate the air channels within the lungs. They are as strong as the benzodiazepines and despite the fact that greater dosages are needed they are generally not considered addicting. Depression can be a serious side effect, and when it occurs it may be necessary to discontinue these types of drugs. These agents have been used in children to treat high blood pressure and irregular heartbeat. A newer use of these agents in children involves the treatment of emotional and behavior problems. These beta-blockers appear to be effective in decreasing aggression and violent behaviors. They may be particularly helpful for children who have developmental delays or autism. Examples of these medications include Inderal (propanolol), Tenormin (atenolol), Visken (pindolol), and Corgard (nadolol).

Biosynthesis: The production of neurochemicals stimulated by enzymes.

Bipolar disorders: A group of mental disorders historically referred to as manic depression or bipolar affective disorder, characterized by extreme fluctuations in mood. There are three major diagnoses that fall in this area, bipolar I, bipolar II, and cyclothymia.

Bipolar I disorders: There are six subgroups of this mental health disorder identified in the *DSM-IV*. Bipolar I involves a recurring illness of elevated mood that impairs psychosocial functioning (a manic episode) and depressed affect that also impairs psychosocial functioning (an episode of depression). Five of these subgroups include criteria to determine if a client is experiencing a single manic episode and the other five describe the most recent episode. The specifiers describe the episode recurrence. The six subgroups included in the *DSM-IV* are: bipolar I disorder single manic episode; bipolar I disorder, most recent episode hypomanic; bipolar I disorder, most recent episode manic; bipolar I disorder, most recent episode mixed; bipolar I disorder, most recent episode depressed; bipolar I disorder, most recent episode unspecified.

Bipolar II disorders: In this mental disorder there are one or more major depressive episodes and the client has no history of a manic or mixed episode. Bipolar II disorders are best described as the alternating experiences that a client has with episodes of major depression and periods of hypomania.

Bipolar disorder not otherwise specified (NOS): A type of bipolar disorder that does not meet all of the criteria described for the bipolar disorders, yet exhibits some of the basic symptoms evident in manic, major depressive, or mixed episodes.

Blood–brain barrier: A wall-like separation between the brain and the bloodstream that carefully modulates what substances, including drugs, cross into the brain.

Blood level: The measure of a drug's presence in the plasma at a given time.

Bromides: Certain medications with a strong sedative effect.

Bupropion (brand name Wellbutrin): An antidepressant drug known to induce seizures and therefore administered with specific recommendations on dosage ranges. It should not be administered concurrently with MAOIs.

BuSpar (buspirone): An antianxiety drug that is not often associated with abuse because of the absence of withdrawal phenomena, cognitive impairment, and sedation. It has a short half-life and therefore must be taken several times daily. It is also said not to have the same addicting or euphoric quality that is often noted in the benzodiazepines. BuSpar is not a benzodiazepine and is referred to as a nonbenzodiazepine. BuSpar is generally prescribed for a limited time to help control the symptoms of anxiety and allows the client to be calmer while learning new ways of coping with anxiety-producing events.

Carbamazepine (brand name Tegretol): Originally developed as an anticonvulsant medication. It is used along with other medications such as valproic acid (Depakote or Depakene) to treat individuals suffering from some type of mood disorder (acute mania and bipolar disorders). It is thought to retard the electrochemical process in the nervous system that can set off either convulsions or manic episodes. Also used to treat alcohol withdrawal, cocaine addiction, and emotional disorders.

Carcinogens: Cancer-causing agents often found in the environment.

Cardiovascular agents: Drugs that have their action on the heart or peripheral blood vessels for the treatment of hypertension (high blood pressure), angina, heart failure, or cardiac arrhythmia (e.g., beta-blockers, nitroglycerin, digoxin).

Catalyst: A substance that influences the rate of a chemical reaction without being permanently changed or consumed in the process.

Celexa (brand name): See citalopram hydrobromide.

Central nervous system: The system of neurons comprising the brain and the spinal cord. It serves as the body's major nerve-control system, directing and regulating all parts of the body to receive stimuli from external and internal environments and interpreting those stimuli that cause the body to react.

Cerebral hemorrhage: Escaping of blood from an artery into the cerebrum; a form of stroke.

Citalopram hydrobromide (brand name Celexa): An antidepressant used to treat major depression. It should not be taken any sooner than 14 days after discontinuing a MAO inhibitor. Some side effects may include abdominal pain, agitation, impotence, loss of appetite, and sweating.

Cerebellum: Controls bodily functions that operate below the level of consciousness including posture, balance, and movement through space. It receives information directly from sense organs, muscles, and joints.

Cerebral cortex: The folded, outermost region of the cerebrum. It is responsible for primary sensory functioning, visual processing, long-term memory, motor and perceptual coordination and integration, language, thinking, and problem solving. It is entirely made up of the so-called gray matter and four lobes (the frontal lobe, the temporal lobe, the parietal lobe, and the occipital lobe) that manage all functions.

Chronic disease: A disease process that often develops slowly and progresses for a long period of time.

Clomipramine (brand name Anafranil): A heterocyclic antidepressant drug that is also effective in the treatment of obsessive-compulsive disorders. This drug should not be taken with the MAOIs.

Clozapine (brand name Clozaril): An atypical antipsychotic drug found to be effective in treating schizophrenia. It is not used generally as a first-line antipsychotic drug because of a small risk of agranulocytosis, a depletion of white blood cells that can be fatal if not monitored. Clozapine has demonstrated effectiveness in treating both the positive and negative symptoms of schizophrenia. One of the most problematic aspects of this drug is for those who live in rural communities because of the regular (usually weekly) monitoring that it requires.

Cold maceration: A process of preparing a mixture (usually tea) by combining it with cold tap water. Generally the preparation is covered and left to stand for 6 to 8 hours and is then strained.

Colocalization: The process created when more than one neurochemical is involved in stimulating a response.

Compliance: The accuracy by which an individual follows the treatment prescribed by a physician or other health care professional.

Cultural bias: Tendency of psychometric tests to include questions involving content or skills more familiar to some cultural groups than to others.

Cyclothymic disorder: A form of depressive disorder typified by mood swings, hypomania and depression. In this mental disorder clients have milder experiences than those who suffer from bipolar disorder, although the symptoms are more consistent and last for approximately 2 years.

Decoction: A process of preparing a mixture (usually tea) by combining with cold water, covering and boiling, and later simmering and straining.

Defense mechanisms: Mental processes that help protect a person from anxiety, guilt feelings, or unacceptable thoughts.

Delusion: A false belief strongly held despite contrary evidence of a different social, commonly agreed upon reality. Common types are persecutory delusions (belief of threat or harm from others), delusions of grandeur (inflated sense of self), delusions of being controlled (external agents impose thoughts or feelings), and delusions of reference (external events are significant or reflective of self).

Dementia: Deterioration of mental processes such as memory, personality changes, abstract thinking, and impaired judgement. There are numerous causes of dementia, the two most common being Alzheimer's disease and vascular dementia (stroke).

Depakene or Depakote (sodium valproate or valproic acid): Medications commonly used as mood stabilizers for the following reasons: (a) inadequate response or intolerance to antipsychotics or lithium; (b) manic symptoms; (c) rapid cycling of the condition; (d) EEG abnormalities; and (e) head trauma. The side-effect profiles for Depakene and Depakote include upset stomach, increased appetite, thinning hair, tremor, drowsiness, and weight gain. Behavioral or emotional side effects involve increased aggression and irritability. Serious but rare side effects are very similar to Tegretol (carbamazepine) except valproic acid has not been noted to decrease the number of blood cells or lead to lung irritation. If this medication is stopped suddenly, uncomfortable withdrawal symptoms may occur and a planned course for discontinuance of this medication should always be implemented.

Depression: A state of sunken mood where an individual feels impairment in daily living and functioning.

Desipramine (brand name Norpramine): A tricyclic antidepressant sometimes prescribed because it is has the fewest anticholinergic effects of the heterocyclic drugs.

***Diagnostic and Statistical Manual of Mental Disorders* (DSM):** A publication developed by the American Psychiatric Association that is used to clarify mental health disorders. The manual identifies the specific symptoms and criteria used to determine the mental health diagnostic impression.

Diastolic pressure: Denotes arterial pressure while the heart is resting between beats.

Diazepam (brand name Valium): A benzodiazepine used to treat anxiety, which may act as a sedative. It provides short-term relief for mild to moderate anxiety and is used to treat epilepsy and alcohol withdrawal symptoms.

Dopamine: A type of neurotransmitter thought to be involved in disorders of cognition (such as schizophrenia), motor control systems, and limbic activity (emotional behavior).

Doxepin (brand name Sinequan): A commonly prescribed heterocyclic antidepressant drug. It is also occasionally used for the treatment of anxiety. This medication should not be used with an MAOI.

Drug agonist: A drug that is capable of combining with receptors to initiate a drug action.

Drug–drug interaction: Adverse drug reaction when a second drug modifies the way the body handles or reacts to the first agent.

Drug tolerance: When a person becomes less responsive to the same dosage of medication as time passes.

Duration: The time in which a substance exists or lasts (e.g., symptoms of an illness; effects of a medication on the human system).

Dysthymia: Depression that is chronic (all day or most of the day) but not acute, and lasts for at least 2 years.

Dystonia: Uncoordinated, involuntary twisting movements of the jaw, tongue, or entire body, produced by sustained muscle spasms generally associated with the neuroleptic medications. Very often clients will complain of having a "thick tongue."

Efficacy: The ability of a drug to address and control an illness based on how well it works and how much is needed to make it work effectively.

Electroconvulsive therapy (ECT): A procedure used in the treatment of severe depression where an electric current is briefly applied through electrodes to one or both sides of the brain. Temporary side effects may include convulsions, unconsciousness, and memory loss.

Elimination: All bodily processes that act to lower the concentration of a drug and other substances in the body.

Enzyme: A protein produced by living cells that catalyzes chemical reactions in organic matter within the cell structure.

Extrapyramidal symptoms (EPS): Numerous negative side effects experienced by clients as a result of taking several types of medications, especially the typical antipsychotic medications used to treat psychotic disorders.

Extracts: Liquid, powdered, viscous, concentrations derived from dried plant parts that can be prepared by either maceration or percolation.

Fat-soluble vitamins: Those vitamins that are soluble in fat such as A, D, K and E.

Fear: An individual's response to a real threat.

Fluoxetine hydrochloride (brand name Prozac): An antidepressant that functions as an SSRI and is prescribed for depression that is severe enough to impair daily functioning. This medication is also used to treat obsessive-compulsive disorder (OCD). It should not be used with an MAO inhibitor. Some common side effects include abnormal dreams, abnormal ejaculation, decreased orgasmic functioning, agitation, and headaches.

Fluphenazine (brand name Prolixin): A high-potency antipsychotic drug used for the treatment of disorganized and psychotic thinking, delusions, and hallucinations.

Fluvoxamine (brand name Luvox): An SSRI often prescribed for obsessive-compulsive disorder.

Gama amino butyric acid (GABA): A general amino-acid type of neurochemical that is often linked to exciting, stimulating reactions within the human body. General neurotransmitters make up the majority of neurotransmissions in the human body. The most common examples are GABA, glycine, and glutamate.

Hallucinations: False sense of perceptions of external objects that do not exist. The most common type is auditory (hearing), followed by visual (sight), tactile (touch), somatic (internal organs), olfactory (smell), and hypersensitivity (hyperacute sight, sound, and smell).

Haloperidol (brand name Haldol): A high-potency antipsychotic drug used for the treatment of schizophrenia that can also be used to treat the neurological condition of Tourette's syndrome, which involves both motor and vocal tics.

Herbal medicines: Products are generally derived from plants, leaves, roots, and flowers.

Hypervitaminosis: An excess of one of more vitamins in the human body.

Imipramine (brand name Tofranil): Often referred to as the grandfather of all antidepressants. It is the oldest tricyclic antidepressant available and has traditionally been used for the treatment of depression and for those who have panic attacks. It is sometimes used now to assist with withdrawal from cocaine addiction and in obsessive-compulsive disorder.

Infusion: A type of preparation for herbal medications that most commonly involves boiling in hot water, steeping, and straining the concoction.

Klonopin (clonazepam): A common medication used as a mood stabilizer often prescribed for the following reasons: inadequate response or intolerance to antipsychotics or lithium, manic symptoms, rapid cycling of the condition, EEG abnormalities, and head trauma. The most common side effects are difficulty with balance and drowsiness. Behavioral and emotional side effects include irritability, excitement, increased anger and aggression, trouble sleeping or nightmares, and memory loss. The most serious side effect is the interaction effect if this medication is combined with alcohol or other drugs, which can result in sleepiness, unconsciousness, and death.

Lag time: The amount of time required for a drug to have its desired effect, depending on factors such as the body's tolerance of the drug, the drug's absorption, protein binding, and metabolizing rate, and individual differences in physiology.

Lithium: The most commonly used mood-stabilizing medication. Lithium is a derivative of lithium salts, which occur naturally, and is relatively inexpensive. With a shorter half-life than most antipsychotics and antidepressants, it must generally be taken more than once a day. As a rule, it is the drug of choice for treating bipolar disorder but can also be used to treat certain types of depression, severe mood swings, and very serious aggression. Caution should be used due to the possibility of toxicity. Therefore, routine lithium levels are considered essential for effective and safe treatment. Lithium is available in several different forms: lithium carbonate tablets (Lithotabs) or capsules (Eskalith or Lithonate); controlled-release capsules or tablets (Eskalith CR or Lithobid); and lithium citrate syrup. Lithium salts are used to treat manic episodes of bipolar disorder. Of note is the recent use of Lithium with all age groups including children and adolescents.

Mania: A psychological and emotional state where an individual experiences increased excitement and persistent elevated mood.

Manic episode: A state of mood that features euphoria, irritability, and the lack of inhibition and is often accompanied by substance abuse. There is a distinct period of consistently elevated or irritable mood followed by significant problems in psychosocial functioning that may require hospitalization.

MAO inhibitors: See Monoamine oxidase inhibitors.

Major depression: A severely depressed mood state featuring a total loss of interest or pleasure in life with a significant change in the usual quality of life functioning. Characteristic symptoms include marked weight changes, daily psychomotor disturbances, sleep disturbances, loss of concentration, loss of energy, and recurring thoughts of death or suicide. Major depression requires two or more major depressive episodes, separated by at least 2 months of regular functioning.

Medication half-life: The time it takes for a medication to fall to 50% of its previous peak level.

Medicinal herbal preparations: Preparations that are said to have some type of therapeutic effect.

Megadoses: Doses of a nutrient or chemical in excess of the normal requirement.

Mesoridazine: An antipsychotic drug with a fairly strong sedating effect that may calm persons who feel highly agitated or violent.

Metabolism: The process by which the body breaks down a drug into chemical form, enabling it to be excreted from the system later.

Mirtazapine (brand name Remeron): An antidepressant that functions as an SSNRI used for the treatment of depression.

Monoamine oxidase (MAO) inhibitors: A class of drugs developed as the first antidepressants. They differ from more recent antidepressants in that they inhibit enzyme actions that metabolize norepinephrine and serotonin in the nervous system. They are not widely used today because of the strict dietary regimens they require. They have been shown to relieve some depressions that are not responsive to other antidepressant drugs.

Monoamines: Biogenic amines with a single amine (an organic compound), this group includes dopamine, norepinephrine, epinephrine (the catecholamines), acetylcholine (quaternary amine), and serotonin (an indoleamine).

Mood disorders: Characterized by disturbances in affect that are typical of psychotic disorders and depression. The disturbances in mood are reflected by severely flattened affect and by extreme emotional ambivalence.

Mood episodes: There are four types of mood episodes that cannot be diagnosed separately as a mental disorder and that constitute the building blocks of the mood disorders. The types of mood episodes that clients may manifest who suffer from the bipolar disorders are manic, hypomanic, major depressive, and mixed episodes.

manic episode: a mood episode where a client's mood is persistently elevated. Other symptoms such as increased psychomotor agitation, distractibility, flight of ideas, decreased need for sleep, and grandiosity may be noted. These symptoms should last for at least a week.

hypomanic episode: symptoms may initially appear similar to the manic episode involving persistently elevated, expansive, or irritable mood. The time frame is approximately 4 days, and it must be clear that the individual is exhibiting signs that remain uncharacteristic of previous levels of functioning. Individuals experiencing a hypomanic mood episode rarely need to be hospitalized, because although the symptoms may impair functioning, marked impairment is not noted. These individuals also do not show evidence of psychotic features even though others are aware that the behaviors they are exhibiting are uncharacteristic.

major depressive episode: involves at least five or more characteristic signs such as appetite disturbances that result in either weight gain or loss, disturbances in sleeping (hypersomnia or sleeping too much; or insomnia, an inability to sleep or disturbance in sleep), daily bouts of depressed mood, markedly diminished interest or pleasure in activities that usually are pleasurable, psychomotor agitation or retardation nearly every day, fatigue or loss of energy, and other related symptoms.

mixed episode: Referred to as mixed because it generally meets the criteria for the manic and the depressive episode. The major difference is that it only lasts for approximately 1 week and not 2. In this type of episode the individual often experiences rapidly alternating moods of feelings of sadness, irritability, and euphoria.

Mood-stabilizing drugs: Drugs that feature actions aimed at keeping mood within a stable range and that lower moods from a manic state. Included in this grouping are the tricyclics, MAOIs (for depression), and lithium (for bipolar disorders). The mood stabilizers work to keep moods regular avoiding extremes of either pole.

Nefazodone hydrochloride (brand name Serzone): An antidepressant that functions as an SSNRI used in the treatment of severe depression. Some side effects include blurred or abnormal vision, dry mouth, nausea, and weakness. This medication may be considered the drug of choice for those with depression who also have a lack of sexual interest and difficulty with performance.

Neuroleptics: A group of medications known as the antipsychotics that used to be referred to as the major tranquilizers. Generally these medications are used to treat psychosis reflective of the symptoms often seen in conditions such as schizophrenia, mania, or very severe depression. These medications can help to reduce auditory hallucinations (hearing voices) and visual hallucinations (seeing things that are not there) as well as delusions (beliefs that are held in view of false or contradictory evidence). These medications can also reduce motor and vocal tics (fast repeated movements or sounds) in conditions like Tourette's syndrome. They are being used now to reduce severe aggression problems such as those seen in children with conduct disorder, mental retardation, and autism. These medications are very powerful and require constant monitoring for side effects. Overall, these medications can help clients to feel less agitated or upset. Examples of brand name medications in this category are Clozaril, Haldol, Loxitane, Mellaril, Moban, Navane, Orap, Prolixin, Risperdal, Stelazine, Thorazine, Trilafon, and Zyprexa.

Neuron: A basic nerve cell.

Neurotransmitters: Chemicals found in the nerve cells that act as messengers, carrying electrical impulses through the cells.

Over-the-counter medications (OTCs): Medications that can be purchased in a pharmacy without a prescription (analgesics, laxatives, cold remedies, etc.).

Parkinsonism: Generally refers to a slowing or rigidity in muscular activity.

Paroxetine (brand name Paxil): One of the new classes of atypical antidepressant drugs that function as a serotonin reuptake inhibitor in producing a therapeutic effect. Also used to treat panic disorder and obsessive-compulsive disorder.

Pharmacokinetics: The management of a drug within the body including absorption, distribution, metabolism, and excretion.

Pharmacotherapy: Medications used to help maximize the physical or mental health and including education in regard to the medication and how it can interact with the counseling support that can be provided.

Phobic avoidance: Attempts avoid coming into contact with a specific object or stimulus in an individual who has severe anxiety and fear in regard to the object or stimulus. It is this type of avoidance behavior that is known as stimulus avoidance.

Photosensitivity: A reaction to the sun.

Placebo: An inactive sugar pill used in research to be compared with new medications that are being tested.

Plant juices: Freshly harvested plant parts that are generally prepared through maceration in water or by pressing.

Polypharmacy: The use of more than one drug for the treatment of the same ailment. This includes the concurrent administration of several psychotropic drugs.

Positive symptoms of psychosis: The presence of bizarre and frequently affect-laden experiences ordinarily absent from a person's normal experience. Symptoms include hallucinations, delusions, and bizarre thinking or behavior.

Postsynaptic membrane: The wall of the dendrite cell body located at the opposite side of the synaptic cleft from the axon, on which receptor sites are located to receive neurotransmitter input and pass the impulse through the rest of the cell.

Postural (orthostatic) hypotension: A drop in blood pressure that occurs after sitting or standing suddenly and resulting in faintness and dizziness.

Potency: A drug's relative strength in standard units of measurement. For example, low-potency drugs such as chlorpromazine are given in higher milligram doses, while high-potency drugs such as haloperidol are given in lower milligram doses. Potency should not be directly linked to the presence or absence of medication side effects.

Psychopharmacology: The study of drugs that affect cognition, behavior, and bodily responses.

Psychotropic drugs: Drugs that alter psychological functioning or mood, thoughts, motor abilities, balance, movement, and coordination.

Pyramidal: One of two long nerve pathways that stretch from the cerebral cortex to the spinal cord (the other is known as extrapyramidal). Pyramidal pathways carry messages to and from the central nervous system and control groups of muscles that contract simultaneously (for instance, grasping an object with the hand).

Reuptake: The process through which a neuron reabsorbs a chemical neurotransmitter.

Rhizome: The bark of a root that is often used in herbal preparations.

Risperdone (brand name Risperdal): An atypical or nontraditional antipsychotic medication used to treat schizophrenia and other types of psychotic features.

SAM-e: A molecule present in the human body that helps to stimulate dopamine and is generally used to treat numerous general symptoms including depression and arthritis.

Schizoaffective disorder: A continuous period of illness during which there are some symptoms of schizophrenia such as delusions, hallucinations, or grossly disorganized behavior, concurrent with either a major depressive episode, a manic episode, or a mixed episode.

Schizophrenia: A major mental disorder lasting more than 6 months and characterized in part by thought disturbances, misinterpretations of reality, mood change (including blunted affect and inappropriate moods), communication problems (poverty of speech and coherence), and bizarre, withdrawn, or regressive behaviors. The five subtypes are disorganized, catatonic, paranoid, undifferentiated, and residual.

Symptoms in schizophrenia:

negative symptoms in schizophrenia: These symptoms are harder to detect than the positive symptoms and often involve blunted affect, emotional withdrawal and poor rapport, passive apathetic social withdrawal, difficulty in abstract thinking, lack of spontaneity, and stereotyped thinking patterns.

positive symptoms in schizophrenia: A positive symptom involves the development of delusions, conceptual disorganization, hallucinatory behavior, excitement, grandiosity, suspiciousness or persecution, and hostility. These symptoms are often very obvious and easy to detect in the assessment process.

Secondary side effect: An adverse reaction that is an indirect consequence of a drug's action but is nevertheless predictable (e.g., lowered potassium with diuretics, nausea with Digoxin, dry mouth with antidepressants).

Selective serotonin norepinephrine reuptake inhibitors (SSNRIs): The newest group of medicines that have successfully been used to treat emotional and behavioral problems such as depression, panic disorder, obsessive-compulsive disorder (OCD), similar to their counterparts, the SSRIs. Some examples of the SSNRIs include Effexor, Serzone, and Remeron.

Selective serotonin reuptake inhibitors (SSRIs): A relatively new group of medicines that have been used successfully to treat emotional and behavioral problems such as depression, panic disorder, obsessive-compulsive disorder (OCD), bulimia, and posttraumatic stress disorder in adults. These medications are now being used to treat the same types of behavior in children. Some examples of SSRIs include: Prozac (fluoxetine), Zoloft (sertraline), Luvox (fluvoxamine), and Paxil (paroxetine).

Serotonin: A specific type of neurotransmitter.

Sertraline (brand name Zoloft): An antidepressant medication that functions as an SSRI prescribed primarily for major depression. It can also be used to treat obsessive-compulsive disorder. Some side effects include difficulty with ejaculation, dry mouth, dizziness, and decreased sex drive.

Side effects: Any unintentional and nontherapeutic effects of a drug on the body. Also called adverse effects, side effects are frequently due to the interaction of the brain, drug, and body.

Short-acting: When a medication is considered to have been eliminated or excreted quickly from the body.

Standardization: The procedures used to evaluate a medication or a treatment. Medications that are standardized have been evaluated for efficacy and safety.

Standardized extract: When the unwanted components of a preparation are removed and what remains is a more concentrated mixture that contains active ingredients (see extract).

Synapse: The bridge between the gap from one nerve cell to the next.

Synthesis: The process that results when a neurochemical is stimulated by an enzyme that in turn stimulates the production of the neurochemical.

Systolic pressure: Denotes the force exerted when the heart beats, sending blood to the arteries.

Tardive dyskinesia: A side effect of the traditional or typical antipsychotic medications thought to be irreversible and serious. Most professionals agree that the longer an individual is on the typical antipsychotic medication, the greater the likelihood of developing tardive dyskinesia. Those who have this disorder often exhibit coordinated but involuntary rhythmic movements such as facial movements, grimacing and lip tremors and involuntary movement of the fingers, hand, and trunk.

Teas: Herbs that are capable of being infused.

Tegretol (carbamazepine): A common medication referred to as a mood stabilizer. This anticonvulsant medication is used as mood stabilizer for the following reasons: (a) inadequate response or intolerance to antipsychotics or lithium; (b) manic symptoms; (c) rapid cycling of the condition; (d) EEG abnormalities; and (e) head trauma. Side effects of this medication include double or blurred vision, sleepiness, dizziness, clumsiness or decreased coordination, mild nausea and stomach upset, hair loss, increased risk of sunburn, and skin rash. Some of the behavioral or emotional side effects include anxiety and nervousness, agitation and mania, impulsive behavior, irritability, increased aggression, hallucinations, and motor and vocal tics. Serious but rare side effects include a decrease in the number of blood cells, lung irritation, worsening of seizures, yellowing of the skin, loss of appetite, increased or decreased urination, dark urine or pale bowel movements, sore throat or fever, mouth ulcers, vomiting, and the development of severe behavior problems.

Therapeutic index: The relative measure of a drug's toxicity or safety level; the difference between the median effective dose the median toxic dose; the safety margin of a drug.

Thorazine: Considered the first antipsychotic drug, discovered more than 40 years ago.

Time-release medication: Medication that is coated so that it can be released in planned graduated doses. Tablets and capsules should not be broken or chewed.

Tincture: Alcohol/hydroalcohol solutions derived from botanicals where the concentration of the herbal product generally remains very low.

Tricyclic antidepressants: Antidepressant drugs that have a central three-ring molecular structure, tricyclics are increasingly grouped under the larger heading of heterocyclic drugs. Tricyclic antidepressants are now used to treat enuresis (bedwetting), attention-deficit hyperactivity disorder (ADHD), school phobia, separation anxiety disorder, panic disorder, obsessive-compulsive disorder (OCD), some sleep disorders such as night terrors, and tricotillomania (compulsive pulling of one's own hair) in children and adolescents. Examples of these medications include Tofranil (imipramine), Pamelor or Aventyl (nortriptyline), Norpramin or Perto-fane (desipramine), Elavil or Endep (amitriptyline), and Anafranil (clomipramine).

Tyramine: An amine found in fermented foods especially cheese. Its effects on the body resemble that of epinephrine and can be dangerous with individuals taking MAO inhibitors by causing an increase in blood pressure.

Valproic acid: A medication first used solely as an anticonvulsant drug that has become commonly used for the treatment of bipolar disorder and sometimes to increase the effectiveness of antidepressant drugs.

Venlafaxine hydrochloride (brand name Effexor): An antidepressant medication that functions as an SSNRI as is used in the treatment of depression. Some side effects include abnormal ejaculation or orgasm, blurred vision, bruising, and impotence.

Volatile oils: Concentrates of active plant parts derived from distillation that tend to evaporate quickly.

Water-soluble vitamins: Those vitamins that can be dissolved in water such as vitamin C and the B complex.

Wellbutrin (Bupropino hydrochloride): A medication that has been successfully used to treat depression in adults. One type of this medication Zyban (bupropion hydrochloride) has been used for smoking cessation. Both of these medications contain bupropin and should not be used together. This medication is not recommended for eating disorders such as bulimia or anorexia nervosa because of the potential for the incidence of seizures.

Withdrawal symptoms: Symptoms that result when a drug or medication is discontinued.

Index

Index

315

362.1042

100981

0999